A LIFEBOAT YEAR

Compiled by
Barry Cox
Honorary Librarian
Royal National Lifeboat Institution

"Without fear or thought of self, the lifeboatmen
have never spared their strength and skill
in helping their brother sailors in distress
from the dangers of the sea and violence of the enemy."

The Admiralty
7 February 1940

To find out about other titles produced by
Historic Military Press visit our website at
www.historicmilitarypress.com.
Alternatively please write to us free of charge at
Customer Services, Historic Military Press,
Freepost SEA 11014, Pulborough, West Sussex, RH20 4BR,
or telephone our freephone number: 0800 071 7419.

HISTORIC MILITARY PRESS

A LIFEBOAT YEAR

First published 2001 by Historic Military Press,
Green Arbor, Rectory Road, Storrington, West Sussex, RH20 4EF.

ISBN 1-901313-13-1

Printed in the United Kingdom by
Selsey Press Ltd., 84 High Street, Selsey, Chichester, PO20 0QH
Telephone: 01243 605234

HISTORIC MILITARY PRESS
Green Arbor, Rectory Road, Storrington, West Sussex, RH20 4EF.
Telephone/Fax: 01903 741941

Front cover: from a painting by Charles Dixon (1872 - 1934) which is in the RNLI collection. It shows a service by Coxswain Henry Blogg of Cromer, to the barge 'Sepoy' in December 1933.

www.historicmilitarypress.com.

DEDICATED

To all those past and present members
and supporters of the
Royal National Lifeboat Institution
to whom so many owe so much.

THE AUTHOR

This book came about as a result of a placement that the author undertook with the RNLI back in 1987.
Now, 14 or so years later, Barry Cox is still there.

It all started when his, then employers, the National Westminster Bank, seconded Barry to the RNLI. As part of a community relations programme, the RNLI asked Barry to sort, arrange and catalogue the impressive library and archives held at the headquarters in Poole. The insight that this work allowed into some of the very important documents within the archives sparked the idea that ultimately led to the creation of this book.

Barry has had a varied career that has included five years in the Royal Air Force and six years at sea with P&O. In 1961 he was the Senior Assistant Purser on the maiden voyage of the 'Canberra' - and was also a passenger on its farewell cruise in 1997. It was in 1963 that he joined the Westminster Bank, serving in large City offices before spending the bulk of his banking career in the International Division.

He retired from the Bank in 1992 and offered to continue assisting the RNLI as their Honorary Librarian. In this capacity he frequently helps researchers from around the world on a variety of subjects - station histories, lifeboat services, family connections, in fact anything to do with the lifeboat service.

Barry has been involved in the creation of a number of articles, and also edited the excellent 'Lifeboat Gallantry', published by Spinks.

CONTENTS

ACKNOWLEDGEMENTS

The majority of the entries in this book have been taken from items in the library of the RNLI at Poole, and, where appropriate, I have quoted the source material.

I would particularly like to thank Jeff Morris, The Archivist of the Lifeboat Enthusiasts Society, for all his help. The archives of his predecessor, the late Grahame Farr, have also proved very useful. My thanks to the members of the RNLI Public Relations Department who have met my many queries with unfailing courtesy.

I am indebted to Mary-Anne Miles who took the time to type out the manuscript - no easy task.

Finally, my thanks to my publishers Martin Mace and Leanne Swannie, and Dave Cassan (a member of the Historic Military Press team) who, incidentally, is a member of the Shoreham Harbour Lifeboat crew.

INTRODUCTION

Since becoming involved with the RNLI in 1987, I have spent many happy and interesting hours in the library amongst the archives of the Institution. These contain many fascinating items covering the history and development of the first national lifeboat organisation in the world. There are minute books from the first committee meetings in 1824: the annual reports and Lifeboat Journals: station histories: books written about or containing references to the RNLI: and much, much more.

From the earliest days, the Institution has been helped by a dedicated band of supporters, whilst countless thousands of fishermen, coastguards and others have manned lifeboats around the coasts of the British Isles. In the early days few crew members were named in the records - unless they were the Coxswains, won medals or paid the ultimate sacrifice of losing their own lives whilst trying to save the lives of others.

The RNLI is 'on call' twenty four hours every day of the year. At stations the Coxswain and Mechanic ensure that their boat is always ready to go out on service at a moment's notice: crews are trained for every eventuality: the supporters and families of the crew help maintain the boathouse and raise funds. At the headquarters in Poole, the Operations Room is staffed 24 hours a day with a duty officer on watch at night, whilst a storekeeper and a driver are on call to meet any needs following incidents at stations.

Since its foundation in 1824, there have been many changes. Rowing and sailing lifeboats have given way to engine power: no longer do boats have to wait at wreck sites in the dark awaiting daylight to effect rescues: radio and radar have improved communications and navigation: tractors help with launching instead of men and women helpers or horses: helicopters can be called in to help with rescues.

This book sets out to illustrate the continuing day to day activity within the Institution and similar organisations, with an incident for each day of a year taken from the RNLI archives. It may be a gold medal rescue service: a development in lifeboat design: mention of those who have helped manage the Institution or raise funds: services which rate only a line or two in the Journal, others several pages: lifeboat capsizes and tragedies: shore boat services (i.e. those where no lifeboat was involved): lifeboats helping in floods.

It is impossible to cover every aspect of the Institution's work, but I trust the following pages will give readers an insight into the achievements of one of the great voluntary organisations of this country, if not of the world.

Barry Cox
Hon. Librarian, RNLI

WHAT MAKES A GOOD LIFEBOATMAN

In 1918, the seventh Duke of Northumberland, President of the Institution, offered a prize for the best essay on a lifeboat theme to be *"written by children still actually attending the senior classes in national elementary schools throughout the United Kingdom"*.

Sadly the Duke died before the first competition, but it was decided to go ahead with what became the *'Duke of Northumberland's Lifeboat Essay Competition'*. The country was divided into six (later eight) districts, and a challenge shield and thirty five individual prizes were offered in each district.

The subject for the 1928 competition was *'Describe the kind of man that a good lifeboatman should be'*. The May Lifeboat Journal of that year announced the results, together with extracts from the essays. Some of the comments made by the children are very apt, others amusing but at times equally appropriate. Judge for yourselves.

The Qualities of the Lifeboatman

One essayist wrote that the lifeboatman *"must be perfect, both mentally and physically, and also have the dexterity of an athlete"*. After that there does not seem much more to be said; but even those essayists who did not ask for perfection set a very high standard. Strict temperance was demanded by a large number of the competitors. Others, again, touched on the question of diet, and the laws of health generally, pointing out the lifeboatman's need for regular and simple meals, no drinking between them, plenty of exercise, and houses in which, as one essayist wrote, *"there should be plenty of fresh air and as much sunlight as the climate we enjoy (or have to put up with) admits"*.

The question of diet brings us naturally to the question of physique. Should the lifeboatman be a heavyweight? On the whole, the children of the British Isles think that he should be. As one writes, *"He must be very heavy and healthy to keep his place in the boat"*. Another describes the *"average lifeboatman"* as *"an old bunch of bone and muscle"*; another says that he is usually *"very fat"*. Others again are for the happy mean. One writes that he must have *"a cool, steady head on a pair of sturdy shoulders. He need not be a heavy hunk, but a middleweight"*. Another gives excellent reasons for a moderate figure: *"A lifeboatman must not be too fat and not too thin; too much flesh is a burden, and his weight would smash fragile things if he trod on them; but a little flesh helps to keep him warm on a cold night"*.

It must not be thought that the competitors have discussed the physical to the neglect of the moral and spiritual side of the lifeboatman. A fair balance is kept between the two. What is most noticeable is the number of writers who have felt that the ability to turn out in the middle of the night is the best proof of courage, good health and unselfishness of the lifeboatman.

As one writer excellently puts it: *"A lifeboatman should always be prepared to give up his beauty sleep for others. But it is not sufficient that he should get up. He must not be awkward with those who have called him"*. A lot seems to lie behind that adjective.

To be cheerful and good tempered, *"and have a jolly face,"* is, in the opinion of several competitors, essential, *"In his weather-beaten face you should find a smile which brave men always possess"*.

Should a Lifeboatman be a Married Man?

This is a question that has exercised the thought of a number of the writers. Some are quite certain that he should be a bachelor - *"Among little things a lifeboatman should not have are wives or a child"*. Others are equally convinced that a wife is an advantage to him, but she must be *"a cheery wife, not one who moans and groans, as it makes him miserable"*. Another goes so far as to say that *"a good wife is the most important of all the qualifications,"* but you would never guess why - *"because she can make hot tea for the rescued"*.

Other Quaint Phrases

Here are some more quaint and original reflections on the character of the lifeboatman:

"A lifeboatman should not grumble, for the harder his life is, the brighter will sparkle his crown in heaven."

"Before the lifeboat service was established millions of people went to a watery grave, unknelled, uncoffined and unknown."

"The lifeboatman should never be brutal to his wife and children, but he himself will get knocked about plenty of times whilst at sea."

"A lifeboatman is a monstrous specimen of humanity and therefore has no difficulty in passing the doctor and becoming a trained member of the crew."

"For men must work and women must weep, and these gallant men do all this for nothing."

"Their hard, brown and horny hands have been set to tasks that the very thought of which would have made a raw 'land-lubber' quail."

"A lifeboatman should be a sea-dog to his last hair."

"The sea and all its vicissitudes must be as familiar to him as the kitchen is to the cook."

"He must not be selfish and grab the best seats."

"He must know the front of the boat from the back."

"Lifeboatmen have very red faces and red noses because they get the very best fresh air."

"A lifeboatman must be a tall man and have the courage of a lion when caught in a pinch."

"He must have good teeth. What use would a lifeboatman be with toothache?"

"He must be strong and muscular, possess great courage, a spirit of self sacrifice and a waterproof hat."

"Courage and wit are another two official things which must be in the lifeboatman's spirit."

Phrases of the Year

One of the phrases of the year comes from a London essayist,
"The sea is called the Briton's Birthright, but it often proves to be his grave".

Another London essayist gives a good motto for a lifeboatman -
"God first, other people second, self last".

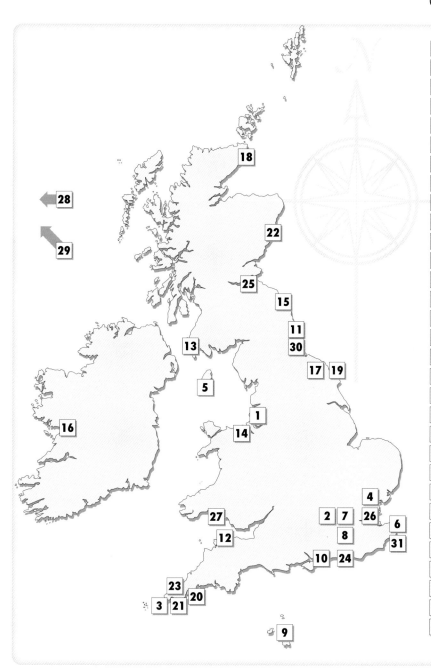

1	January 1st	1944	New Brighton
2	January 2nd	1984	London Boat Show
3	January 3rd	1923	Penlee
4	January 4th	1894	Clacton-on-Sea
5	January 5th	1847	Douglas
6	January 6th	1881	Ramsgate
7	January 7th	1875	London
8	January 8th	1852	London
9	January 9th	1825	Jersey
10	January 10th	1920	Hayling Island
11	January 11th	1913	Tynemouth
12	January 12th	1899	Lynmouth
13	January 13th	1932	Portpatrick
14	January 14th	1991	West Kirby
15	January 15th	1922	Holy Island
16	January 16th	1962	Galway Bay
17	January 17th	1928	Whitby
18	January 18th	1958	Wick
19	January 19th	1881	Whitby
20	January 20th	1940	Falmouth
21	January 21st	1939	Penlee
22	January 22nd	1930	Aberdeen
23	January 23rd	1939	St Ives
24	January 24th	1944	Shoreham Harbour
25	January 25th	1992	Queensferry
26	January 26th	1990	West Mersea, Essex
27	January 27th	1883	The Mumbles
28	January 28th	1915	United States of America
29	January 29th	1928	Iceland
30	January 30th	1790	South Shields
31	January 31st	1919	North Deal & Ramsgate

1st JANUARY   NEW BRIGHTON, CHESHIRE, **1944**

Shortly after one in the afternoon, the flag-officer-in-charge, Liverpool, requested the services of a lifeboat to land a soldier who was dangerously ill in one of the forts near the Burbo Bank in the Mersey estuary. The fort was one of a group built on massive concrete piles, connected by bridges. On it was mounted heavy anti-aircraft artillery. The piles, which incline inwards, were without fenders and dangerous to approach in bad weather.

The case was urgent and owing to the very rough sea, with a strong west-south-west wind, no other boat could make the passage with any degree of safety. At 1.45 p.m. the Barnett class motor lifeboat *William and Kate Johnston* was launched and arrived at the fort at 3.15 p.m. The bridges were 70 feet long - some ten feet longer than the lifeboat - and about 40 feet above sea level. The sick man was lashed in a stretcher and lowered by ropes from one of the bridges. It was a very slow and difficult operation, and one moment the lifeboat would be in position and the next swept away or lifted 15 feet by the seas. The greatest skill in manoeuvring, and the greatest patience, were required, and the man was embarked safely, with only trifling damage to the lifeboat. She landed him at Woodside Pier, Birkenhead, and reached her moorings again at 6.30 that evening.

The anti-aircraft battery made two donations, one to the crew, the other to the Institution, in appreciation of "the valiant show", and as a contribution to a worthy cause.

2nd JANUARY   LONDON BOAT SHOW, **1984**

Storm Force, a support group for everyone under 16, was launched at the London Boat Show. Two members of the cast of the TV series 'Grange Hill' became the first members - Erkan Mustafa (who played Roland Browning) and Simone Nylander (who played Janet St. Clair).

The purpose of Storm Force is to inform children about the work of the RNLI and to give them the idea of belonging to and supporting the cause, although direct fund raising is not intended. Members receive Storm Force News, the club's magazine, four times a year. They have their own mascot - Stormy Stan. Visits to lifeboat stations may be arranged. There are now over 20,000 members.

3rd JANUARY   PENLEE, CORNWALL, **1923**

The new Watson class motor lifeboat *The Brothers* had only been on station for a week or two before she was called to the *s.s. Dubravka* of Dubrovnik which had lost her propeller and was in danger of dragging on to the Runnelstone, one mile south of Gwennap Head, near Land's End, with a worsening strong westerly gale and darkness coming on. The lifeboat took off 27 of the 31 crew, so close to the rocks that the seas were breaking over her. In the event the steamer survived to be towed away. According to Coxswain Frank Blewett the new motor lifeboat approached the *Dubravka* so fast that the crew took fright, thinking she was a whale.

4th JANUARY   CLACTON-ON-SEA, ESSEX, **1894**

The following service report appeared in the Lifeboat Journal of August 1894:

"On the morning of the 4th January, while a whole gale was blowing, with a very heavy sea, the Coxswain of the lifeboat saw a vessel stranded on the Buxey Sand. The crew of the lifeboat **Albert Edward** *were summoned and the boat put off to the assistance of the vessel, the masts of which had already fallen over her side. The lifeboat steered for the wreck, and, on nearing her, the crew could be seen clinging to the deckhouse and other*

The lifeboat Albert Edward launching from Clacton Pier. Taken from a postcard in the Gordon Campbell collection.

portions of the vessel, the heavy seas breaking over them. The lifeboat kept to windward, let go her anchor, and slacked away until she came to the end of her cable, but she could not get near the vessel. It was then decided to lift the anchor and drop down again, but it was discovered the anchor had fouled something in the sand and could not be raised. The cable was therefore cut and sail was made, but, on getting to the lee side of the stricken ship, her masts and gear, which were lying alongside, rendered it impossible to get near her in the heavy sea.

"Signs were made to the ship's crew to attach to a rope something which would float, and slack away until it reached the lifeboat, but this attempt to obtain communication was frustrated, for the object veered by the men fouled some of the wreckage.

"The lifeboat then sailed to windward and again making for the vessel threw the grapnel into the rigging. Three of the crew then crawled out on the mast, and a rope was thrown to them to make fast; unfortunately the first man instead of doing so clung to the boat and was dragged into her. The grapnel becoming unhooked, the lifeboat was again driven away, and the other two men crawled back to the ship. Once more the lifeboat men strove to get to the vessel, and having thrown the grapnel on board, were enabled to haul the boat between the spars to the wreck, thereby enabling five men to jump into her. The Master being too much exhausted to do so, a rope was thrown to him and he fastened it around his body. But, as the Coxswain was about to lift him into the boat, a heavy sea came and, there being so much ice in the boat, he missed his foothold and was thrown overboard between the wreck and the boat. Fortunately he had hold of one end of the rope attached to the Captain, and was hauled into the boat; he, however, received a severe blow and cut over one of his eyes. The Captain was dragged through the surf by means of the rope and was also taken into the boat.

"The whole of the wrecked crew - seven men in all - having thus been rescued, sail was made, and at 2.30 p.m. the lifeboat arrived at Clacton pier after a fearful journey, the boat and those on board her being covered with ice. The wrecked vessel was the brigantine **St. Alexei**, *of Copenhagen, bound from Valberg for Stranraer with a cargo of wood."*

The King of Denmark awarded a silver medal to Mr. W. Schofield, Coxswain of the lifeboat, and the sum of £10 to the crew of the boat in acknowledgment of their brave services on this occasion.

5th JANUARY   DOUGLAS, ISLE OF MAN, **1847**

On the 28th February 1823, Sir William Hillary published a powerful appeal for the setting up of a national organisation for

saving lives from shipwreck. He had often witnessed, whilst living on the Isle of Man, many harrowing scenes following the loss of vessels and their crews. As a result of his appeal, a general meeting was held at the London Tavern in Bishopsgate, in the City of London, on the 4th March 1824. The outcome was that the National Institution for the Preservation of Life from Shipwreck was founded and established on a permanent basis.

A portrait of the founder of the Institution, Lieut-Col. William Hillary, Bt. The original is held by the RNLI at Poole.

Sir William himself took a very active part in the lifeboat service in the Isle of Man. He was awarded three gold medals for services in lifeboats, as well as an honorary gold medal as Founder of the Institution. He died at Woodville, Douglas, Isle of Man on the 5th January, 1847.

6th JANUARY   RAMSGATE, KENT, **1881**

A service, which exemplifies the tenacity, courage and endurance of lifeboat crews in the days of rowing and sailing boats, began on the 5th January 1881 and ended 26 hours later on the 6th. The service is well described by Jeff Morris, Archivist of the Lifeboat Enthusiasts Society, in his history of Ramsgate station.

At 2.20 a.m. on Wednesday January the 5th 1881, the 1,238 ton barque *Indian Chief* ran aground in extremely heavy seas and a full north-easterly gale, on the Long Sands. She had 29 people on board and was bound for Yokohama from Middlesborough. The lifeboats from Clacton, Harwich, Aldeburgh and Ramsgate were all called out. The *Bradford* left harbour at noon, in-tow of the tug *Vulcan*, after news of the wreck had been brought to Ramsgate by fishing smack. The 12 men on board the *Bradford* were soon soaked to the skin, the men on the tug faring little better, Coxswain Fish later stating that the spray was going clean over the tug's funnel.

After checking with the crew of the Kentish Knock light vessel, the tug and the lifeboat battled on, into the teeth of what was generally agreed by the lifeboat-men to be the worst seas they had ever encountered. It was dark by the time they reached the reported area of the wreck and, although they searched for some hours and burned hand flares, nothing could be seen of a wreck.

The lifeboatmen decided to remain in the area through the night and continue the search at daybreak and this message was passed to the men on the tug. Her Master, Alfred Page, kept the *Vulcan* heading slowly into the heavy seas, maintaining his position by skillful use of his engines, the lifeboat lying astern of the tug, at the end of her towline. The 12 lifeboat-men huddled together, dragging spare sails over themselves for some protection, but it was a desperately long, bitterly cold, wet night for them all. By 1.00 a.m. they were all suffering greatly from the cold and so they had a nip of rum, all that is, except Coxswain Fish, who did not drink. During the night, the violent seas washed away the tug's sponsons and damaged one of her deckhouses, but the crew of 7 gallantly stuck to their task and fortunately, no one was injured.

In the faint grey light of dawn, the lifeboat-men slowly began to stir and looked around for any signs of the wreck. Suddenly young Thomas Cooper shouted *"there she is!"* They all peered through the heavy spray and could just make out a single mast, visible about 3 miles away. Within minutes, the towline had been slipped, the foresail raised and Coxswain Fish was steering the *Bradford* straight towards a seething, boiling mass of white water. The anchor was dropped to windward of the wreck and the lifeboat veered down towards the remains of the *Indian Chief*. Only 12 men remained alive on the wreck and, one by one, they dropped onto the ship's deck, from the mast where they had spent a fearful night. They threw a line to the lifeboat-men, who hauled the *Bradford* close to the wreck. Coxswain Fish was

The survivors from the Indian Chief having been landed ashore by the Ramsgate lifeboat Bradford.

stunned by the sight that greeted them, with the dead bodies of other members of the barque's crew either floating in the water close-by, or lying amongst the debris on the deck. With outstanding skill, he manoeuvred the lifeboat beneath the high stern of the barque and the 12 men dropped down into the arms of the lifeboat-men. The rope was cut, sail was made and Coxswain Fish took the *Bradford* out into deeper water, to the waiting tug, which towed them back to Ramsgate, arriving at 2.00 p.m. on the 6th, 26 hours after they had set out.

Sadly, during the journey back to Ramsgate, one of the men from the *Indian Chief* died, despite all the efforts of the lifeboat-men.

Coxswain Charles Fish was awarded the Institution's gold medal and the 11 members of his crew each received the silver medal. Silver medals were also awarded to the Master, Alfred Page, and the 6 crew of the tug *Vulcan*.

7th JANUARY   LONDON, **1875**

The minutes of the meeting held this day recorded that two models of lifeboats to be presented by the English residents of St. Petersburg to the Duke of Edinburgh and the Grand Duchess Marie of Russia, (on the occasion of their wedding), were shown to the Committee of Management. The models were presented to them at the Annual General Meeting on the 11th May 1875 at the Mansion House. The two lifeboats, *Alfred* and *Marie* were handed to the Russian Shipwreck and Lifeboat Society. The lifeboats, with their carriages and equipment, were built in London and were placed on station, one in the Baltic, the other in the Black Sea.

8th JANUARY   LONDON, **1852**

The Committee of Management decided that all boathouses should be built with doors at each end. This would facilitate the launching and the return of lifeboats on their carriages.

A typical early design of lifeboat house - though it is not known with certainty whether this buidling was fitted with doors at both ends.

9th JANUARY   JERSEY, CHANNEL ISLANDS, **1825**

The French boat *Fanny* of St. Malo was seen to strike on rocks off Jersey in thick, hazy weather. Four gentlemen put off in a boat that was kept for the purpose of helping vessels in danger. In two trips thirteen people were saved from the wreck before it broke into pieces.

The dangerous swell of the sea was so great that a pilot boat, which also arrived on the scene, would not venture through the surf breaking over the *Fanny*. Messrs. Francis, Jean and Philip de St. Croix each received a gold medal: Philip Nicolle received a silver medal.

10th JANUARY   HAYLING ISLAND, HAMPSHIRE, **1920**

In May 1914, a new lifeboat was sent to Hayling Island - the 35ft self-righter *Proctor*, named after its donor, the late William J. Proctor of Newcastle.

The *Proctor* had to wait until 1920 before answering her first service call. On the morning of Saturday, January 10th, a schooner was seen to be dragging her anchors about 3 miles off the entrance to Chichester Harbour, in very heavy seas and a full west-south-westerly gale. The *Proctor* was launched at 10.50 a.m., the boat having to be hauled out through the very heavy surf by using a hauling-off warp. The casualty was the 900-ton *Monte Grande*, of Le Havre, which had been sailing, in ballast, from her homeport to Haiti. At the request of the Master the lifeboat-men stood-by for nearly 5 hours. The Selsey lifeboat was also launched, but returned to her station when further assistance proved unnecessary.

The Hayling Island lifeboat Proctor on her launching carriage is hauled along the sea-front by the horses used to launch her.

As the *Proctor* stood-by, the schooner continued to drag her anchors in the violent seas, becoming dangerously close to the shore. It was then decided to take the crew off the *Monte Grande* while it was still light and so Coxswain Cole took the lifeboat alongside and the crew of 15 was rescued. One of the lifeboatmen injured his hand during the rescue - the lifeboat receiving slight damage. Great skill was required on the part of Coxswain Cole when, as the heavily laden lifeboat entered Chichester Harbour, huge waves repeatedly swept clean over her. However, they crossed the Bar safely and the rescued men were landed. The *Monte Grande* eventually became a total wreck.

The Master of the *Monte Grande* later wrote a letter of thanks to Coxswain Cole and his crew, the letter being published in the local newspaper. The translation reads thus:

TO THE CREW OF THE LIFEBOAT PROCTOR.

Dear Friends,

I could not leave England without offering you my warmest thanks for the notable manner in which you hastened to our assistance. It was thanks to your efforts and in spite of the heavy seas running, that we were able to save the entire crew. Be sure that the men of the Monte Grande will ever remember the brave crew of the Proctor.
Once more, thanking you all and with my best remembrance,

L. Richard.
Captain of the wrecked ship,
Monte Grande.
Chichester, January 18 1920.

11th JANUARY   TYNEMOUTH, NOTHUMBERLAND, 1913

Trials with motor lifeboats had started in 1904, and the first motor lifeboat was stationed at Tynemouth in 1905. The *J. McConnell Hussey*, a 38-foot self-righter was built in 1893 and fitted with a motor in 1904. She was on station there until 1911.

A service that proved the efficiency of motor power occurred at Tynemouth in 1913. The s.s *Dunelm*, of Sunderland was wrecked close to Blyth east pier. Because it was low water it was impossible for the Blyth pulling and sailing lifeboat to reach the

vessel. A telephone message was sent to Tynemouth, 10 miles to the south, asking that their lifeboat be sent to help. The self-righting motor lifeboat *Henry Vernon* set out and reached the wreck one and a quarter hours later. The lifeboat was frequently buried in the seas, working against tremendous difficulties of wind and weather. As reported in the Lifeboat Journal of February 1914, the motor lifeboat *"showed splendid qualities and proved beyond question the value of this type of boat"*.

Captain H.E. Burton, R.E., Honorary Secretary, and Coxswain Robert Smith of Tynemouth were each awarded the Institution's silver medal. Rocket apparatus and a shore boat in fact saved the crew of the *Dunelm*. Coxswain Anthony Nixon of Cambois (Blyth No. 2) station, who had helped in the rescue from shore, also received a silver medal.

12th JANUARY   LYNMOUTH, NORTH DEVON, 1899

The Lifeboat Journal of November 1899 reported the following on the exploits of the Lynmouth lifeboat *Louisa* in January of that year.

Telegrams were received at about 7 p.m. on the 12th January asking for assistance to a vessel showing signals of distress off Gore Point. Almost immediately after the messages had been received the wires were blown down and it was impossible to obtain any further information. A whole gale was blowing from the west-north-west, the weather was thick and the sea so heavy as to render it impossible to launch the lifeboat *Louisa* at Lynmouth. It was therefore decided to take the boat on her carriage by road to Porlock. The course taken was over two of the steepest hills in England, the road rising 1500 feet in two miles. In fact, on parts of the route the lifeboat had to be taken on skids, the carriage being taken through fields (gates and posts having to be pulled down), the road being too narrow for the wheels to pass. The men were obliged sometimes to haul, and at other times to hold the boat back, so that their strength was greatly taxed. The undertaking even in daylight would be beset with danger to life or limb, but on a dark and stormy night, when it was difficult for a man even to stand in exposed places, it was only just possible to accomplish the work. However, in the uncertainty as to the danger of the vessel and in the absence of any other means of getting to her, it was decided to make the attempt. Horses were procured and the crew with 28 helpers started with the lifeboat.

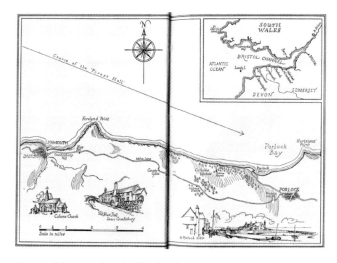

The route of the Lynmouth overland launch on the 12th January 1899. (By kind permission of C. Walter Hodges).

The journey, which occupied ten and a half hours, ended without a casualty, and at six o'clock on the following morning the lifeboat was launched at Porlock and proceeded to the vessel, which proved to be the full-rigged ship *Forrest Hall*. Of and for Liverpool, from Bristol in ballast, 1900 tons register, with a crew of 15 men; she was lying at anchor disabled. It appeared she had been in tow of a steam-tug, and when westward of Ilfracombe the hawser parted and the tug collided with her and disabled the steering gear. Shortly after the arrival of the lifeboat two steam-tugs came up and took the ship in tow, the lifeboat-men assisting to get the anchors up. The lifeboat remained by her, as she was in an unmanageable state owing to the loss of her steering gear, besides which the weather had become very bad. She was ultimately towed to a safe anchorage outside Barry, and the lifeboat crew, who had been without food for twenty-four hours, landed at Barry Dock to obtain refreshment. On the following day they returned to their station, a steamer kindly giving them a tow part of the way, arriving there at 11.30 a.m. The carriage was brought back by road, having covered a distance of twenty-eight miles.

13th JANUARY PORTPATRICK, WIGTOWNSHIRE, **1932**

The 520-ton s.s *Camlough* had left Belfast on the morning of the 12th January bound for Birkenhead. Developing engine trouble off the Isle of Man, the Captain decided to return to Belfast. On the morning of the 13th January a gale blew up, and the *Camlough* was driven towards the Wigtownshire coast. For six hours she was helpless in the gale until sighted by the s.s. *Moyalla*. A tow was established at 11.30 a.m. Six times the tow parted, only to be made fast again.

Answering a distress wireless message received by the Portpatrick coastguard at 8.25 p.m., the Watson class lifeboat *J and W* put out through the notoriously difficult entrance to the harbour, reaching the casualty at about 11.30 p.m. Coxswain Campbell decided to stand by until the steamers were in safe waters. For five hours the seventh tow held, whilst the *Moyalla* made for the comparative safety of Luce Bay. There the tow failed again. The *Camlough* dropped both anchors but they would not hold and the ship was quickly carried towards the rocks. The lifeboat anchored and then dropped down, stern first, to the weather side. A line was fired and a heavy rope then used to haul the lifeboat alongside, enabling the eight crew of the *Camlough* to jump into the lifeboat. This operation took 50 minutes, but so skillfully was she handled that she had not even scratched her paint.

For this service, Coxswain John Campbell was awarded the Institution's bronze medal.

14th JANUARY WEST KIRBY, CHESHIRE, **1991**

West Kirby's D class inflatable took the term Inshore Lifeboat literally on the 14th January 1991, when the crew took her 14 miles by road and through the Mersey Tunnel to rescue a boy and his dog from a park lake in Liverpool.

Thirteen year old Fred Allen and his dog Buster had fallen through ice on the lake, said to be up to 50 feet deep, during the cold spell which swept the country. Although they had struggled ashore on an island, police and firemen could not reach them as the temperature plunged to -4°C. The police contacted the coastguard, who in turn contacted West Kirby's Honorary Secretary. He then set off the pagers to initiate one of the station's more unusual services. At 8.45 p.m., with police escort and blue lights flashing, the lifeboat started her 'passage' to the middle of Liverpool - where it took eight lifeboat-men to lift the

D class over the park railings. With two of the crew using their 'wellies' over the bow as ice-breakers the inflatable finally reached the lad and his dog and ten minutes later had handed them over to the police and ambulance crews.

Although taken to hospital suffering from hypothermia Fred was later allowed home, and with the lifeboat safely back on station at 9.48 p.m. Honorary Secretary Bob Jones told a newspaper:

"This was an unusual call - we're not called an inshore lifeboat for nothing!"

15th JANUARY   HOLY ISLAND, NORTHUMBERLAND, **1922**

At 8 p.m. in a strong south-easterly gale, heavy sea and a snow storm, the trawler *James B. Graham* went ashore on the rocks off False Emmanuel Head on the north side of Holy Island, off the Northumberland coast. The whole village turned out in the dark and snow to launch the lifeboat - it needed 60 helpers, and women waded out waist deep into the sea to help. When the self-righting lifeboat *Lizzie Porter* arrived at the site of the wreck, the trawler was found lying in a perilous position by rocks and iron remnants of an older wreck. An unsuccessful attempt having been made to reach the wreck, Coxswain Cromarty lay off for two hours for the tide to rise, but the next attempt also failed. After another hour, he veered his boat carefully down, took off the nine men and returned to station at 2 a.m. on the 16th.

For this service, Coxswain George Cromarty received the second service clasp to his silver medal, whilst Second Coxswain William Wilson and Bowman Thomas A. Stevenson each received a bronze medal. The lifeboat *Lizzie Porter* is now on display at the RNLI exhibition in the Historic Dockyard at Chatham.

16th JANUARY   GALWAY BAY, CO. GALWAY, **1962**

The Rotterdam coaster s.s *June* ran aground in a gale on the reefs off Mutton Island, near the entrance to Galway docks. At 12.30 p.m., the Watson class lifeboat *Mabel Marion Thompson* put out from Kilronan, 24 miles from the casualty. The coaster was found with a 20° list to port with her bows on a rock but, as the weather was improving, her Master decided not to abandon her.

The lifeboat put into Galway docks but set out again at 7.15 p.m. when the weather deteriorated. She towed with her a small boat and carried an extra man with local knowledge and the owner of the *June*. The gale was now gusting to strong gale with rough seas, hail and rain squalls, and the *June's* crew had taken refuge on Mutton Island. Coxswain Coleman Hernon took the lifeboat as close to the lighthouse landing as possible and Bartley Mullen and Thomas Joyce then brought off six survivors in the small boat. Patrick Quinn replaced Bartley Mullen and several attempts were made to return to the landing. Eventually, after twice being swamped, two other men and a dog were taken off. All survivors were landed at Galway at 11 p.m.

Coxswain Hernon, Assistant Mechanic Mullen and crewmembers Joyce and Quinn each received the bronze medal of the Institution.

17th JANUARY   WHITBY, YORKSHIRE, **1928**

The Whitby self-righting motor lifeboat *Margaret Harker-Smith* was kept busy this day escorting and helping local fishing vessels, a regular feature of its work at this port. First, the motor fishing boats *Irene*, *Faith*, *Diligence*, *Remembrance*, *Lady Kitchener* and *Pilot Me* were escorted into the harbour. Then she was called out to the *Fortuna* and *Guide Me*. Both boats were saved, together with their nine crewmembers.

18th JANUARY   WICK, CAITHNESS-SHIRE, **1958**

At 9.50 on the night of the 18th January 1958, the coastguard informed the Honorary Secretary that a fishing vessel was ashore in Sinclair Bay. At 10.15 p.m. the Watson class lifeboat *City of Edinburgh* was launched in a moderate sea. There was a fresh northerly gale, with heavy snow showers, and it was high water. The lifeboat found the steam trawler *Jean Stephen* of Aberdeen. With a crew of thirteen, her decks were awash and heavy seas were breaking over her.

The lifeboat tried a number of times to come alongside, but without success, so she stood by until the trawler's crew eventually scrambled ashore with the help of the coastguard. On the way back to her station the lifeboat embarked an injured man from the trawler *Strathdee* and landed him at Wick at 4.15 a.m.

ON THE COAST — THE WHITBY LIFEBOAT ON ITS WAY TO ROBIN HOOD'S BAY

The Whitby lifeboat going by road to Robin Hood's Bay on the 19th January 1881. (By kind permission of A.F. Humble).

19th JANUARY   WHITBY, YORKSHIRE, **1881**

This day the Whitby men took part in one of the most outstanding launches in lifeboat history. It had been snowing for days, with a southeasterly gale piling the snow into deep drifts. At 10.30 a.m. on the 19th, a telegram was received by Captain Robert Gibson, Harbour Master at Whitby and Honorary Secretary of the Lifeboat Station, reporting that a ship had sunk off Robin Hood's Bay. It went on to say that her crew had taken to the ship's boat, but had had to drop anchor, as they were unable to land because of the very heavy seas. The wind had veered to northeasterly, churning up an exceptionally heavy sea at Whitby and it was quite impossible to take the lifeboat to Robin Hood's Bay by sea. But undaunted, the Whitby men decided on the only other alternative - take the lifeboat overland and launch it from Robin Hood's Bay. It was over 6 miles to the Bay, the road being very narrow and rising in parts to over 500 feet above sea level. The snow was up to 7 feet deep in places, but Captain Gibson sent a telegram back, saying that they were bringing the lifeboat by road and asking for some men to set out from Robin Hood's Bay to meet them.

About 60 Whitby men were given shovels and they began to clear the snow from the road out of town, the horses were hitched to the carriage and the *Robert Whitworth* set off on her historic journey. More men joined in the snow clearing operation, until over 200 were involved. Additional horses were obtained from farmers along the way, until 18 were hauling the lifeboat and carriage up over the moors. Progress was slow but steady and, eventually, they met up with the men from Robin Hood's Bay. They then began the long and dangerous descent down the steep road into the Bay. As they neared the bottom, there was very little clearance between some of the houses but, just over 2 hours after leaving Whitby, the *Robert Whitworth* arrived at Robin Hood's Bay.

The crew of the lifeboat had worked as hard as anyone to clear the snow, but, despite being very tired, they immediately manned the lifeboat and set off towards the shipwrecked sailors. For over an hour, they struggled desperately to reach the small boat, but when six of the oars and the steering oar were broken by an exceptionally heavy wave, they were forced to return ashore. While the oars were being replaced, Coxswain Freeman called for volunteers to double-bank the oars. So, with 18 men on board, the *Robert Whitworth* was launched for a second time and after battling for an hour and a half, they reached the small boat and rescued the 6 sailors, landing them at 4.00 p.m. The men were from the Whitby brig *Visitor* and they had to be carried ashore and given urgent medical attention, some of them being almost unconscious. The lifeboat-men also suffered greatly and several of them needed medical attention, one man being so exhausted that he was unable to return home for some time. The rest of the Whitby men returned home by road, going back to Robin Hood's bay a few days later when conditions improved to sail the *Robert Whitworth* home.

20th JANUARY   FALMOUTH, CORNWALL, **1940**

At 11.20 a.m. the Coastguard at St. Anthony reported that a vessel was flying a distress signal three miles south-west of St. Anthony. A fresh south-south-east wind was blowing with a nasty swell. The Watson class motor lifeboat *Crawford and Constance Conybeare* launched at 11.35 a.m. She found the tanker *Caroni River* of London, a motor vessel of 8,000 tons, sinking rapidly after striking a mine. She had just left harbour to undergo tests. Twenty-seven of the crew were rescued by the lifeboat, the remainder by a drifter. The lifeboat returned to station at 1.30 p.m.

21st JANUARY   PENLEE, CORNWALL, **1939**

Early in the morning the Belgian trawler *Paul Therese*, of Ostend, broke from her moorings in Newlyn Harbour and drifted out to sea. Her crew of six were asleep and unaware of their danger. A southwesterly gale was blowing, with a rough sea, and the weather was thick. The news was received from the Coastguard, and the Watson class motor lifeboat *W and S* was launched at 4.35 a.m. She found the trawler near the rocks between Penzance and St. Michael's Mount and one of the lifeboat crew boarded her. He roused her crew and the lifeboat towed her out of danger. Her crew then got the engine going and she followed the lifeboat clear. She returned to Newlyn Harbour, and the lifeboat arrived back at her station at 7.15 a.m.

22nd JANUARY   ABERDEEN, ABERDEENSHIRE, **1930**

Returning from a successful fishing trip the 101 ton steam trawler *John G Watson* came too close to shore and became trapped between two sandbanks off the coast to the north of Donmouth. The trawler grounded near the Black Dog, some three miles north of the river mouth and six miles from the port of Aberdeen.

The No.1 Aberdeen Barnett class lifeboat *Emma Constance* left her moorings at 3.00 a.m., making the wreck area half an hour later. The Acting Coxswain, Thomas Walker, (normally the Bowman) thought that it was too dangerous to attempt to take the deep-draught Barnett through heavy breaking seas over the sandbank to reach the trawler. He therefore returned to Aberdeen, and the smaller self-righting No. 2 (pulling) lifeboat *Robert and Ellen Robson* was drawn by tractor overland to a site opposite the wreck. The lifeboat was launched through heavy surf to be tossed about like a cork. At 7.55 a.m. the trawler was reached, a rope thrown and ten crew scrambled into the lifeboat. The return to shore was very quick - at 8.00 a.m. the lifeboat and rescued men were on shore!

According to the station history *'The Lifeline'*, written by Norman Trewren, *"the actual rescue had taken exactly three minutes, and was accomplished with the loss of three blue (port side) oars, two tins of chocolate, and two bottles of rum!"*

23rd JANUARY   ST.IVES, CORNWALL, **1939**

In the early hours of the morning, the Coastguard reported a vessel in a dangerous position about eleven miles from St. Ives, and it was decided to launch the St. Ives motor lifeboat, the 35 ft. self-righter *John and Sarah Eliza Stych* (on temporary duty from Padstow).

Leaving the shelter of St. Ives Head, the lifeboat met mountainous seas, and the Coxswain decided to keep clear of Clodgy Point to the west of St. Ives. Turning to westwards, so facing into the gale, the lifeboat sheered as she came down a sea. The next sea struck her on the starboard bow, and she capsized. She righted almost immediately, but four of her eight crew had been carried away, including the Coxswain. Attempts were made to restart the engine, without success, and the reduced crew could not raise the mast. Drifting eastwards across St. Ives Bay, the lifeboat capsized and righted a second time, but one more crew member was washed away. By this time the lifeboat was fast approaching the rocky shore of Godrevy. Another huge sea hit the lifeboat, and for a third time she capsized. William

Freeman thus found himself alone in the lifeboat, and three minutes later she struck the rocks. Freeman managed to get ashore and reach a nearby farmhouse.

As is typical of this tight-knit lifeboat community, the seven dead men of the crew included the Coxswain, Thomas Cocking, his son John, and son-in-law Richard Stevens: and two brothers Matthew and William Barber.

24th JANUARY   SHOREHAM HARBOUR, SUSSEX, **1944**

About 2.30 p.m., the naval authorities asked, through the Coastguard, for the lifeboat to go to the help of two landing craft about a mile south of Shoreham. A strong southerly wind was blowing, with a rough sea.

The Watson class motor lifeboat *Rosa Woodd and Phyllis Lunn* launched at 2.40 p.m. Meanwhile, one of the vessels the *LBV33* had got into harbour. The *LBV42* fouled the east pier and went ashore on the East Side of the pier. The lifeboat passed a rope to her, towed her off, and brought her into harbour at 3.40 p.m.

25th JANUARY   QUEENSFERRY, LOTHIAN, **1992**

Tiffany, Timothy, Chocolate Drop, Snuffles and Gem were five goats who had got quite used to their lonely existence on the Isle of Inchkeith in the Forth estuary. When the Allandale Animal Sanctuary moved to Lanarkshire from the isle, sanctuary trustee Mrs. Allan had been unable to capture them and was forced to leave them behind to their own devices.

In fact they were so used to it, they didn't want anything to disturb their tranquil existence. And they were quite unaware of Mrs. Allan's growing concern for their safety, particularly after spent cartridges were found on the island from the guns of uninvited guests. The animal sanctuary formed a volunteer group of students to transport the five goats to safety. This day in January, 42 volunteers took the *Spirit of Fife* ferry journey on a mission of 'goat rescue'.

But the goats had seen them coming - and promptly scarpered out of reach. It wasn't long before Snuffles was caught. But two of the five - in desperation - plunged into the sea and swam a short distance to perch precariously on a rock, way out of safety's reach. Predictably, the waves were soon threatening to engulf the goats and drown them - something drastic would have to be done to save them! Following word from the ferry captain, Queensferry's inshore lifeboat launched to the rescue. With one of the goats on board and the other being towed behind the lifeboat, Queensferry's Atlantic 21 transported the two deserters to safety.

Back on the island and with their minds firmly fixed on freedom, the two survivors at once made off again - without a word of thanks.

26th JANUARY   WEST MERSEA, ESSEX, **1990**

West Mersea's Atlantic 21 lifeboat carried out a somewhat unusual rescue on the 26th January when she was called to a taxi stranded on the causeway to a nearby island. Thames coastguard had been alerted after the vehicle broke down on the winding causeway and the driver radioed for help.

The cab's lights were still shining under water which helped locate the casualty, and at 9.10 p.m. the lifeboat arrived alongside. The tide rises rapidly in the estuary in which the car was stranded and there is considerable depth of water over the road at high water. The driver and his passenger had taken to the roof of the vehicle, and water was lapping around their shoes as they were taken aboard the lifeboat. The men were unhurt but suffering from shock.

Writing to the station's Honorary Secretary after the event the Coastguard sector officer praised the way the crew had found their way through the shorter route in the shallows behind the island to reach the men. *"To run aground in that area at that state of tide was the easy part,"* he said, *"to stay afloat was almost impossible - except for West Mersea lifeboat."* In official reports of the service there is a section for the Port of Registry of the casualty - the Honorary Secretary duly completed it: 'DVLC Swansea.'

27th JANUARY   THE MUMBLES, GLAMORGANSHIRE, **1883**

In the early hours of Saturday the 27th January 1883 the north west gale which had been blowing for a day backed to the south west and increased to storm force. Three vessels were lost on the Glamorgan coast: the steamers *Agnes Jack* at Port Eynon and *James Gray* off Porthcawl were lost with all hands, the barque *Admiral Prinz Adalbert* of Danzig dragged ashore on Mumbles Head after the tug *Flying Scud* failed to tow her into Swansea Bay.

The 33 ft. self-righting lifeboat *Wolverhampton* was launched at about 10 a.m. with Coxswain Jenkin Jenkins at the helm. His crew consisted of twelve men including four of his sons, his son-in-law and a nephew. The lifeboat was rowed through the sound and anchored to windward of the wreck. John Williams, the Bowman and a nephew of the Coxswain, veered the boat towards the barque and two of the German crew were taken off by breeches buoy.

As the ship's carpenter was being hauled out, a large sea struck the lifeboat parting her anchor cable and capsizing her. The *Wolverhampton* was now driven towards the outer sound, repeatedly righting and capsizing until all of her crew had been thrown out. Only the two Germans remained aboard clinging below the thwarts.

John Williams was thrown by the next big sea on to the poop of the wreck and escaped with bruising. Coxswain Jenkins dragged himself on to the middle head and his sons Jenkin and George swam into Bob's Cave below the lighthouse. John Thomas and William Rosser clung to the lifelines of the *Wolverhampton* and were dragged from the sea by the combined efforts of Gunner Hutchings (from the lighthouse fort), and Margaret and Jessie Ace, daughters of the lighthouse keeper. The German crew were able to come ashore when the wreck dried, but John and William Jenkins, sons of the Coxswain, William Macnamara, his son-in-law, and William Rogers were drowned. The latter's body was not recovered but the others were buried at the parish church where their gravestones and a memorial window and plaque may be seen. Coxswain Jenkins received the Institution's silver medal and Gunner Hutchings the Thanks of the Institution on Vellum. The Ace sisters received gold brooches from the Empress of Germany.

28th JANUARY — UNITED STATES OF AMERICA, **1915**

The following is an extract from an article in the Lifeboat Journal

of December 1958 by Captain R.L. Mellen, Chief, Public Information Division, United States Coast Guard.

"Maritime safety in the United States took a giant step forward on 28 January 1915, when two historic agencies, the Revenue Cutter Service and Lifesaving Service, were merged into a single organisation know as the United States Coast Guard. Both organisations had long and proud traditions of humanitarian service reaching far back to the early days of the Republic. The Revenue Cutter Service, direct ancestor of the Coast Guard, had been in existence for more than a century and had already achieved a distinguished record both as a fighting force and as a highly versatile law enforcement and maritime safety agency. Similarly, the Lifesaving Service had won itself an honoured place in the affections of the American public for its effective and heroic actions on behalf of distressed vessels and persons at sea.

In approving the merger of the two agencies, President Wilson was putting into effect the principle of 'organisation and combination' developed several years before by President Taft. Prior to that time, the work of maritime safety had been carried out by a number of agencies with considerable duplication of function. The consolidation of the two principal maritime safety organisations, therefore, was designed to eliminate this confused, irrational, and uneconomic pattern. By this action, the resources, facilities and skills of two outstanding safety organisations were fused into a new unit of incomparably greater utility and efficiency. For the United States, the establishment of the new agency was truly the beginning of a modern era in maritime safety".

29th JANUARY — ICELAND, **1928**

The National Lifesaving Association of Iceland (Slysavarnafjelag Iceland) was founded in 1928, and its first lifeboat came from the RNLI. This was the *George and Mary Berrey*, a 35ft self-righter that had been stationed at Banff in Scotland from 1901 to 1924 and then Whitehills from 1924 to 1928. She was renamed the *Porsteinn* and stationed at Sandgeroi.

More recently the 70-ft Clyde class lifeboat *Grace Paterson Ritchie* was sold to Iceland in 1989 and was renamed *Henry H. Halfdanssen*. This lifeboat had been in service at Kirkwall from 1967 until 1988.

30th JANUARY   SOUTH SHIELDS, DURHAM, **1790**

Henry Greathead was a ship's carpenter, born at Richmond, Yorkshire, in 1757. In 1789, he replied to an advertisement from the Gentlemen of the Lawe House. This was a private club at South Shields, who had offered a prize of two guineas for the best model of the kind of boat which might have been of use in saving the crew of the ship *Adventure*. This vessel had been wrecked at the mouth of the Tyne with the loss of all her crew. However, his design was not accepted. Another South Shields man, William Wouldhave, also entered a design which, although considered the best, was awarded only half the prize - one guinea!

Two members of the adjudicating committee continued to experiment, and they subsequently asked Greathead to build a boat based on their ideas. This he did, incorporating modifications of his own and incorporating some of the principles of Wouldhave. The result was the lifeboat named the *Original*. The first service by the *Original* took place on the 30th January 1790, when the crew of a vessel, wrecked on Herd Sand, were rescued. The boat remained in service until 1830.

A lifeboat designed by Henry Greathead at sea during a rescue - note the stricken vessel in the top right corner. Greathead, whose cameo can be seen in the insert, was a ship's carpenter born at Richmond, Yorkshire, in 1757.

31st JANUARY   RAMSGATE & NORTH DEAL, KENT, **1919**

The Ramsgate and North Deal lifeboats combined on a very fine service on the 31st January 1919. The North Deal lifeboat *Charles Dibdin (Civil Service No. 2)* was launched at 10.30 p.m. on the 29th, going to the aid of the s.s. *Piave*, of New Jersey, which had run aground, in rough seas and a blinding snow-storm on the Goodwin Sands. The steamer had a crew of 96, and some of the lifeboat-men boarded the vessel and helped to jettison some of the cargo. But, at 5.30 p.m. on the 31st, a loud crack was heard and it was found that the steamer had broken her back, the vessel then slowly rolling over on to her side.

The Ramsgate lifeboat *Charles and Susanna Stephens* then arrived on the scene, having been called out when extra help was requested. She rescued 23 of the steamer's crew, another 29 being saved by the North Deal lifeboat, the remaining men being able to reach tugs in their own ship's boats. For their gallantry on this occasion, the President of the U.S.A. awarded gold watches to Coxswain William Cooper, of the Ramsgate lifeboat and to Coxswain William Adams, of the North Deal lifeboat. Inscribed binoculars were also awarded to Second Coxswain Thomas Read, of Ramsgate and to the Second Coxswain of the North Deal lifeboat.

The President awarded gold medals to the members of the crew of both lifeboats, similar awards being made to the Master and crew of the tug *Aid*.

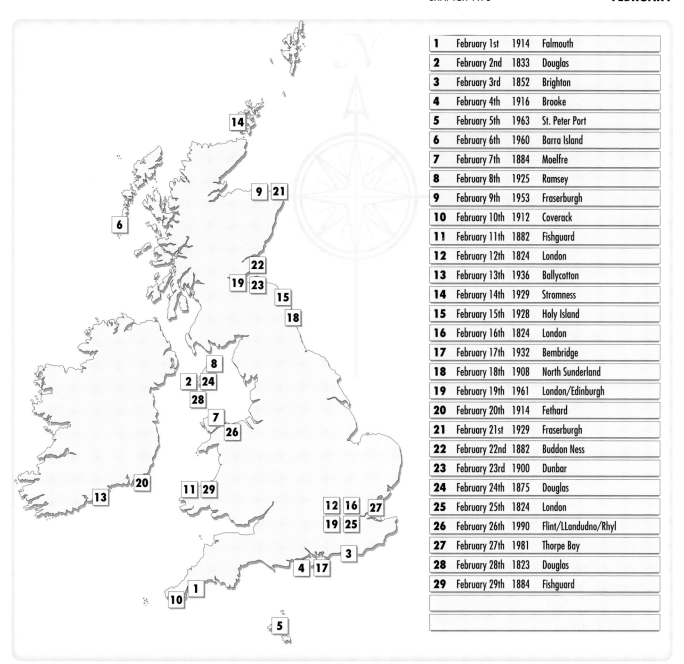

1	February 1st	1914	Falmouth
2	February 2nd	1833	Douglas
3	February 3rd	1852	Brighton
4	February 4th	1916	Brooke
5	February 5th	1963	St. Peter Port
6	February 6th	1960	Barra Island
7	February 7th	1884	Moelfre
8	February 8th	1925	Ramsey
9	February 9th	1953	Fraserburgh
10	February 10th	1912	Coverack
11	February 11th	1882	Fishguard
12	February 12th	1824	London
13	February 13th	1936	Ballycotton
14	February 14th	1929	Stromness
15	February 15th	1928	Holy Island
16	February 16th	1824	London
17	February 17th	1932	Bembridge
18	February 18th	1908	North Sunderland
19	February 19th	1961	London/Edinburgh
20	February 20th	1914	Fethard
21	February 21st	1929	Fraserburgh
22	February 22nd	1882	Buddon Ness
23	February 23rd	1900	Dunbar
24	February 24th	1875	Douglas
25	February 25th	1824	London
26	February 26th	1990	Flint/LLandudno/Rhyl
27	February 27th	1981	Thorpe Bay
28	February 28th	1823	Douglas
29	February 29th	1884	Fishguard

1st FEBRUARY   FALMOUTH, CORNWALL, **1914**

The Falmouth lifeboat *Bob Newbon* rescued five men at about 3 a.m. from the German barque *Hera*, of Hamburg, which was totally wrecked near the Gull Rock when bound from Pisagua, Chile to Falmouth with a cargo of nitrate of soda. As soon as signals of distress were reported immediate steps were taken to despatch the lifeboat, but before she arrived the barque foundered and nineteen of the crew unfortunately perished. The rescued men were taken, with much difficulty, from one of the vessel's spars which remained above water.

Owing to the darkness considerable difficulty was experienced in finding the wreck, and the men saved owed their rescue to the Boatswain, who was lashed to the spar, blowing his whistle. A strong south-south-westerly gale was blowing, with a heavy sea, and the water was thick and cloudy. As soon as the men had been saved and, all hope of picking up any others had been abandoned, the lifeboat was towed back to Falmouth. Here the shipwrecked men were landed in a very exhausted condition.

2nd FEBRUARY   DOUGLAS, ISLE OF MAN, **1833**

On her maiden voyage from Douglas to Liverpool, the 500-ton ship *Parkfield* ('the largest and finest vessel ever built in the Isle of Man') suddenly encountered a storm when ten miles out. Her ballast of large paving stones shifted, at one time bringing the ship on her beam-ends. The Captain decided to return to Douglas Bay, reaching there shortly after midnight. There the ship struck on St. Mary's Rock - site of the then recently completed Tower of Refuge. She let go of her anchors but, in half an hour, was driven on to the Black Rocks. The plight of the ship was seen from the shore and Sir William Hillary was informed. As soon as a crew could be mustered, he sent off 'the lesser lifeboat' following himself shortly after in 'the larger lifeboat'. Waiting for high tide, the entire complement of 60 crew and passengers (including women) were taken off and landed at the pier before sunrise. All this without the loss of a single life. Sir William commended the services of the Coxswain, Isaac Vondy, who was exceptionally awarded a silver medal and a silver boat.

Sir William himself had frequently been off in the Douglas lifeboats and is credited with saving over 300 lives. This was his last active service in a lifeboat.

The Tower of Refuge had been built in 1832 at a cost of £250 - of which more than a quarter had been given by Sir William. He had proposed the building of the Tower and he laid the foundation stone.

3rd FEBRUARY 1852   BRIGHTON, SUSSEX, **1852**

The Lifeboat Journal of March 1852 reported on the trial of a lifeboat designed by James Peake, Assistant Master Shipwright at Woolwich Dockyard. The trial took place at Brighton in a strong south-west breeze. The Duke of Northumberland, President, Mr. Thomas Wilson, Chairman, and the various other officials attended.

"This boat has both ends alike, a long flat floor, sides straight in a fore-and-aft direction, slightly raking stem and stern-post, is diagonally built of rock elm, and copper-fastened. Length, extreme 30 feet; length of keel, 24 feet; breadth of beam, 8 feet;

A lifeboat design by Mr. James Peake, Woolwich, that appeared in the Lifeboat Journal in 1901.

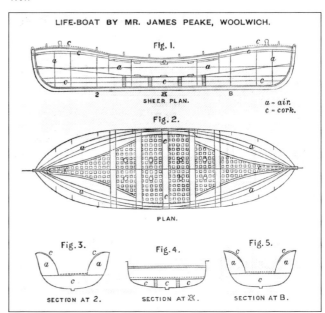

depth, 3¹/₂ feet; sheer of gunwale, 28 inches; rake of stem and stern post, 6¹/₂ inches in a foot; straight keel, 4 inches deep; and bilge pieces with openings in them to lay hold on each side of the bottom. The boat pulls 10 oars, double banked, (or 12 if required,) with eyebolts, (not thole pins,) and rope grummets, and steers with a sweep oar. She has side air-cases under the thwarts, and raised air-cases 4 feet long in the extremes, up to gunwale height; the tops covered with a good coating of cork to prevent their being stove, if jumped upon.

"The air-cases are built of the material patented by Mr. J.T.Forster, R.N., consisting gutta-percha between two layers of thin wood, at once light, tough and watertight. But as most of the so-called air-tight cases admit water, a small disc valve, the invention of Mr. George Wells, of 15, Upper Smithfield, has been introduced into each of the cases. This is so that any water that gets in may be run out, and the cases be aired, which will tend much to their preservation. The means provided for freeing the boat of any water she may ship, are 8 tubes, 6 inches diameter each, through the deck and bottom; closed by self-acting valves. For ballast, and to assist her in righting, the boat has an iron keel of about 7 cwt., and with this included, weighs 46 cwt. Draft of water when light, 15 inches, with crew on board, 18 inches.

The results of the trial showed:
1st. That the boat having been hove keel up by a crane, righted herself on two occasions in about 7 seconds of time.
2nd. That she freed herself of water entirely when light, in about 55 seconds.
3rd. That on taking the beach through heavy rollers, the boat showed great buoyancy and stability, and brought her crew on shore without shipping water.
4th. That she will carry 30 persons with ease besides her crew, or 42 in all."

The boat on her trial was manned by coastguard men, of the Brighton District, and was under the charge of Commander Ward, R.N., Inspector of Lifeboats, who volunteered his services to go out in her.

4th FEBRUARY   BROOKE, ISLE OF WIGHT, **1916**

In a south-westerly gale, the Norwegian barque *Souvenir* of Trevisand was wrecked to the south-east of Brooke, Isle of Wight.

She had already become derelict and unmanageable in the violent gale off St. Catherine's and drifted through the darkness. Eventually she stranded hard and fast on the Great Stag Ledge in an area of comparatively shallow water studded with rocks.

The self-righting lifeboat *Susan Ashley* launched just before 8.30 a.m., but was unable to get alongside the wreck. The barque's crew therefore donned lifebelts and jumped into the sea. Although they were carried in different directions, the lifeboat succeeded in picking up the nine crew members, although the steward died shortly afterwards from exhaustion. The Master refused to leave his ship and stayed in his cabin. The vessel broke up before the lifeboat could return to try to save him, and his body was recovered the next day. Coxswain Benjamin Jacobs was awarded the Institution's silver medal for this service.

5th FEBRUARY   ST PETER PORT, GUERNSEY, **1963**

The relief lifeboat ON912 Euphrosyne Kendal photographed at Exmouth on the 20th September 1978.

The Barnett class lifeboat *Euphrosyne Kendal* left her moorings in St. Peter Port at 3.45 p.m. on the 5th February in a near gale from the south, rough seas and overcast weather. The 1,995-ton Norwegian m.v. *Johan Collett*, 14 miles west-north-west of Les Hanois lighthouse at the southwest corner of Guernsey, in passage from Tunis to Ghent, Belgium, was in difficulty; her cargo of zinc concentrates had shifted. Fourteen of her crew had been transferred, and a South African frigate was standing by. When the lifeboat reached her at 6.30 p.m. they found the motor vessel lying stopped, beam on to the wind and waiting for a tug. In four runs, Coxswain Petit took off the Chief Engineer and two apprentices before the tug arrived. After the tow had been connected and the wind force had risen to Beaufort strength ten, the Coxswain made six more runs and saved the remaining six men. All survivors were landed at St. Peter Port at 6.45 a.m. on the 6th February.

For this service, Coxswain Hubert Ernest Petit received the Institution's gold medal: Mechanic Eric Clifford Pattimore and crew member John Hubert Petit (son of the Coxswain) each received the bronze medal.

6th FEBRUARY   BARRA ISLAND, OUTER HEBRIDES, **1960**

In the sparsely inhabited parts where lifeboats are stationed, particularly on the west coasts of Scotland and Ireland, it is not uncommon for lifeboats to act as floating ambulances, especially when conditions at sea are too bad to prevent other boats from being used. Twice in three days in February 1960 the Barra Island lifeboat *R.A. Colby Cubbin No. 3* was launched to convey people to hospital. On the first occasion, on the 5th February, the lifeboat put out at 11.10 at night. The sea was calm at the time and there were only light variable airs. The patient to be transported was an expectant mother, and the woman's husband and a nurse accompanied her. The birth occurred sooner than had been expected and the baby was actually born on board the lifeboat. So far as is known, this is the first occasion on which a birth has actually occurred in a lifeboat. The birth was successful, and the mother and child were taken to hospital when the lifeboat reached South Uist. The lifeboat then returned to her station, arriving at six o'clock in the morning.

Rather more than twenty-four hours later, at 12.45 early on the morning of the 7th February, the same lifeboat put out, to take an elderly man suffering from a strangulated hernia to hospital. He too was landed successfully, and the lifeboat returned to her station at seven o'clock in the morning.

7th FEBRUARY   MOELFRE, ANGLESEY, **1884**

The minutes of the meeting of the Committee of Management, held on the 7th February 1884, confirmed the award of the silver

medal to Coxswain Rowland Hughes of Moelfre. It stated that he *"at the advanced age of eighty-two years, was retiring from the post after 34 years' service, having assisted to save forty-nine lives"*. In that period he served in three successive lifeboats and services to 17 wrecks, among them being incidents involving the brig *Carrs* and the schooner *Emma* (1852), the schooner *Douglas Pennant* (1868), the schooner *John* (1876) and the smack *Frens* (1883).

Coxswain Hughes received his medal from the Princess of Wales at Marlborough House on 3 March. The Prince of Wales (later King Edward VII), President of the RNLI, was also present. Coxswains now retire at age 55.

8th FEBRUARY   RAMSEY, ISLE OF MAN, **1925**

The Lifeboat Journal of May 1925 reported the following life-saving service at Ramsey:

"On Sunday morning, 8th February, the Ramsey lifeboat went out to a ketch which was seen to be flying signals of distress a little way outside the harbour. A strong breeze was blowing, but the sea was smooth and the weather fine. The ketch was found to be the Amis Reunis, of Falmouth, manned by a family crew, which consisted of the father and mother, a daughter of nineteen, and two sons of seventeen and fifteen. With them was a goose.

"The ketch was bound from Killough, in Northern Ireland, to Portmadoc, in Wales, with potatoes. She had had a terrible night in a southwesterly gale, had been compelled to run back to Ramsey for shelter from ten miles off Holyhead, and was making water very fast. The lifeboat brought her and her crew into harbour".

So much for the actual service! The more domestic side of the story is best told in the following account which has been received from Ramsey:

"It appears that the skipper of the ketch was a Dutchman, who was married to a Welshwoman, and the whole family spoke Welsh. They had bought a goose for their dinner, but, running into very heavy weather, all their thoughts of a meal passed away, and the whole family was occupied in pumping operations, so much so that, practically, they were rescued at their last gasp

The crew of the Amis Reunis rescued, goose and all, on the 8th February 1925 by the Ramsey lifeboat on the Isle of Man.

(including the goose). Subsequently, as you are aware, the ketch itself was brought in. The unhappy experiences of the whole family, including the goose, were such that, instead of the latter being used for the purposes of sustaining life, it has become a family pet, and now plays the part of a faithful watch-dog."

If it were the practice of the Institution to include geese in the record of lives saved, we might very justly claim this goose as having been saved twice.

9th FEBRUARY — FRASERBURGH, ABERDEENSHIRE, **1953**

The Watson class motor lifeboat *John and Charles Kennedy* launched at about 1 p.m. to escort local fishing boats into the harbour as there was a very heavy swell breaking across the harbour mouth. Having seen two vessels safely into port, the lifeboat went out a third time only to find its help not needed. Putting about to return to harbour, the lifeboat was travelling at full speed just off the end of the north pier when a very heavy swell lifted her stern and broke alongside her amidships. Shortly after, a second and even bigger swell reared up astern. It broke right aboard her. It filled the cockpit and flung the six crew men under the canopy and against the engine controls. Coxswain Andrew Ritchie was thrown clear of the boat but was struck on the head by a piece of wreckage and drowned.

Of the six men trapped under the canopy, only Second Coxswain C.G. Tait escaped, being washed up alive on the rocks to the south of the harbour. The Institution pensioned the six widows, as if the men had been servicemen killed in action, with allowances for six children under the age of 16. It gave £500 to the Provost of Fraserburgh's fund for the dependents.

10th FEBRUARY — COVERACK, CORNWALL, **1912**

The four-masted barque *Pindos* of Hamburg, with a crew of 28, went ashore at Mear Point, to the south west of Coverack, in a whole gale. The Liverpool class lifeboat *Constance Mélanie* had launched at 9.45 p.m. shortly before the barque was wrecked.

Seas were breaking over the barque, and the first four men were taken off before lines between the lifeboat and the *Pindos* broke. Because of the darkness, it was decided to cease operations until daylight. In the meanwhile, however, a powerful new acetylene lamp, recently supplied to the station by the Institution, was carried to the scene and enabled the rescue to proceed. An endless whip was formed by lines and a life-buoy bent on. By this means, the remaining 24 men on the *Pindos* were brought into the lifeboat.

Coxswain John Corin received the Institution's silver medal. The German government sent a pecuniary reward to each of the lifeboat crew.

11th FEBRUARY — FISHGUARD, PEMBROKESHIRE, **1882**

A small screw steamer and a schooner had been at anchor in Fishguard roadstead for some days. They had been unable to go round St. David's Head owing to the strong westerly winds. On the night of the 10th February the wind suddenly shifted to north-north-east, and blew a strong gale with a heavy sea. As the two vessels were in bad anchorage, and riding heavily, a good look out was kept, and soon after 11 o'clock on the following morning they exhibited signals of distress.

The Fishguard No. 2 lifeboat *Helen of Foxley* went to the steamer, which proved to be the *Udea* of Llanelly, bound from Ayr to Llanelly with a cargo of pig-iron, and took off her crew of ten men. She then proceeded to the schooner, the *George and Mary*, of Barrow, bound from Ardrossen to Newport with pig-iron, which had parted both chains and had drifted on Goodwick Sands. A tremendous sea was washing over her, and tossing her about fearfully, so that it was with the utmost difficulty that her crew of five men were taken off; but happily all were saved. The schooner became a total wreck.

12th FEBRUARY   LONDON, **1824**

A preliminary meeting to discuss the setting up of a National Shipwreck Society, as proposed by Sir William Hillary, was held at the City of London Tavern, Bishopsgate, in the City. Eighteen persons attended, including Sir William. Thomas Wilson, M.P. for the City of London, took the chair. It was resolved that a meeting of 'the Nobility, Gentry and Merchants, Traders and others' be held on the 25th February *at 12 o'clock for 1 precisely'*, or on such other convenient day.

A provisional Committee of 20 was formed. The Chairman was requested to approach the Earl of Liverpool, the Prime Minister, to be President. King George IV was to be asked to be Patron and seven royal dukes to be Vice Patrons.

13th FEBRUARY   BALLYCOTTON, CO. CORK, **1936**

In a south easterly gale, verging on hurricane force, the Daunt Rock lightship, with eight men aboard, broke her moorings and, early on the 11th was reported drifting towards Ballycotton, Co. Cork. In intolerable conditions, Coxswain Sliney took out the Barnett class motor lifeboat *Mary Stanford*. The morning was spent searching, and the lightship was found at noon with two ships standing by her. One of the vessels left, but the lifeboat stood by for three hours before returning to Cobh. The other ship, the destroyer, H.M.S. *Tenedos*, remained all night but, when the lifeboat returned early on the 12th, she left the scene. The lifeboat then stood by for 25 hours. After refuelling at Cobh early on the 13th, the lifeboat returned to find the Irish Lights vessel *Isolda* present. At 8 p.m. a huge wave carried away one of the lightship's warning lights. The vessel was drifting towards Daunt Rock and, at 9.30 p.m., with the Rock only 60 yards away, Coxswain Sliney commenced the rescue.

With seas sweeping over the casualty, which was plunging

The Ballycotton lifeboat standing by the Daunt Rock Lightship.

After seventy-six arduous hours the Ballycotton crew return to dry land. Left to right are: M.C. Walsh; Motor Mechanic T. Sliney; Second Coxswain J.L. Walsh; J.S. Sliney; Coxswain Patrick Sliney; T.D. Walsh and, lastly, W. Sliney.

wildly, he took his boat alongside more than a dozen times. Six of the crew jumped into the boat, but two had to be dragged off as they were transfixed with fear. The lifeboat returned to Cobh after being away for 76 hours, on service for 63 hours and at sea for 49 hours. The crew had been without food for 25 hours, and had sustained salt-water burns and other injuries.

Coxswain Patrick Sliney was awarded the Institution's gold

medal: Second Coxswain John Lane Walsh and Motor Mechanic Thomas Sliney, the Coxswain's brother, received the silver medal. The four other crew members each received the bronze medal, including William Sliney, son of the Coxswain.

14th FEBRUARY   STROMNESS, ORKNEY, **1929**

The Barnett class lifeboat *J.J.K.S.W.* left Stromness harbour, at 4.35 a.m. in a strong south-westerly breeze over a heavy sea and in bitterly cold weather. The Grimsby trawler *Carmania II* had gone ashore on Kirk Rocks in Hoy Sound, out of range of rocket apparatus. There was no hope of reaching her from seaward with seas breaking up to 150 yards before they reached her. Also the water was too shallow until the tide rose. After waiting for three hours, the lifeboat managed to get two lines on board the wreck, and five men were brought off. Then in spite of the lifeboat being swept by heavy seas, the remaining seven men were saved. Coxswain Johnston withdrew with great skill, landing everybody after a five hour service.

For this service, Coxswain William Johnston received a second service clasp to the Institution's bronze medal which he was awarded in 1922.

15th FEBRUARY   HOLY ISLAND, NORTHUMBERLAND, **1928**

The Holy Island Watson class motor lifeboat *Milburn* was on service between 11.45 a.m. to 7 p.m. helping fishing boats in difficulties in a south-westerly whole gale with very heavy seas. Firstly two men were rescued from the motor fishing yawl *Nellie* of Holy Island which was in trouble 3 miles east of the harbour. Then three yawls from Seahouses were reported in trouble 1$^1/_2$ miles east-south-east of the Longstone light. In all, eleven crew were saved from the *Water Lily*, *Blossom* and *Marquis of Lossie*.

16th FEBRUARY   LONDON, **1824**

A further meeting of the provisional committee (see 12th February) was held to consider the resolutions to be proposed at the General meeting now to be held on the 4th March. The first resolution would propose the formation of *"a National Institution (to be supported by voluntary donations and annual subscriptions)"*. Other resolutions suggested included one that *"the subjects of all nations be equally object of the Institution, as well in War as in Peace"*.

17th FEBRUARY   BEMBRIDGE, ISLE OF WIGHT, **1932**

An unusual service by the Bembridge lifeboat was reported in the June 1932 Lifeboat Journal:

"Shortly after 9.30 a.m. on 17 February, the Coastguard telephoned that a seaplane had made a forced descent at sea, about a mile east of Foreland Lookout. Signals for help were also seen. The motor lifeboat **Langham** *was launched into a fresh easterly wind with a moderate sea. She found that the seaplane was a Government machine, S.1502 carrying out experiments, and that she had been damaged and disabled when she alighted.*

"Three men were on board her, and the pilot asked the lifeboat to tow her out of broken water. With the machine in tow the lifeboat made for Lee-on-Solent. Air Force launches met her, but the pilot declined to change his tow, as he feared it would be dangerous owing to the damaged state of the seaplane. The Commanding Officer at Lee-on-Solent thanked the lifeboat crew. He also sent a letter of thanks".

The *Langham* served at Bembridge from 1922 to 1939. In all she launched from there 61 times, saving 62 lives. She was then placed in the reserve fleet, launching a further 35 times and saving 38 lives. The lifeboat was paid for from the legacy of Mr. T.G. Langham *'of London and Great Wigston, Leicester'.*

18th FEBRUARY   NORTH SUNDERLAND, NORTHUMBERLAND, **1908**

The following service was reported in the Lifeboat Journal of August 1908:

"The steamer **Geir**, *of Bergen, whilst bound for Blyth in ballast, stranded on the Knavestone Rock, Farne Islands, on the night of the 18th February, during a northerly gale and heavy sea. Information reached the North Sunderland Lifeboat Station about 7.00 p.m., and within a few minutes the lifeboat* **Forster Fawcett** *was launched.*

The ON.557 Forster Fawcett. This 35ft, 10-oared self-righting lifeboat was on station at North Sunderland from 1906 to 1925

"On arriving at the scene of the wreck, it was necessary for the lifeboat to use the greatest caution in approaching her, on account of the exceedingly dangerous nature of the locality. Even in fine weather the sea is heavy there, and the tide and current are very strong. To go alongside the steamer to rescue the crew was not possible. The Coxswain, James Robson, therefore, after fully considering the matter, decided to land on an adjoining small rock, taking a life-buoy with him. When he had safely accomplished this, the lifeboat was pulled out into a safer position. By means of lines, the crew of the steamer, fourteen in number, got to the rock on which the Coxswain stood, and then, placing themselves in the life-buoy, they were one by one hauled through the sea to the lifeboat, the Coxswain being the last man to go aboard. The conduct of the Coxswain who was only twenty-eight years of age, in acting in the manner he did, was both gallant and praiseworthy, and a large number of people who awaited the lifeboat's return, loudly cheered the crew when she entered the harbour about 11 p.m."

The Committee of Management, in recognition of the gallant conduct and zeal displayed by the Coxswain, awarded him the silver medal of the Institution. The Chairman of the local committee made the presentation publicly, about a month later. On the same occasion a framed certificate of service was presented to Michael Robson, his father, who had recently relinquished the post of Coxswain Superintendent in favour of his son following many years of faithful service. The King of Norway also presented Coxswain Robson with a silver medal. The station has recently been renamed Seahouses.

19th FEBRUARY   LONDON & EDINBURGH, **1961**

On Sunday the 19th February 1961, the BBC broadcast the first television appeal on behalf of the RNLI. Mr Wynford Vaughan Thomas made the appeal to viewers in England, Wales and Northern Ireland. In Scotland, the appeal was made by the Reverend James Wood.

The September 1961 Journal reported the results of the appeals.

The response to Mr Wynford Vaughan Thomas was £3,496. 11s. 8d, whilst in Scotland the sum of £736. 19s. 8d. was donated - a total of £4,233. 11s. 4d.

20th FEBRUARY   FETHARD, CO. WEXFORD, **1914**

During a south-south-west gale and strong tide, the Norwegian schooner *Mexico*, bound from South America to Liverpool with a cargo of mahogany logs, lost her bearings and drove into Bannow Bay, Co. Wexford. There she struck on South Keeragh Island. About 3 p.m. on the 20th, the Fethard self-righting lifeboat *Helen Blake* put off to her assistance. Within 50 yards of the schooner, the lifeboat was struck by a heavy breaker and filled to the thwarts. The anchor was let go, but before it could bring her up three or four following seas struck her and hurled her against the rocks, where the lifeboat was smashed to pieces. Of the 14-man crew, nine were washed away and drowned. The five survivors managed to scramble on to the island and, by means of rope helped eight of the *Mexico's* crew on to the island. Two other men from the *Mexico* had got away in a ship's boat and were washed ashore.

As soon as news of the disaster reached London, Commander Thomas Holmes, the Chief Inspector of Lifeboats, was ordered to Fethard, and arrived there at 3 p.m. on Sunday the 22nd. In the meantime the lifeboats from Wexford, Kilmore and Dunmore East had made unsuccessful attempts to rescue the survivors. Shortly after his arrival, Commander Holman led another unsuccessful attempt in the Dunmore East boat. At 6 a.m. on Monday the 23rd, they set out again, came close to the island and got a line ashore by rocket. Two men were then dragged through the water to the lifeboat. The Wexford lifeboat arrived on the scene about 8.15 a.m., and two of her crew, James Wickham and William Duggan, volunteered to go off in a strong punt which they veered down on to the rocks. In five trips, bringing two men at each time, they brought off the remaining survivors. During the second trip the punt was holed on the rocks which the men stopped with a loaf of bread and some packaging. The two lifeboats were then taken in tow by a tug, which had originally brought out the Wexford lifeboat, and returned the men and boats to their various stations.

During the whole time the survivors were on the island all they had to eat was two small tins of preserved meat and a few limpets. Their only drink was a small quantity of brandy and half a pint of wine, which the Captain of the *Mexico* had taken with him. With no shelter, they were exposed to a biting wind and were drenched by rain and spray. One of the *Mexico* crew, a Portuguese sailor, died from exposure.

Silver medals were awarded by the Institution to Commander Holmes, Coxswain Edward Wickham, William Duggan and James Wickham of the Wexford lifeboat and Coxswain Walter Power of Dunmore.

21st FEBRUARY   FRASERBURGH, ABERDEENSHIRE, **1929**

Awards for gallantry are normally awarded within a reasonable period after the service concerned. In the early days of the Institution, when the Committee meetings were held more frequently, some medals were awarded very promptly. In two cases, medals were voted only two days after the event. A service at Padstow, on the 2nd April 1872, was reported to the Wreck and Reward Committee on the 4th April. A medal was recommended. The Committee of Management, on the same day, confirmed this. Medals for services at Ramsey on the 7th and 11th November 1890 were awarded on the 13th November.

Whilst some services require deeper consideration before awards are recommended, the long gap between a service in January 1912 and the award of a medal on the 21st February 1929 is exceptional. The Honorary Secretary, because of a serious illness, did not report the full circumstances of a service by the Fraserburgh lifeboat at the time. The matter was brought to the attention of the RNLI Secretary during a visit in 1928. This resulted in the belated award of a silver medal to Coxswain James Sim for helping to save seven crew from the Dundee trawler *Clio*.

22nd FEBRUARY   BUDDON NESS, ANGUS, **1882**

Before the advent of wireless and telephone, other means of communication were used, as indicated by this report in the Lifeboat Journal of May 1882:

"At about 11 a.m. signal guns were fired from the lightship, indicating that a vessel was ashore on the South bank at the

mouth of the Tay, or in imminent danger. The Buddon Ness lifeboat **May** *proceeded to the spot as soon as possible, and found a schooner ashore on the elbow end of the sands. The wind was blowing a strong gale from the northeast, with a heavy sea. The lifeboat, with difficulty, after breaking two oars in the attempt, and besides losing a grapnel, succeeded in getting alongside the vessel. This proved to be the schooner* **Oscar**, *of Leith, bound from Dundee to St. Felin de Guixols, in Spain, with a cargo of yarns. She had on board a crew of six men and a pilot, all of whom were taken into the lifeboat and safely landed. The sea was breaking over the vessel, and by the time the lifeboat left her she was full of water, and soon became a total wreck".*

23rd FEBRUARY   DUNBAR, EAST LOTHIAN, **1900**

The 34ft self-righting lifeboat *Sarah Pickard* was on station at Dunbar from 1893 to 1901, during which time she launched only 8 times, saving 24 lives.

The November 1900 Lifeboat Journal described the service in which those 24 lives were saved.

"While a moderate easterly gale was blowing, accompanied by a heavy sea and thick weather, intelligence was on the morning of the 23 February received that a large vessel was stranded on the Chapel rocks, at Skateraw Point, between Dunbar and Cockburnspath. She was subsequently ascertained to be the four masted barque **Ecclefechan**, *bound from Calcutta for Dundee with a cargo of jute. The Dunbar and Thorntonloch Life-saving Brigades proceeded to the rescue, but the vessel was too far distant from the shore to allow communication being made by means of their apparatus, all the rockets fired falling short.*

"The Dunbar lifeboat **Sarah Pickard** *was therefore launched at 9.45 a.m. and in two trips rescued twenty-four of the crew. The captain and three of the crew declined to leave the ship in spite of repeated warnings from the Assistant Coxswain, who was in command of the boat in the absence of the Coxswain, but they were afterwards taken off by a steam tug, the vessel becoming a total wreck. On the first trip fourteen men were taken into the lifeboat and were landed at Skateraw harbour. On the second occasion ten men were rescued and landed at Dunbar, the arrival of the lifeboat being greetd by loud cheers from a large number of people who had assembled to witness the proceedings."*

24th FEBRUARY   DOUGLAS, ISLE OF MAN, **1875**

Reading the reports of services in the early magazines, some of the phrases used are quite picturesque. For instance, a service was reported at Douglas, Isle of Man, on the 24th February 1875 when the lifeboat *John Turner-Turner* put off to the assistance of the smack *Britannia* which was riding very heavily in a dangerous position in Douglas Bay during a gale. As the smack was in peril of breaking her moorings, the smack's three crew *"availed themselves of the services of the lifeboat and were brought safely ashore"*. Rather like waiting for a No. 11 bus!

25th FEBRUARY   LONDON, **1824**

Lionel Lukin was a London coachbuilder, but he also experimented in finding ways in which he might increase the safety of boats.

On the 2nd November 1785 he patented an *'unimmergible boat'* which incorporated buoyancy gunwales to the sides and watertight bulkheads within. In 1786 he converted a coble for Bamburgh, Northumberland, which was therefore probably the first place to have a craft specifically adapted for the task of saving life at sea.

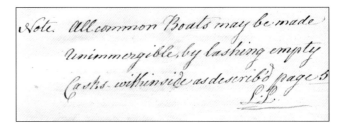

The handwriting of the London coach-builder Lionel Lukin with one very important notation.

When he saw the notice in the Morning Herald of the meeting to form the Institution, he immediately wrote to Mr. Wilson from Southampton, sending him a copy of his own pamphlet of 1807. This is still in the RNLI archives, and the final page is marked in his own hand; *"Note - all common boats may be made unimmergible by lashing empty casks within as describ'd page 5. L.L."*

26th FEBRUARY LLANDUDNO, RHYL AND FLINT, **NORTH WALES, 1990**

Severe flooding hit North Wales in late February, and the lifeboats and personnel from Llandudno, Rhyl and Flint were in operation from the 26th February to the 1st March. Working in difficult, dangerous and extremely un-comfortable conditions they helped some 580 people and countless pets to safety after the failure of the sea wall at Towyn in hurricane force onshore winds and exceptionally high tides. Many of those evacuated were elderly, sick or disabled, and all had to be taken by lifeboat or by Llandudno's tractor or Flint's Land Rover to a place of safety.

From the first alert in the late morning of the 26th February until the highest tides had passed nearly five days later, virtually every lifeboatman and helper in the area was involved, some spending up to 19 hours a day in the floodwater.

27th FEBRUARY
THORPE BAY, ESSEX, **1981**

While sailing his 11ft 6in Laser dinghy off Thorpe Bay Yacht Club at 3.55 p.m. on Friday February 27th, 1981, 16 year old Carl Palmby saw someone on the beach waving to alert him to a casualty. He immediately headed for the position indicated to try to help.

Seeing an overturned 8ft rowing dinghy with someone clinging to it, Carl gibed and made for the capsized boat. As he approached he shouted to the man in the icy water, a fisherman, to let go of the dinghy and come aboard the Laser on her starboard side. The man was too cold and exhausted to help himself, so Carl tried to lift him on board. Before he could pull the fisherman in, the Laser capsized throwing them both into the water.

AN APPEAL

TO THE

BRITISH NATION,

ON THE

HUMANITY AND POLICY

OF FORMING

A National Institution,

FOR THE PRESERVATION OF

LIVES AND PROPERTY FROM SHIPWRECK.

BY SIR WILLIAM HILLARY, BART.

LONDON:
PRINTED FOR G. AND W. B. WHITTAKER,
AVE-MARIA-LANE.
1823.

Carl immediately righted the boat, grabbed the fisherman again and pulled him aboard over the stern. He then tried to tack into the beach but, with the survivor on board, there was not enough room in the little single-handed racing dinghy for the helmsman to be able to sail his boat effectively and no ground could be made. He therefore waved his lifejacket to people on the beach to indicate that further help was needed, then sat with the survivor, taking care of him.

At 4.15 p.m. Southend-on-Sea lifeboat station was alerted. The station's Atlantic 21 rigid inflatable lifeboat launched at 4.19 p.m. The Laser was quickly reached and the fisherman transferred to the lifeboat but, because of his condition, helicopter assistance was requested. He was lifted off at 4.22 p.m. by a helicopter from RAF Manston and taken to Southend Hospital. Carl Palmby sailed back to Thorpe Bay Yacht Club and the lifeboat returned to station. For this service Carl J. Palmby was awarded the Thanks of the Institution on Vellum together with an inscribed wristwatch.

28th FEBRUARY
DOUGLAS, ISLE OF MAN, **1823**

Sir William Hillary's pamphlet entitled *"An Appeal to the British Nation on the Humanity and Policy of forming a National Institution for the Preservation of Lives and Property from Shipwreck"* was published in Douglas on the 28th February 1823.

The pamphlet set out Sir William's ideas on the purpose and organisation of such an institution. He proposed, inter alia, central committees to manage the organisation and raise funds, with local committees to help maintain and crew lifeboats.

It says much for the farsightedness of the author that the majority of his proposals were adopted and retained as permanent features of the RNLI.

29th FEBRUARY   FISHGUARD, PEMBROKESHIRE, **1884**

Early in the morning, during a fresh gale from the southeast and a rough sea, the coastguard watchman at Fishguard reported that a vessel was burning signals of distress in the roadstead. The Coxswain of the lifeboat immediately assembled his crew, who launched the No. 1 lifeboat, *Sir Edward Perrott*, and found that the signals were shown by the smack *Rapid*, of and for Cardigan, from Milford, with a cargo of culm (coal-dust).

She had entered the roadstead under close reef canvas, and anchored about half a mile to windward of the smack *Topaz*. Both her anchors were let go, and all possible chain was given, but she drove right across the bows of the *Topaz*, and coming in contact with that vessel's chain, the *Rapid* started her rudder case, and began to leak badly. After getting clear, it was found impossible to keep her afloat. Her crew of three men were therefore taken into the lifeboat and safely landed, the vessel soon afterwards going down.

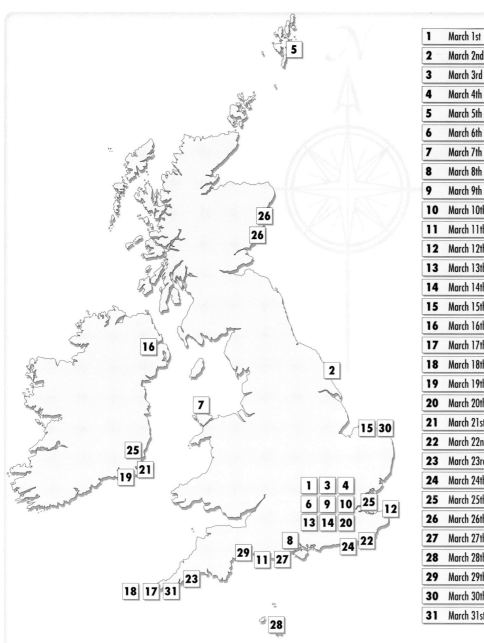

1	March 1st	1852	London
2	March 2nd	1937	Flamborough
3	March 3rd	1824	London
4	March 4th	1824	London
5	March 5th	1947	Lerwick
6	March 6th	1824	London
7	March 7th	1835	Cemaes Bay, Anglesey
8	March 8th	1824	Christchurch
9	March 9th	1824	London
10	March 10th	1825	London
11	March 11th	1993	Poole
12	March 12th	1876	Broadstairs
13	March 13th	1824	London
14	March 14th	1901	London
15	March 15th	1942	Cromer & Sheringham
16	March 16th	1842	Belfast
17	March 17th	1907	The Lizard
18	March 18th	1967	Isles of Scilly/Penlee
19	March 19th	1950	Kilmore
20	March 20th	1824	London
21	March 21st	1951	Rosslare Harbour
22	March 22nd	1937	Eastbourne
23	March 23rd	1947	Fowey
24	March 24th	1910	Newhaven
25	March 25th	1901	Southend/Wexford
26	March 26th	1898	Gourdon & Johnshaven/Montrose
27	March 27th	1879	Poole
28	March 28th	1962	Alderney
29	March 29th	1878	Sidmouth
30	March 30th	1917	Cromer
31	March 31st	1955	The Lizard

1st MARCH   LONDON, **1852**

The first edition of the Lifeboat Journal was published on the 1st March 1852 and priced at 1½d. The decision to proceed with the publication had only been taken on the 5th February 1852.

The Journal was planned to set out to inform readers about lifeboat design, new lifeboats and lifeboat stations, reports of the local committees and associations, medal and other awards and to act as an open forum by encouraging *"all correspondence bearing on the subject of saving life from shipwreck"*. Originally planned to be a monthly publication, it soon became quarterly, reaching its 500th edition in the summer of 1987. During the Second World War, a quarterly one page Bulletin only was issued.

2nd MARCH   FLAMBOROUGH, YORKSHIRE, **1937**

Fifty launchers, many of them up to their chests in the sea, helped get the motor lifeboat *Elizabeth and Albina Whitley* afloat so that she could go to the aid of the 15 strong crew of the Grimsby steam trawler *Lord Ernle*. This vessel had gone ashore under Bempton Cliffs, north of Flamborough Head.

Reaching the wreck shortly before midnight on the 2nd, Coxswain George Leng veered the lifeboat down and succeeded in getting a rope on board. Only one man had been rescued when the rope parted. Twice more communication by rope was re-established before all 15 crew were brought into the lifeboat. At one point, a heavy sea swept the lifeboat on to the trawler but fortunately she slid off again, although her rudder had been split and half of it torn away. For this service, Coxswain Leng received the Institution's silver medal.

3rd MARCH   LONDON, **1824**

A Provisional Committee Meeting was held at the City of London Tavern, Bishopsgate, to finalise arrangements for the General Meeting to be held the next day.

It was announced that King George IV had agreed to be Patron. Since the letter of request to him had only been sent on or after the 12th February, it is gratifying to note the ready response. The letter of acceptance, datelined *"Whitehall, February 25th 1824"*,

and signed by Robert Peel, the then Home Secretary, is in the RNLI Archives at Poole. The Committee had earlier learned that the Earl of Liverpool, the Prime Minister, had agreed to be President although he felt he would not be able to devote much time to the post. He sent a donation of 50 guineas and a subscription of £5. He remained President until 1828 when he died. Only in 1851 was the office filled again (see 2nd May).

The letter from Robert Peel, at the time the Home Secretary, indicating the acceptance by King George IV of the post of Patron of the RNLI.

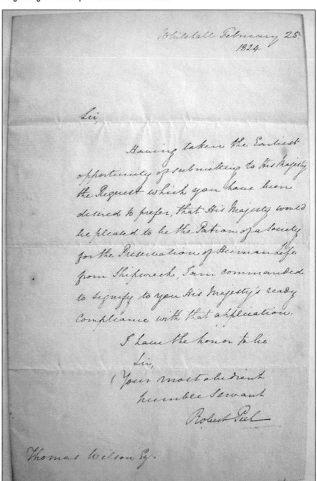

4th MARCH   LONDON, **1824**

The inaugural meeting of the Institution was held at the London Tavern, Bishopsgate, in the City of London. Dr. Manners Sutton, Archbishop of Canterbury presided. Twenty resolutions were passed. The first, moved by the Archbishop himself, proposed the formation of the *"National Institution for the Preservation of Life from Shipwreck"*.

William Wilberforce M.P., the anti-slavery campaigner, moved the second resolution. He proposed that *"medallions or pecuniary rewards be given to those who rescue lives in cases of shipwreck"*.

Resolution 18 thanked Sir William Hillary for his *"zealous endeavors to promote the establishment of the Institution"*.

5th MARCH   LERWICK, SHETLAND, **1947**

Heavy snowfalls meant that many roads were blocked, and alternative means of transport had to be found in cases of emergency.

At 10.55 p.m. on the night of the 5th March 1947, a doctor was urgently needed for a maternity case at Aithsetter, and he asked that the lifeboat take him as the roads were impassable. The Lerwick lifeboat *Lady Jane and Martha Ryland* left at 11.43 p.m., and landed the doctor at Aithsetter by means of a small boat. Two hours later, after a baby girl had been born, the small boat brought the doctor back to the lifeboat which reached Lerwick again at 3.46 a.m. on the 6th. The Department of Health for Scotland paid the cost of the service, amounting to the sum of £11.

6th MARCH   LONDON, **1824**

Wasting no time, the first meeting of the Committee of Management was held. Thomas Wilson M.P. was elected as Chairman of the Institution - a post which he held until 1852.

Two sub-committees, one for Correspondence, and the other for Finance and Subscriptions were formed. These were to be summoned for Monday 8th March and Tuesday 9th March respectively. The main Committee would meet every Saturday at 11 a.m. until further notice. This it did until Saturday the 24th July, after which the meetings were switched to Wednesdays.

7th MARCH   CEMAES BAY, ANGLESEY, **1835**

The Belfast smack *Active*, anchored in Ramsey Bay, Isle of Man during a north-westerly gale, started to drag her anchors. As soon as they had been hauled up she started to drift out to sea. Many hours later, the smack drifted into Cemaes Bay, Anglesey, where she tried to anchor but grounded a long way from the shore with every successive wave breaking over her. The Reverend James Williams of Llanfairynghornwy arrived after several unsuccessful attempts had been made to launch a boat and, ignoring the mountainous seas, rode a horse into the surf and drew near enough to throw a grappling hook over the smack's bowsprit. It was then possible to launch a boat and pull out to the wreck whose crew of five were found in the cabin, too exhausted to move. All were landed safely.

A period engraving entitled 'The Rescue'. In pounding waves, a horse is used to try and effect a rescue from the floundering ship.

For this service the Reverend Williams was awarded a gold medal on the 7th October 1835. The Committee also took into consideration a service on the 18th September 1835 when he directed the rescue operations in which the crew of the Liverpool ship *Sarah* were rescued.

8th MARCH

CHRISTCHURCH, HAMPSHIRE, **1824**

Only four days after the founding of the Institution, Captain Charles Howe Fremantle R.N. was involved in a rescue which resulted in the award of the first gold medal. The 'Hampshire Telegraph and Sussex News', of Monday the 15th March 1824, reported the rescue.

*"The Swedish brig **Carl Jean**, from Alicante to Gefle, laden with salt and four casks of wine, went on shore on Monday, at Whitepit, about ten miles to the East of Poole, and in about two hours went to pieces. The crew of the Coast Guard, stationed near where the accident happened immediately rendered every possible assistance to the unfortunate people on board. Captain Fremantle, R.N., Inspecting Commander of the District, was the first to attempt getting to the wreck, in doing which he nearly lost his life, by the sailors on board not throwing him a rope; but, at length, through his exertions and his boat's crew, the men were all saved."*

The award was voted on the 10th July 1824, before the final design of the medals had been agreed. He did not receive his medal until June 1825.

9th MARCH

LONDON, **1824**

The first meeting of the Sub-committee of Finance and Subscription was held at No.33 New Broad Street in the city. Mr. Cock, a member of the Sub-committee, was empowered *'to employ a person to make the necessary applications to the Bankers, to deliver letters and generally to assist in the business of the Institution'*.

10th MARCH

LONDON, **1825**

The Committee of Management awarded Sir William Hillary the gold medal in recognition of his work in founding the Institution. After this Honorary award, Sir William subsequently won three gold medals for services in the Douglas lifeboats.

11th MARCH

POOLE, DORSET, **1993**

The Rother class lifeboat *Osman Gabriel* left the Institution's Poole depot by road for Felixstowe where she was loaded aboard

The lifeboat Osman Gabriel, (O.N.998). One of the Rother Class, she was sent to Port Erin in 1973. She was in fact the first of the improved, and slightly lengthened, by six foot, Oakley lifeboats that became known as the Rother Class. She is seen here at Cardiff on her delivery voyage.

a ship bound for Estonia. The Estonian Lifeboat Service, Eesti Vetelpaasteuhingu, wished to add to its existing fleet of five rescue cruisers.

The *Osman Gabriel* which saw service at Port Erin from 1973 to 1992 had been built by William Osborne Limited of Littlehampton in 1972. In fact this was the first of the new Rother Class lifeboats. She was presented to the Estonian service in Tallin on the 18th March by the British ambassador, Brian Low. His wife, Mrs Anita Low, named the boat *Anita*.

12th MARCH   BROADSTAIRS, KENT, **1876**

This fulsome report appeared in the August 1876 Journal:

*"At 5 p.m., 12 March, the schooner **Lion**, of Goole, bound from Hull to the Isle of Wight, was observed driving before a heavy gale at north, with signals of distress flying. The signal guns of the station having failed to assemble the proper number of men, the lifeboat **Samuel Morrison Collins** was launched with part of the crew only, the place of one being filled by Major Elyard, of 2nd Royal Surrey Militia, an active member of the Local Committee.*

*"Stretching off under sail, the lifeboat succeeded in boarding the disabled vessel about 5.30 p.m. She was found to be in deplorable condition, especially aloft. The lifeboat's crew, however, succeeded in carrying her safely into Dover Harbour on the following day, at which time they had been twenty-four hours without breaking their fast. The **Lion** had a crew of four men. Major Elyard has long been distinguished in the lifeboat service - which he culminated on this occasion.*

"Accordingly, at the monthly meeting of the Institution in April last, it was decided to present him with its gold medal, which is the highest honour in the power of the Society to bestow, in recognition of his series of gallant services in the Broadstairs lifeboat. He had been out in the lifeboat altogether 18 times on service, and has assisted to save 49 lives from different wrecks.

"By order of Major-General Sir Garnet Wolseley, G.C.M.G., K.C.B., the Inspector-General of Auxiliary Forces, the gold medal was presented to Major Elyard at the head of his regiment on a brigade field-day held on the Queen's Birthday."

13th MARCH   LONDON, **1824**

At the Committee of Management meeting on Saturday the 13th March 1824, it was reported that a subscription of £500 had been received from Trinity House.

It was also resolved unanimously that *'no Gentleman to address the Committee, otherwise than standing'*.

14th MARCH   LONDON, **1901**

The Committee of Management 'learned with great satisfaction that His Most Gracious Majesty (Edward VII) had consented to be Patron in succession to her late Majesty Queen Victoria, and that His Royal Highness the Duke of Cornwall and York (later the Prince of Wales) had consented to become President of the Institution'.

The Institution has always enjoyed excellent relations with the Royal family over the years. The current Patrons are Her Majesty Queen Elizabeth the Queen Mother, and Queen Elizabeth II. The President is His Royal Highness the Duke of Kent K.G., who is ably assisted by the Duchess of Kent.

15th MARCH   CROMER AND SHERINGHAM, NORFOLK, **1942**

On the night of the 14th March and on the morning of the 15th, a convoy was attacked by German E-boats (torpedo firing fast attack craft). The E-boats were in turn attacked by destroyers and by HMS *Vortigern*, which sank three of them and damaged two more. HMS *Vortigen*, however, was also hit by two torpedoes and sank.

Cromer lifeboat *H. F. Bailey* launched at 7.57 a.m. after receiving a message from the Flag Officer in charge at Great Yarmouth that two vessels had sunk ten miles north east of Cromer. By 9.45 a.m., *H. F. Bailey* was at the scene where the rescue boats were already in action. The lifeboat found a lot of wreckage and picked up 11 bodies. Sheringham lifeboat *Forester's Centenary* had also been called out, and she found one body and a barrage balloon.

After returning to their respective stations, smothered in oil, the lifeboats transferred the bodies to a motor boat that took them to Lowestoft.

16th MARCH   BELFAST, **1842**

The exploits of two of the youngest persons to be awarded medals were reported to the Committee of Management on the 16th March 1842.

On the 3rd February 1842, at 3 p.m., a lighter working its way up to Belfast was seen to founder off Whitehouse between Mandon Point and White Abbey. There was scarcely enough time to place a ladder against the mast so that the crew could take refuge, as water was already up to the shrouds.

Master John Sewell, aged 14, the son of Lieutenant H.F. Sewell, R.N., and Master John Kennedy, aged 12, the son of Commissioned Boatman P. Kennedy, launched the Whitehouse Coastguard station punt and rowed three quarters of a mile to save two men from the sunken barge. Each boy received the silver medal of the Institution.

17th MARCH   THE LIZARD, CORNWALL, **1907**

What was described in the Lifeboat Journal as *'a disaster of such magnitude as seldom occurs on the coast of the United Kingdom'* took place near the Lizard on the night of the 17th March 1907. The report continues: *'thanks to the prompt action of the lifeboats in the neighbourhood and the splendid discipline maintained on board it was happily unattended by loss of life'.*

In a dense fog the 12,000-ton White Star liner *Suevic* ran on to the Maenheere Reef off the Lizard. Homeward bound from Australia, there were 524 persons on board. During the rescue operations, lifeboats from the Lizard, Cadgwith, Coverack and Porthleven were involved. Two of the *Suevic's* seamen carried children down rope ladders and dropped them into the arms of lifeboatmen in boats rising up and down on the waves.

In all, Cadgwith's *Minnie Moon* saved 227: The Lizard's *Admiral Sir George* Back 167: Coverack's Constance *Mélanie* 44: and Porthleven's *John Francis White* 18 - a total of 456.

18th MARCH   ISLES OF SCILLY, **1967**

When the 61,000-ton Liberian tanker *Torrey Canyon* went aground on the Seven Stones near the Isles of Scilly, lifeboats from St. Mary's and from Penlee were called out.

During operations associated with this maritime disaster the St. Mary's lifeboat under Coxswain Matthew Lethbridge was at sea for a total of 54 hours. On the 19th March, fourteen men had been transferred by lifeboat to the Trinity House tender *Stella*, and later took off a further nine men. The *Guy and Clare Hunter* was at sea continuously from 9.30 a.m. on the 18th to 6.35 p.m. on the 19th, and again from 5 p.m. on the 20th to 7.15 a.m. on the 21st. The Penlee lifeboat *Solomon Browne* was at sea for 30 hours, standing by the *Torrey Canyon* continuously for 24 hours (with a three hour journey in each direction) whilst the St. Mary's boat returned to station.

19th MARCH   KILMORE, CO. WEXFORD, **1950**

The Kilmore lifeboat is often called out to help the crew of the Coningbeg Light-vessel. On this occasion, at 2.05 p.m. a message was relayed by the Valentia radio station to the lifeboat station requesting assistance. A man on board the vessel was ill, suffering from a perforated ulcer. The lifeboat *Ann Isabella Pyemont* launched at 2.15 p.m. to take the sick man to a waiting ambulance on shore. This prompt action probably saved the man's life.

20th MARCH   LONDON, **1824**

A reproduction of the minutes of the meeting of the Committee of Management relating to the granting of the prefix 'Royal' to the Institution by King George IV.

The Committee of Management was advised by Dr. Manners Sutton, Archbishop of Canterbury (who had presided at the inaugural meeting), that King George IV had most graciously commanded *that the Institution be hereafter authorised to take the name of the Royal National Institution for the Preservation of Life from Shipwreck'*.

At a special meeting held on the 5th October 1854, the title was changed to the *'Royal National Life-boat Institution - founded in 1824 for the Preservation of Life from Shipwreck'*. The change was due partly to avoid confusion with the Shipwrecked Fishermen and Mariners' Royal Benevolent Society who also at that time operated some lifeboats. These were taken over by the RNLI (see 29th November).

Although now 'lifeboat' is generally written as one word, the title of the RNLI retains the hyphen 'life-boat'.

21st MARCH   ROSSLARE HARBOUR, CO. WEXFORD, **1951**

The summer 1951 Journal headed this next service under the title "R.N.L.B. to ex R.N.L.B."

At 6.45 in the morning the lifeboat watchman reported a lifeboat in a bad position in the bay. At 7.30 a.m. the lifeboat *Mabel Marion Thompson* left her moorings. The sea was rough with a strong south-easterly breeze blowing. She found the ex-R.N.L.B. *Elsie* (which had recently been sold out of the service) with a crew of two, on passage from Troon to Highbridge. She was at anchor, but her sails had been damaged and the two men could not start the engine. The lifeboat therefore towed her to Rosslare and got back to her station again at 8.30 a.m. The owner made a gift to the lifeboatmen and another to the funds of the Institution.

The *Elsie* had seen service at St. Mary's, Isles of Scilly, from 1919 to 1930, Helvick Head 1930 to 1946 and in the Relief fleet until sold out of service in 1951. She had then been renamed *Happy Return*. She was last seen in Tahiti in 1955.

22nd MARCH   EASTBOURNE, SUSSEX, **1937**

The first permanent lifeboat museum was opened on the 22nd

March 1937, in Eastbourne in the old lifeboat-house. The building commemorated William Terriss, one of the handsomest and most popular actors of his time who was stabbed to death by a fellow actor outside the stage door of the Adelphi Theatre in London in 1897. A year later the *'William Terriss Memorial Lifeboat-house'* was built in Eastbourne out of a fund raised by the 'Daily Telegraph'.

23rd MARCH   FOWEY, CORNWALL, **1947**

With Coxswain John Watters in charge, the Watson class reserve lifeboat *The Brothers* launched at 4.40 a.m. in a whole gale, a dark night and heavy seas. The auxiliary m.v. *Empire Contamar* had run on to Callyvardor Rock, Par Bay, Cornwall, but the Coxswain had to search the bay before he found her, fast on the Rock with only her bow and poop visible. The seven-man crew was waist deep in water on the poop.

In a difficult operation a line was got on board, the men were taken off and all landed at Fowey, 50 minutes after the lifeboat had reached the wreck. At one time the lifeboat was washed right into the waist of the ship. She was washed out again with her bows damaged. For this service, Coxswain Watters received the Institution's bronze medal.

24th MARCH   NEWHAVEN, SUSSEX, **1910**

The Newhaven lifeboat *Michael Henry* was responsible for saving seven men from two fishing vessels on the 24th March 1910.

At 6.30 p.m., in a south-south-west gale, the *Spes* of Brixham and the *Rialto* of Ramsgate were wrecked trying to reach the harbour. The *Spes* had struck to the eastward of the East pier. In a first operation, three men were rescued. Then the lifeboat proceeded to the *Rialto*, which had struck the bar, and rescued four men from her. Both vessels subsequently became total wrecks.

25th MARCH   WEXFORD, CO. WEXFORD AND SOUTHEND-ON-SEA, ESSEX, **1901**

In 1894, James Stevens of Birmingham left a legacy of £50,000 to the RNLI, the largest it had ever received until then. An incredible twenty lifeboats were built from this legacy, each subsequently being named after Mr. Stevens.

Two of 'his' boats were called out on the 25th March 1901. At Wexford, *James Stevens No. 15* (a 40ft Watson class) stood by the local schooner *Perseverance* homeward bound from Dublin. She had stranded on Raven point and the lifeboat stood by until she floated free and reached harbour safely.

At Southend-on-Sea, *James Stevens No.9* (a 38ft Norfolk and Suffolk class) also stood by a vessel, the barque *Grethe* which had run aground on the Nore Sand. She also later floated free.

26th MARCH   MONTROSE, ANGUS, GOURDON AND JOHNSHAVEN, KINCARDINESHIRE, 1898

The East Coast of Scotland was being swept by a gale whipping up heavy seas that threatened local fishing vessels. Lifeboats from three stations in Angus and Kincardineshire were called out to help them.

At Montrose, about forty-five boats were at sea. Ten of the boats returned without shooting their lines, the others, which had shot their lines, would be in danger in crossing the bar. The lifeboat *Robert Henderson* therefore put to sea and escorted each of the boats as they came in over the bar.

Meanwhile, further up the coast, Gourdon's *Theophilus Sidney Echalaz* helped fourteen fishing vessels. From Johnshaven, the lifeboat *Meanwell of Glenbervie* aided four vessels.

27th MARCH   POOLE, DORSET, 1879

The first lifeboat at Poole was the *Manley Wood*, named after the donor's father, a clergyman in Devon. The boat was delivered to Poole free by the London and South Western Railway in January 1865.

The last service of this first Poole lifeboat was on the 27th March 1879. The iron full-rigged ship *Martaban* of Greenock, stranded during the night on Hook Sands on the east side of the Swash Channel at the entrance to Poole Harbour. The lifeboat launched at 2 a.m. and on reaching the wreck found that six of the ship's crew had already left in their own boats. The *Manley Wood* then stood by for eleven hours. Finally the *Martaban's* captain decided to abandon ship, and the remaining eleven men were taken off and landed at Poole. The ship was later re-floated and brought into the harbour for repairs.

28th MARCH   ALDERNEY, CHANNEL ISLANDS, 1962

The motor vessel *Ridunian*, loaded with 150 tons of grit and gravel, had sailed from Alderney for St. Peter Port, Guernsey, despite bad weather and poor visibility. Passing close to the Corbet rock to avoid the worst of the sea, the vessel struck the Barsier rock at 7.20 p.m. As it was too rough to launch the ship's boats, and two attempts to use inflatable rafts failed, the seven-man crew took to a ten-man raft which the *Ridunian* was transporting.

Following receipt of a mayday call, the St. Peter Port lifeboat was launched. Captain Jennings, Harbour Master of Alderney, was also informed. He decided to launch the Trinity House pilot cutter *Burhou* and at 8.20 p.m. he set out with a crew of four men to search the area. As the pilot cutter had no radio there would have been serious problems if the cutter herself struck the rocks.

Fortunately, at 9.10 p.m. the raft was eventually sighted and the seven men brought safely to the cutter and landed at Alderney harbour at 9.45 p.m.

Captain Arthur Jennings received the Institution's bronze medal for this service.

29th MARCH   SIDMOUTH, DEVON, 1878

A lifeboat was stationed at Sidmouth from 1869 to 1912. The first boat there was the 33ft self-righter *Rimington*, which was on station from 1869 to 1885, launched 6 times and saved 32 people.

On the 29th March 1878, the smack *Lady of the Lake*, of Portsmouth, was seen to show signals of distress. A strong gale with snow showers was blowing at the time. The *Rimington* launched to her aid. Three crew members had taken to the smack's small boat, which was drifting, shoreward into heavy

The Sidmouth lifeboat being beached, taken from a postcard in the Gordon Campbell Collection.

breakers. The lifeboat rescued these three men then proceeded to the *Lady of the Lake* where only the Master remained. He refused to leave. After standing by for some time, the *Rimington* left. Because of the gale the lifeboat had to sail to Exmouth to land the rescued men.

30th MARCH   CROMER, NORFOLK, **1917**

At a meeting held in London on Friday the 9th March 1917, the Committee of Management decided to institute a bronze medal, to be awarded to crews of lifeboats and others in recognition of conspicuous gallantry in life-saving.

The first bronze medals were awarded on Friday the 30th March

1917, to the twelve men who crewed the Cromer lifeboat *Louisa Heartwell* on the 9th January 1917 in the service to the s.s. *Fernebo*.

For this service, Coxswain Henry Blogg won the first of three gold medals, and Acting Second Coxswain William Davies won the silver medal. These medals had been awarded on the 9th February 1917.

31st MARCH   THE LIZARD, CORNWALL, **1955**

At 2.23 p.m., the lifeboat Honorary Secretary saw an Avenger aircraft, with a crew of four, from the Royal Naval Air Station at Culdrose, crash into the sea half a mile south-west of Lizard

Point. He at once sent off a small rowing boat, manned by two members of the lifeboat crew and a lighthouse keeper.

By this time the remaining crew of the lifeboat *Duke of York* had also assembled, and at 2.44 p.m. the lifeboat was launched in a slight sea. There was a moderate easterly breeze, and the tide was half ebb. The rowing boat found one airman in a rubber dinghy and another man in the sea. She rescued the man from the sea, and then the lifeboat arrived and rescued the man in the dinghy. She took on board the men in the rowing boat, took the boat in tow, and made for her station. A helicopter had reached the position just after the lifeboat, but made for the shore again and landed on the cliff top near the lifeboat station. The lifeboat came ashore at three o'clock and landed the survivors, who were then taken by the helicopter to Culdrose. The lifeboat put to sea again, searched for the two missing airmen, but did not find them.

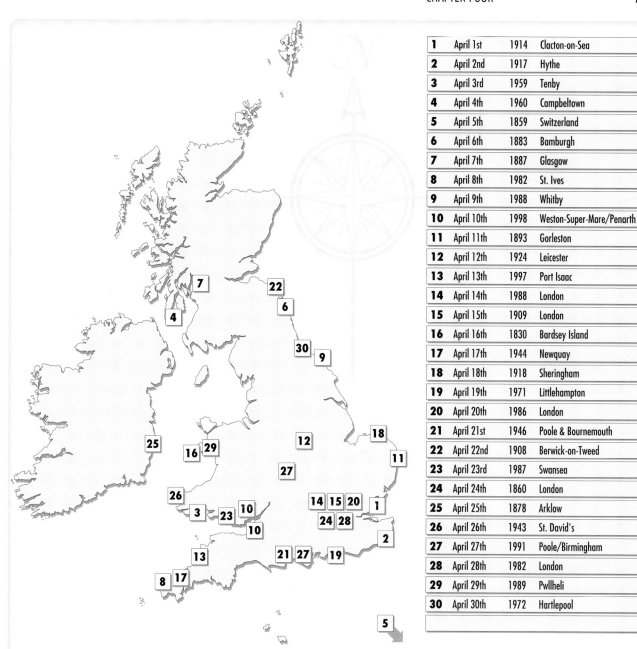

1	April 1st	1914	Clacton-on-Sea
2	April 2nd	1917	Hythe
3	April 3rd	1959	Tenby
4	April 4th	1960	Campbeltown
5	April 5th	1859	Switzerland
6	April 6th	1883	Bamburgh
7	April 7th	1887	Glasgow
8	April 8th	1982	St. Ives
9	April 9th	1988	Whitby
10	April 10th	1998	Weston-Super-Mare/Penarth
11	April 11th	1893	Gorleston
12	April 12th	1924	Leicester
13	April 13th	1997	Port Isaac
14	April 14th	1988	London
15	April 15th	1909	London
16	April 16th	1830	Bardsey Island
17	April 17th	1944	Newquay
18	April 18th	1918	Sheringham
19	April 19th	1971	Littlehampton
20	April 20th	1986	London
21	April 21st	1946	Poole & Bournemouth
22	April 22nd	1908	Berwick-on-Tweed
23	April 23rd	1987	Swansea
24	April 24th	1860	London
25	April 25th	1878	Arklow
26	April 26th	1943	St. David's
27	April 27th	1991	Poole/Birmingham
28	April 28th	1982	London
29	April 29th	1989	Pwllheli
30	April 30th	1972	Hartlepool

1st APRIL   CLACTON-ON-SEA, ESSEX, **1914**

The Clacton lifeboat *Albert Edward* was one of the first to be fitted with an engine, a four cylinder petrol engine of 40 b.h.p., giving a top speed of just over 7^1/$_2$ knots.

On the 1st April 1914 the lifeboat was called out to the assistance of an aeroplane - a seaplane en route for Harwich which had crashed into the sea off St. Osyth beach. The pilot and co-pilot were taken on board a passing barge but the *Albert Edward* picked them up and then towed the remains of *Seaplane No.11* back to the beach at Clacton.

Three weeks later another seaplane was forced to land off the town. On board was Winston Churchill, then First Lord of the Admiralty. Another aircraft picked him up, but again Clacton's lifeboat helped in the recovery of the seaplane.

2nd APRIL   HYTHE, KENT, **1917**

The ketch *Mazeppa*, of Harwich, a small vessel of seventy-two tons, came to anchor in Hythe Bay about midnight on the 1st-2nd April. At about 2.30 a.m the vessel dragged her anchors and drifted towards the shore, and the Master, realising the danger, made signals of distress. In response the lifeboat *Mayer de Rothschild* was launched. The vessel had been kept under observation, as it was feared she would come to grief in the prevailing gale, and directly the signals of distress were made the boat proceeded to her assistance.

It was, however, only with considerable difficulty that the lifeboat reached the ketch. Endeavours were made to save the crew of two hands by throwing ropes on board, and one man who jumped into the sea with the rope attached was successfully hauled into the lifeboat. Before the other man could be taken off, the lifeboat had to stand clear of the wreck as the dangerous seas made it impossible to remain near her. The lifeboat veered down to the ketch a second time, and this time the other man aboard was also saved, by being dragged through the sea to safety. As soon as the man had been picked up, the lifeboat's cable was cut, in order to get her clear of the wreck, and then she returned ashore. The Committee of Management awarded the bronze medal to Coxswain L. James Dearman. They also gave the bronze medal to Wright Griggs, an ex-Second Coxswain, who volunteered to go out on this occasion and act as Second Coxswain.

3rd APRIL   TENBY, PEMBROKESHIRE, **1959**

At 8.30 p.m. on the 3rd April 1959, the Honorary Secretary of Tenby Lifeboat Station received a message that three pedigree

The Henry Comber Brown stationed at Tenby, Pembrokeshire.

cows had fallen over the cliff at Manorbier. Two of the cows were in a position that was inaccessible from the shore, and the other one had been killed. A request for the assistance of the lifeboat was received by the Honorary Secretary, and at 8.40 p.m. the lifeboat *Henry Comber Brown* was launched. She took a dinghy in tow. The weather was fine with a calm sea and a gentle off shore breeze; the tide was ebbing.

The lifeboat made for Swanlake Bay, and when she reached the position given two members of her crew manned the punt. In very heavy surf the punt capsized twice, and it was decided to postpone any attempt to rescue the animals until first light, when it would be nearly high water. The lifeboat returned to harbour to set out again at 5.30 a.m. The two cows were taken in tow to another beach, and the lifeboat returned to her station at 10.52 a.m. The farmer expressed his thanks. The R.S.P.C.A. awarded a framed certificate of merit to the Coxswain and crew *"for their courage and humanity"*.

4th APRIL   CAMPBELTOWN, ARGYLLSHIRE, **1960**

At 10.15 on the night of the 4th April 1960, the Coxswain told the Honorary Secretary that the keeper of the Davaar lighthouse had reported a submarine ashore at the entrance of Campbeltown Harbour. At 10.35 p.m. the reserve Watson class lifeboat *City of Bradford 11* put out. It was low water and the weather was overcast with squally showers. A south-south-westerly gale was blowing, and the sea was choppy.

The lifeboat found H.M. Submarine *Narwhal* aground on the Millbeg bank and at the Captain's request the Coxswain read the submarine's draft fore and aft and gave him his bearing and distance from the Fairway Buoy. The lifeboat returned to her station at 11.50 p.m. as no further help was needed. The *Narwhal* was eventually refloated with the assistance of two tugs at 7.10 on the morning of the 5th April. The Coxswain received a letter of thanks from the Captain of the Third Submarine Squadron at Faslane.

5th APRIL   SWITZERLAND, **1859**

The Finance Committee Minutes record that on the 5th April 1859 it was *'reported the completion of the Geneva Lake lifeboat*

and that her harbour trials had been satisfactory'.

The 'Engineer' magazine of the 28th January 1859 had reported that a Monsieur Antoine Mermilliad had been sent by the government of the canton of Geneva to find a lifeboat suitable for Lake Geneva. The lifeboat was built by Forrestt of Limehouse, who had built many such boats for the Institution.

Later the Société Internationale de Sauvetage du Léman was inaugurated on the 6th September 1885. It is still very active on Lac Léman (normally referred to as Lake Geneva), with rescue craft based in Switzerland and in France. Conditions on the lake can be very treacherous with sudden winds from the Jura Mountains or the Alps.

6th APRIL   BAMBURGH, NORTHUMBERLAND, **1883**

Grace Darling's part in the rescue of survivors from the s.s *Forfarshire* on the 7th September 1838 has been well publicised and much has been written of her exploits. The coble in which she and her father set out from the Longstone lighthouse is now on display in the Grace Darling Museum at Bamburgh.

In the RNLI archives is a letter, dated the 6th April 1883, from George Darling, her brother, addressed to a Mr. John Scott. Regarding the boat, in this letter he states:

"I can assure you of her being built at Tweedmouth vis Berwick on Tweed by Mr Little Jones and named The Darlings, and built as near as I can recollect to the year of 1828 and used by my father up to 1856 or 7. As I was the youngest in the family and in the ship and boat building trade he gave her to me".

7th APRIL   GLASGOW, **1887**

On April the 7th 1887, George Lennox Watson, the yacht designer of Glasgow, was appointed Consulting Naval Architect to the Institution, a post which he held until his death in 1904.

In an appreciation of his work written for the October 1937 Lifeboat Journal it was stated that *"one can say that Mr. Watson's appointment was one of the outstanding events in the development of the lifeboat.*

A picture of Mr. G.L. Watson, the Consulting Naval Architect to the Institution from 1887 to 1904.

"When Mr. Watson was appointed, all but a very few of the lifeboats were of the self-righting type. His appointment was made shortly after the disaster on the Lancashire coast when the lifeboats at Southport and St. Anne's capsized. Both were self-righting lifeboats. The Southport lifeboat failed to right herself. What exactly happened to the St Anne's lifeboat is unknown, as all her crew were drowned. As a result a sub-committee of the Institution carefully examined the whole question of the design and construction of its lifeboats, and among its recommendations was the appointment of a consulting naval architect.

Mr. Watson's first act was to design a new sailing lifeboat, 42ft long by 13feet 3 inches wide, and the following year this boat was stationed at Southport. She was the first of the Watson type. This was the beginning of a new policy in design. Mr. Watson himself in giving evidence before a Select Committee of the House of Commons ten years later explained it. "In the case of the smaller pulling boat, certainly, and possibly even in the case of the larger pulling boats, too, it would be unwise and unsafe to abandon the self-righting principle. With the larger sailing boats I think we can get a better boat by abandoning the self-righting principle."

"That has been the steady policy of the Institution ever since - to set aside the self-righting principle. Whilst it might enable a boat to right itself, it also makes her less easy to handle, and more liable to capsize. Therefore, in the case of the large lifeboats intended to go well out to sea, the aim has been at greater buoyancy, stability and speed than is possible in self-righting boats.

"During his seventeen years as consulting naval architect, Mr. Watson designed many lifeboats of different sizes, of which the outstanding boat was his large sailing lifeboat, 43 feet long by 12 feet 6 inches. When he died in 1904, there were 203 self-righting lifeboats in the Institutions fleet and 82 which were not self-righting. Of these, 31 were of the Watson type".

8th APRIL   ST. IVES, CORNWALL, **1982**

Two youths and two young men in a sailing dinghy, leaving St. Ives harbour in a strong northerly breeze and rough broken seas, got into difficulties a mile clear of the harbour, heading towards Hayle Bar. The dinghy capsized and the crew were seen clinging to her. The St. Ives D Class inflatable lifeboat launched at 4.35p.m. The course was set and full speed maintained although, while approaching, she was taking on more water than her self-bailers could clear. Within minutes of arrival, all four survivors were on board, but the water in the lifeboat was level with the top of her sponsons.

As she tried to clear the casualty, a halyard fouled her propeller. Crew member Allen jumped overboard to hold the bow head to sea, while efforts were made to free the propeller. This done, the lifeboat set out to return to St. Ives. Crew member Thomas treated the survivors for hypothermia. An increased speed caused Allen to fall out of the lifeboat, but he was quickly recovered. The harbour was reached at 4.55 p.m., and the four survivors and Allen were taken to hospital.

For this service, Helmsman Eric T. Ward was awarded the Institution's bronze medal.

9th APRIL   WHITBY, YORKSHIRE, **1988**

The yacht *Cymba* was driven towards the shore after capsizing off Whitby harbour. The Class D inflatable lifeboat *Gwynaeth* launched at 8.40 a.m. followed by the Waveney class lifeboat *The White Rose of Yorkshire*. After negotiating heavy breaking seas at the harbour entrance, Helmsman Botham turned west towards the casualty. In very rough broken water, the inflatable lifeboat picked a man from the water but, sadly, on examination found him to be dead. Meanwhile, Coxswain Thomson had taken the Waveney inshore because the yacht was being driven inland with a survivor in the water on the stern side, apparently attached to her in some way.

Two large seas struck the Waveney as it headed in towards the *Cymba*. This incident persuaded the Coxswain to take her in stern first through atrocious sea conditions. He managed to secure the man at the third approach, and the survivor was dragged alongside the lifeboat, lifted in and later landed at Whitby. The lifeboat then went back to sea to escort fishing vessels into harbour - a regular duty.

Coxswain/Mechanic Peter N. Thomson and Helmsman Nicholas S. Botham were each awarded the Institution's bronze medal.

10th APRIL   SOUTH MIDLANDS, **1998**

At 8.15 a.m. on Good Friday, the 10th April 1998, Weston-super-Mare and Penarth lifeboat stations received information from RNLI headquarters that urgent assistance was requested due to the severe flooding in the South Midlands. Crew members from both stations were rapidly assembled and prepared to travel to Worcester to assist the local emergency services. Meanwhile at headquarters in Poole, three D Class inflatables were being loaded, complete with engines and equipment, on to fleet transport for immediate delivery to the stricken area.

All units arrived on the scene at 1.30 p.m. and commenced operations in conjunction with the fire, ambulance and police services. Houses in the Blanket Estate area were flooded to a depth of six feet on the ground floors and there were many submerged obstacles such as cars and vans which hampered the rescue operations. During the next 20 hours the lifeboats succeeded in evacuating some 30 people and a further six were 'medivaced' with the assistance of local paramedics who were transported to the casualties by the lifeboat crews.

As the floods began to subside on the Saturday morning, the crews were released to return home. This certainly was a rescue operation with a difference but does illustrate the flexibility of the RNLI and its crews to operate wherever and whenever they are needed, even if it is some 50 miles inland from the coast!

While these teams were away, their colleagues left at Weston-super-Mare and Penarth provided normal cover for the local area.

11th APRIL   GORLESTON, NORFOLK, **1893**

The difficulties of communication before the advent of wireless are well illustrated by the report of a service which appeared in the November 1893 Lifeboat Journal:

*"Signal-guns having been fired by the St. Nicholas light vessel on 11 April, the lifeboat **Mark Lane** was launched at 11 p.m., spoke to the lightship and found that the guns had been fired in response to those fired by the Cockle light. The lifeboat thereupon made for the Cockle and, en-route, fell in with the steam-tug **Yare** which took her in tow.*

*"The crew of the Cockle stated that they had fired in answer to signals from North Hasborough lightship, but they had observed flares burning in the Wold. Shaping their course N. 1/2 W. the lifeboat and tug found the barque **Vanadis**, of Cimbrishamn, sunk about three miles S.W. of North Hasborough light vessel. No trace of her crew could be found, and the lifeboat therefore proceeded in tow of the steamer to the North Hasborough lightship and ascertained that the crew of fifteen men and the Master's wife had taken refuge there. They were taken into the lifeboat and landed at Great Yarmouth."*

The lifeboat Robert & Catherine setting out from Leicester on her epic 2,400 mile fund-raising tour of the United Kingdom.

12th APRIL   LEICESTER, **1924**

As part of the celebrations to commemorate the centenary of the Institution in 1924, the reserve lifeboat *Robert and Catherine* set out on tour from Leicester on the 12th April. The tour lasted five and a half months, and in that time the boat travelled 2,400 miles and visited 160 cities and towns and hundreds of villages in sixteen counties in the Midlands and Wales.

Messrs. Foden Ltd., of Sandbach, Cheshire, undertook the cost of transport, providing a tractor to draw the lifeboat, paying the wages and expenses of the driver, and supplying the fuel for the whole tour, which ended in Cardiff on the 24th September.

In five places the boat not only took part in Lifeboat Day processions, but was also launched on rivers or lakes. At Birmingham, the lifeboat display included a rescue from a burning wreck.

13th APRIL   PORT ISAAC, CORNWALL, **1997**

The following 'service' report appeared in the Storm Force magazine:

"The Port Isaac inshore lifeboat crew had to grin and bear it when sightings of a body a few hundred metres from the shoreline turned out to be a 1.2m Winnie the Pooh balloon. It was thought to have got out there as the result of a balloon race that fizzled out. Winnie was, unfortunately, the same brilliant yellow colour, popular among fishermen for wellington boots and waterproofs. When the lifeboatmen got there they told the Coastguard "We have recovered an inflatable Winnie the Pooh bear." To which the reply came over the radio, "Christopher Robin will be pleased." The deflated teddy was taken on board, but one of the lifeboatmen refused to give him the kiss of life - he didn't approve of bears!"

14th APRIL   LONDON, **1988**

A new £530,000, 47ft Tyne Class lifeboat was named at St. Katharine Docks, London on the 14th April 1988 by the Lord Archbishop of Canterbury, the Most Reverend and Right Honourable A.K.Runcie. The proceeds of a national ecumenical appeal to churches, a number of generous bequests and contributions of special projects had funded this boat.

The appeal brought in funds from churches up and down the country. It was therefore appropriate that the lifeboat, to be named *Good Shepherd* in her role in the relief fleet of the Royal National Lifeboat Institution, should stand in at stations operating Tyne Class lifeboats all around the coast, when the station boats are sent away for survey and maintenance.

15th APRIL   LONDON, **1909**

The August 1909 Lifeboat Journal described in detail "The Adventures of a Lifeboat Flotilla".

"A flotilla of three lifeboats, in two of which motor engines had been installed, were dispatched by the Royal National Lifeboat Institution from the London Docks en route by sea for Thurso (Caithness), distance 728 miles, and for Stromness and Stronsay in the Orkneys, distant 768 and 808 miles respectively. Commander Howard F. J. Rowley, R.N., the Institution's Inspector of the Northern District, was in command. He had for his lieutenant and petty officers Mr. Small, the Motor Surveyor of the Institution, and two Motor Mechanics, each of the three boats being manned by a crew of five selected fishermen. The boat for Thurso was a sailing boat of the Watson type, a very powerful boat, and 40ft long by 11ft wide. The boat for Stronsay was of the same type, but with a length of 43ft and 12¹/₂ft beam, in which was installed a 40 B.H.P. motor; while the Stromness boat was of the self righting type, 42ft by 11¹/₂ft, fitted with a 30 B.H.P. motor. The crews who will man them as those in which they felt the most complete confidence had specially selected the type of these three boats.

The little fleet left the London Docks at 8.50 a.m. on the 15th April for Harwich, where the first halt was to be called, a run of 73 miles. The Stromness boat led with the Stronsay in tow, the Thurso coming last, in tow of the Stronsay boat, and this order

was observed throughout the voyage until the Pentland Firth was reached.

The last boat reached her station at Stronsay on the 1st May, so ending as the Journal reported *"A unique voyage of 17 days, the experiences of which will prove most useful not only to all on board the three lifeboats, but also to the Institution. The crews were of the opinion that the boats behaved wonderfully, and that they stated that they could not have credited lifeboats with such remarkable powers."*

16th APRIL   BARDSEY ISLAND, WALES, **1830**

The Institution's silver medal was awarded to David Griffith, a seaman of Beaumaris, for his part in the rescue of a number of emigrants from a wreck.

The emigrant ship *Newry* was wrecked at Bardsey Island, off the Lleyn Peninsula, whilst on passage from Newry, Co. Down, Northern Ireland to Quebec with 400 emigrants on board. At the time of the disaster, the passengers were in their berths, most of them seasick. Confusion and terror resulted. The Master ordered the mainmast cut down to form a bridge between the ship and the shore but, as soon as this had been done, his entire crew, except for the Mate and one seaman, fled without thought for their passengers. As they vanished, David Griffith crossed the makeshift bridge and commenced rescuing the freezing men, women and children, taking them ashore using ropes. Three hundred and seventy-five survivors were saved - 40 to 50 of them by Griffith with the help of three labourers.

17th APRIL   NEWQUAY, CORNWALL, **1944**

Early in the morning of the 17th April 1944, the coastguard heard a crash, but the weather was foggy and he could see nothing. He made enquiries but learnt nothing. At 9.33 a.m. the lifeboat Honorary Secretary at Newquay heard from the flying control officer at St. Mawgan aerodrome that wreckage and a dinghy could be seen off Watergate Bay. The weather was fine, but still foggy, with visibility about three-quarters of a mile.

At 9.50 a.m. the motor lifeboat *Richard Silver Oliver* was

launched and found the wreckage of a British Warwick aeroplane. Her crew of four and twelve passengers had been killed. She picked up eleven bodies, and took in tow some wreckage in which another body was entangled. She also picked up a quantity of mail, including a packet of one hundred dollar bills worth approximately £45,000. She then made a careful search, but found neither survivors nor bodies, and returned to her station at 1.45 that afternoon.

18th APRIL   SHERINGHAM, NORFOLK, **1918**

Hand written records of all lifeboat services were maintained in the Rescue Records Section of the RNLI Headquarters from 1850 until computer based records were started in 1970. Details of each service and payments made to those involved are listed.

On the 18th April 1918, the Sheringham lifeboat *J. C. Madge* went out at 4.35 p.m. to the Dundee registered s.s. *Alice Taylor*. The ship was one mile west of the station and five miles out at sea. There was a N.E. strong gale blowing with a very heavy sea.

It would appear that the *Alice Taylor* and her 18 crew were saved, the ship being taken in to Gorleston by a tug escorted by the lifeboat. The costs involved were listed as:

25 men at 35/-	£ 43	15	-
Helpers	£ 10	-	-
Signalmen	£ -	7	6
Telephone man	£ -	8	6
Tug (Yarmouth)	£ 1	-	-
25 men returning boat to station @ 5/-	£ 6	5	-
25 men loss of time 2 days @ 30/-	£ 37	10	-
Helpers	£ 5	-	-
Refreshments at Yarmouth	£ 6	11	3
Provision for return	£ 1	-	-
	£111	17	3

19th APRIL   LITTLEHAMPTON, SUSSEX, **1971**

The prototype of the new Arun class lifeboat was demonstrated to the press at William Osborne's yard at Littlehampton. The new boat had achieved a speed of 18 knots, was 52 feet in length, with a beam of 17 feet, and was self-righting.

The prototype of the new Arun Class lifeboats powering through the waves off Littlehampton, West Sussex, on the 19th April 1971.

The hull was designed by Mr. J. A. McLachlan of G. L. Watson & Co. of Glasgow, and the general arrangement by the staff of the RNLI. Whilst the prototype was constructed in cold moulded wood, future boats were built of glass reinforced plastic (G.R.P.).

This lifeboat entered service in the Reserve Fleet later in 1971 with the name *Arun*, then at St. Peter Port from 1972 to 1973, before going to Barry Dock in 1974. The design of the Arun lifeboat won a Design Council Award in 1982 (see 28th April).

20th APRIL   LONDON, **1986**

Many and varied are the ways in which groups and individuals raise funds for the RNLI. One favoured way is for a sponsored run, and the London Marathon is often chosen for that purpose.

In the Marathon of 1986, Mr. Stanley Thompson of Gateshead chose to support the RNLI in this way. Mr. Thompson was 71 at the time! A keen sailor for many years, Mr. Thompson was once rescued by the RNLI when his sailing dinghy capsized. An RNLI inflatable lifeboat picked up Mr Thompson and his daughter. Mr. Thompson only took up running 4 years before the Marathon but he had already run in the Newcastle, Paris and Windermere marathons.

A launch of the Thomas Kirk Wright, (ON.811). She was a 32' Surf Type Motor lifeboat, serving from January 1939 to 1962. She launched 64 times and saved 15 lives. She was one of those lifeboats that took part in the Dunkirk evacuation.

21st APRIL   POOLE AND BOURNEMOUTH, DORSET, **1946**

The pleasure boat *Skylark* sank in Poole Bay about a mile off Alum Chine on Easter Sunday afternoon. There were more than 70 people on board. A number of boats put out from Bournemouth and rescued everyone but one man, a member of the crew, who had put on a lifebelt and jumped overboard.

Among the rescuers were two schoolboys, Tony Dryansky, aged 14, and James Salisbury, aged 15. Each rowed out single handed and rescued five lives. James Salisbury also went overboard from his boat to try to rescue the crew member who, unfortunately drowned. The two boys were each awarded £1 and an inscribed silver watch.

The Poole and Bournemouth (as Poole station was then called)

lifeboat *Thomas Kirk Wright* arrived at the scene when the rescue from shore had almost been completed. The lifeboat did pick up one more from a raft and put him on board one of the other rescue boats.

The *Thomas Kirk Wright* served at Poole from 1939 to 1962 and is now on display in the old lifeboat house on Poole Quay.

22nd APRIL   BERWICK-ON-TWEED, NORTHUMBERLAND, **1908**

During a heavy gale from the S.W. the yacht *Bitterne*, of Berwick, was observed being rapidly driven seawards. The gale was increasing in violence, and it was considered necessary to launch the lifeboat, the self-righting *Matthew Simpson*, to save the three men on board. By this time the yacht was out of sight, but a careful bearing had been taken of her last position, and the lifeboat followed her under a double-reefed foresail. When clear of the land the sea was very heavy, and frequently broke on board.

About 7.45 p.m., just before dark, the yacht was sighted,

evidently in a bad plight and shipping water. Two of her occupants were taken into the lifeboat, and two lifeboat men were placed on board with the third. She was then taken in tow by the lifeboat, which made for land. Half an hour later a tug came up and offered to tow them in, and this was accepted, the harbour being reached about 10.30 p.m., after a very wet passage.

23rd APRIL   SWANSEA, GLAMORGANSHIRE, **1987**

The Officers, Committee and Lifeboat Crew of The Mumbles lifeboat station received the Freedom of the City of Swansea at a ceremony in the Council Chamber. The presentation took place on the 40th anniversary of the disaster, when, on the 23rd April 1947, *The Edward Prince of Wales* lifeboat was capsized and wrecked with the loss of all eight of her crew. The lifeboat had gone to help the s.s. *Santampa* off Sker Point.

Among those attending the ceremony were three widows of lifeboatmen lost in 1947.

24th APRIL   LONDON, **1860**

On the 20th March 1824, King George lV granted the pre-fix Royal to the Institution. On the 24th April 1860, Queen Victoria granted a Royal Charter of Incorporation to the Institution.

In the preamble to the Charter, it is stated that the reason for requesting its granting is *"to secure the property of the said Society, to extend its operations, and to place it on a more permanent basis"*. The Charter sets out in detail the powers and authority of the Committee of Management. One restriction that was placed on the Committee was that it could not sell or otherwise dispose of property without the agreement of a General Meeting of the Institution. This particular clause was cancelled by a Supplementary Charter granted by King George V on the 2nd May 1932, which gave the necessary authority to the Committee to act as it saw fit.

25th APRIL   ARKLOW, CO. WICKLOW, **1878**

The November 1878 issue of the Lifeboat Journal printed the following report of a service written by Richard Warden, the

Coxswain of the Arklow lifeboat *Out Pensioner*. The vessel involved in the rescue was the barque *Broughton* of Swansea, and the service extended over two days.

"24 April 1878, at 5 p.m., Arklow Coastguards reported that a vessel was on the Arklow Bank. The lifeboat was launched, and taken through a very heavy sea over the bar, the wind being E.N.E. and the tide being ebb. She then proceeded to Mizen Head, where she was anchored about midnight. At about 1.30 a.m. got sail on the boat and proceeded to Arklow Bank, where, at daybreak, the vessel was seen about two miles to leeward. The lifeboat went outside the bank to the barque, and anchored under her port quarter, when a sea filled the boat. The vessel's crew then veered out a cork fender, but the line broke. A second fender was then veered out, to which a hawser was attached, but the lifeboat filled a second time, when she attempted to get close to the vessel, and shipped a sea fore and aft, washing the Coxswain overboard. He was not missed for a time, but happily though with some difficulty, he was eventually rescued. The boat was afterwards again overwhelmed by the heavy seas, and the crew, believing it to be impossible for them to reach the vessel then, from the state of the sea and the long exposure they had undergone, it was considered best to return ashore and get a fresh crew.

"The boat reached Arklow at about 9.30 a.m. when a fresh crew immediately manned her, and proceeded under a double reefed foresail to Arklow Bank on the first of the flood tide, the wind still blowing very hard from the E.N.E. The boat was again filled twice in attempting to cross the bank. Her head was then turned to the shore, five tacks were made, and eventually she was got through the Mizen Wash, then ran before the wind to the barque, and let go her anchor under the vessel's quarter. The boat was filled twice, the crew being drenched, but they succeeded in getting a grapnel astern and a line from the ship, and in this manner were enabled to take on board the vessel's crew, consisting of 15 men, and safely land them at Arklow, at 6.15 p.m."

26th APRIL   ST. DAVID'S, PEMBROKESHIRE, **1943**

Two tank landing craft foundered during the night of the 25/26 April 1943 off St. Ann's Head, Milford Haven, when caught in a full on-shore gale. The nearest lifeboat at Angle was off service on overhaul, so the St. David's motor lifeboat *Civil Service No.6* was launched at 10.45 p.m. on the 25th. It faced a journey of 18 miles through the gale. An added danger was caused by the floating mines in the area.

The lifeboat reached the scene of the disaster about 1 a.m. on the 26th, but could find nothing. Then at 1.20 a.m., in the pitch darkness, the crew heard a shout. The lifeboat steered towards it, and, in the beam of a search light from a naval vessel, she saw a man swimming towards her. He was picked up, covered in oil, and collapsed as soon as he was rescued. This was the only survivor from over 70 men lost from the landing craft.

The rescued man was stripped of his clothing, massaged and then reclothed in one of the emergency suits carried in the boat. He was then put in the engine room with bags as a pillow and an oilskin over him. The lifeboat continued to cruise around until daylight but found no other survivors. Just before daybreak, a floating mine was sighted a few yards ahead and avoided - just in time. After a rough passage back to the station, the lifeboat was re-housed, with great difficulty, on the slipway by 9.15 a.m. Coxswain William Watts H.Williams was awarded the Institution's bronze medal.

27th APRIL   POOLE, DORSET, and BIRMINGHAM, WARWICKSHIRE, **1991**

This was a big day for Laura Scaife of Barnsley. She won the chance in a competition to name an InterCity 125 locomotive *Storm Force*. The ceremony was carried out at 8.50 a.m. at Poole Station. Laura then joined 175 other Storm Force club members along the train's route to Birmingham, where a further 70 members waited.

At the National Exhibition Centre, a D class inflatable lifeboat carried out three "rescues" as part of a special presentation during a rally for members of the RNLI's junior club. The club had been founded in 1985 (see 2nd January) to encourage the support of school children and give them regular information about the Institution's work.

28th APRIL   LONDON, **1982**

His Royal Highness The Duke of Edinburgh presented the Design Council Award for the Arun class lifeboat to Mr. P. Denham Christie, Chairman of the RNLI Boat Committee and Lt. Cdr. H.

E. Over, Chief Technical Officer. At the special ceremony in the Barbican Centre, awards were made to 34 different products, in six classes, between them forming a cross section of fine British design and craftsmanship.

In presenting its entry, the RNLI gave as the essential principle of the Arun that the hull, machinery and equipment is so arranged that a whole host of operations can be carried out in a comparatively small but highly complex vehicle without overdue interference by one operation with another. Also was the fact that all operations could be performed, when necessary, in extreme conditions of wind and sea.

At the time the entry was made, at the end of the summer 1981, Arun lifeboats had been at sea on service for more than 3,000 hours, rescuing 455 people and landing 256. Although rescues had been performed in winds up to hurricane force and tremendous seas, no Arun has capsized and no crew member lost or seriously disabled. Three services for which gold medals have been awarded had been carried out on Arun lifeboats.

The Design Council judges studied all aspects of the lifeboat's design and fitting out and visited the Arun at Yarmouth, Isle of Wight, where they were taken on a demonstration run, before making the award '...for the excellence of the design'. After the ceremony the Duke of Edinburgh inspected the Arun lifeboat *Duchess of Kent* which had been named in London by the Duchess herself the previous day.

29th APRIL   PWLLHELI, GWYNEDD, **1989**

A new D class lifeboat was dedicated at Pwllheli lifeboat station on Saturday the 29th April 1989. The ceremony followed traditional arrangements for such dedications (see the 11th June for a description of such a ceremony).

The lifeboat costing £9000 was entirely funded from an appeal run by District 105 BS of Lions International. The appeal for this lifeboat was launched in June 1987 and was supported through various fund raising events organised by 49 branches comprising District 105 BS, in Manchester, Cheshire, Staffordshire and North Wales. Pwllheli's new lifeboat was one of a number funded by various Lions Clubs, including those stationed at Brighton, Filey and Selsey.

The current D Class stationed at Shoreham in West Sussex. This boat was paid for by funds raised by the Forest Row Choir, from whom the lifeboat draws its name. (By kind permission of Mr. D. Cassan).

D class lifeboats were first introduced by the RNLI in 1963 and have proved to be fast and effective rescue craft, able to work in shallow water and among rocks. Overall length is 16ft 3in (4.95m) and the beam is 6ft 7in (2.01m). The hull is flexible and the inflatable sponsons are divided into 7 compartments.

The fabric is extremely tough, being nylon coated with hypalon. The 40 hp engine gives a top speed of 20 knots and the lifeboat can remain on service with its crew of 2 or 3 for at least three hours without refuelling. Equipment includes VHF radio, first aid kit, flares, anchor, compass and flexible fuel tanks.

30th APRIL   HARTLEPOOL, DURHAM, **1972**

The first Atlantic 21 rigid inflatable lifeboat entered service at Hartlepool on the 30th April 1972, having been developed by the RNLI from a design originated at Atlantic College, South Wales.

She is 22ft 10in long and with twin 60hp waterproof engines is capable of speeds of up to 29 knots, making her the fastest lifeboat in the RNLI fleet. She normally carries a crew of three and, in the unlikely event of capsize, can be righted by the release of gas into a buoyancy bag.

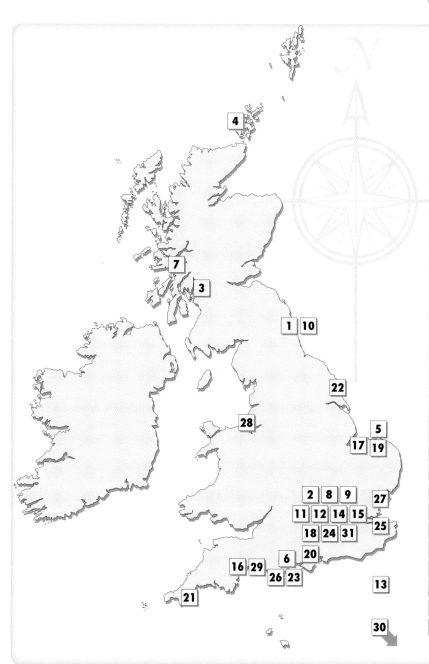

1	May 1st	1905	Tynemouth
2	May 2nd	1851	London
3	May 3rd	1938	Glasgow
4	May 4th	1957	Stromness
5	May 5th	1943	Wells
6	May 6th	1976	Poole
7	May 7th	1983	Oban
8	May 8th	1923	London
9	May 9th	1883	London
10	May 10th	1998	Tynemouth
11	May 11th	1923	London
12	May 12th	1853	London
13	May 13th	1971	English Channel
14	May 14th	1825	London
15	May 15th	1984	London
16	May 16th	1970	Exmouth
17	May 17th	1896	Hunstanton
18	May 18th	1933	London
19	May 19th	1963	Wells
20	May 20th	1973	Portsbridge
21	May 21st	1899	Porthoustock
22	May 22nd	1965	Bridlington
23	May 23rd	1920	Swanage
24	May 24th	1928	London
25	May 25th	1996	Chatham
26	May 26th	1890	Weymouth
27	May 27th	1963	Walton and Frinton
28	May 28th	1975	New Brighton
29	May 29th	1991	Lyme Bay
30	May 30th	1940	Dunkirk
31	May 31st	1889	London

1st MAY   TYNEMOUTH, NORTHUMBERLAND, **1905**

The first lifeboat to be fitted with a motor was placed on station at Tynemouth on the 1st May 1905. This was the 38ft self-righter *J McConnell Hussey* which had been in service at Folkestone since 1893.

As the February 1911 Lifeboat Journal reported *"steadily onwards may be said to be the policy of the Institution in regard to the installation of motive power in its fleet of lifeboats"*. By 1907, trials with four experimental converted boats had proved so satisfactory that the Committee of Management ordered four more boats specially built to be power operated. Two of these went to Stronsay and Stromness (see 15th April). The other two were for Broughty Ferry and Donaghadee. By the time of the 1911 Lifeboat Journal report, eight more motor lifeboats had been or were due to be placed on station. These included the *Henry Vernon* which replaced the first motor lifeboat at Tynemouth in 1911 (see 11th January).

2nd MAY   LONDON, **1851**

After an enthusiastic start in 1824, the Institution went into a period of declining income and interest. Matters improved in 1850, and on the 2nd May 1851 Algernon, 4th Duke of Northumberland was appointed President, a post vacant since the death of the Earl of Liverpool in 1828.

The Duke, an Admiral and later First Lord of the Admiralty, had interested himself in lifeboat work on the coast of Northumberland. The Minutes of the Committee of Management record that in July 1850, the Duke had called on the Chairman, Mr. Wilson, to express his *"greatest anxiety"* in ascertaining the best lifeboat that could be built.

On the 12th September 1850, it was recorded that the Committee could not itself grant any reward for the best lifeboat. If a lifeboat is approved by his Grace, then they would be willing to contribute 100 guineas or thereabouts, for such a boat to be placed on the coast of Northumberland.

The Duke's notice about the competition is dated October 1850 (see 1st June), and on the 21st November the Committee noted that the Chairman had written to the Duke on the 8th November,

acknowledging his liberality and trusting that the Duke's laudable exertions would be crowned with success.

On the 2nd January 1851, the Committee Minutes record that the Chairman should ask the Duke to become President. There then followed an exchange of correspondence in which the Duke suggested various changes in the Institution, and, on the 3rd April, the Committee suggested that the Duke should be ready to assist in carrying them out, either by serving on the Committee or by accepting the office of President.

On the 2nd May 1851, the resolution to appoint the Duke as President was carried unanimously. The Jury, appointed by the Duke to adjudicate on the best lifeboat plan, submitted its report on the 1st June 1851.

3rd MAY   GLASGOW, **1938**

King George VI and Queen Elizabeth opened the Empire Exhibition at Belhouston Park, Glasgow, on the 3rd May 1938. The Institution had its own pavilion at the Exhibition. As reported in the June 1938 Lifeboat Journal:

"The principal exhibit in this pavilion is a motor lifeboat of the Watson cabin type, the type named after Mr. G. L. Watson of Glasgow, the Institution's consulting naval architect from 1887 until his death in 1904. She is a modern development of the first of the Watson pulling and sailing lifeboats which he designed immediately on his appointment. She is 46 feet by 12 feet 9 inches. On service, with crew and gear on board, she weighs $19^{3}/_{4}$ tons. She is divided into seven water-tight compartments, she is fitted with 142 air-cases. She has twin screws, and is driven by two 40 h.p. diesel engines. The engine room is a water-tight compartment, and each engine itself is water-tight so that it could continue running even if the engine room were flooded. Her speed is $8^{1}/_{4}$ knots, and she carries enough fuel to travel some 200 miles at full speed without refuelling. She carries a crew of eight, and in rough weather can take ninety five people on board. She has a line-throwing gun and an electric searchlight, and is lighted throughout with electricity.

She has been built on the Clyde by Messrs. Alexander Robertson, of Sandbank, and has been equipped by the Scottish firm, Coastal Radio of Edinburgh, with radio-telephony.

The boat has cost about £8,000 and has been built out of a gift from Miss Margaret Lithgow, of Glengorm Castle, Tobermory, and at Miss Lithgows's wish will have the name **Sir Arthur Rose**. *When the Exhibition closes the boat will go to the new station which the Institution is establishing at Tobermory."*

4th MAY   STROMNESS, **ORKNEY**, **1957**

At 1.15 early on the morning of the 4th May 1957, the Kirkwall coastguard telephoned to say a message had been received that a vessel was ashore in Hoy Sound. The Barnett class motor lifeboat *Archibald & Alexander M Paterson* put out at 1.20 a.m. in a smooth sea. There was a strong northerly wind blowing and it was high water. The lifeboat found the fishing vessel *Snurp VII*, of Bergen, with a crew of nine at the Point of Ness. A rope was made fast, but before the fishing vessel had begun to be pulled off the rope parted.

The lifeboat stood by until the *Snurp VII* had settled down on the ebb tide, and as the vessel was in no immediate danger the lifeboat returned to her station, arriving at 5.45 a.m. She put out to sea again at 9.30 a.m. and returned to the fishing vessel. A tow rope was put aboard and with the help of the fishing boat *Fame*, which had also come to help, towing operations started at 12.15 p.m. Shortly afterwards the fishing boat *Diligent* also arrived and helped with the tow. The *Snurp VII* refloated on the flooding tide at 12.34 p.m. and all four boats made for Stromness harbour, the lifeboat arriving at 12.55 p.m

5th MAY   WELLS, NORFOLK, **1943**

During the Second World War, trials were carried out to find additional ways of rescuing air-crew who had had to ditch their aircraft at sea.

On the 5th May 1943, an air-borne lifeboat was used for the first time when 'she' was dropped to a Halifax bomber which had come down 50 miles out in the North Sea. The crew of the Halifax got aboard her and made for Wells but, when they were within 12 miles of the coast, the engines failed. The Wells lifeboat *Royal Silver Jubilee 1910-1935* went out to their help, but before she arrived a motor launch had taken the air-borne lifeboat in tow.

The air-borne lifeboat was 23ft by 5ft 6ins and was carried under the fuselage of the aeroplane. With two engines and fitted with air-cases, she was so designed that if she struck the water upside down, she would right herself at once.

An airborne lifeboat was first used on the 5th May 1943, when it went to the aid of a British Halifax bomber that had crashed into the North Sea. This lifeboat, 23ft by 5ft 6inches, was carried under the fuselage of the mother aircraft, and when dropped was deployed safely by parachutes.

In the picture below, the lifeboat has been dropped to the aid of an American B-17 Flying Fortress bomber that has also crashed into the North Sea following an attack over Germany. The bomber's crew have already taken to rubber dinghies.

The rescued airmen have transferred to the airborne lifeboat and have erected the sail.

6th MAY   POOLE, DORSET, **1976**

The new Headquarters of the Institution was formally opened by the President, H.R.H. The Duke of Kent on Thursday the 6th May 1976. In his speech the Duke said " *The decision to move to Poole can only be described as bold and, I am quite confident, a wise one...*

There are a number of reasons for making the change. Perhaps the most important was that the offices in Grosvenor Gardens were on a long lease, which was in itself a diminishing asset. I think it is evidence of the wise financial management of the RNLI that after buying the land on which the new head office is built as a freehold property and completing the building it was able to report that the Institution's reserves stood somewhat higher than they had a year earlier..."

The Duke also called attention to the importance of change in that for a century and a half London had been the site of the RNLI's head office. In its earlier years the RNLI was accommodated in the City of London, first in Austin Friars and later in Great Winchester Street.

A move to the City of Westminster occurred in 1851. The head office was then off the Adelphi. Half a century later there was a move to Charing Cross Road, and in 1931 the RNLI acquired the buildings in Grosvenor Gardens. The main administration during the last war was carried on in the Depot at Borehamwood, but meetings continued to take place in Grosvenor Gardens.

The Depot also moved to Poole and so, for the first time in the history of the RNLI, Headquarters and Depot were together in the same town (see also 2nd September).

7th MAY   OBAN, ARGYLLSHIRE, **1983**

The first 33ft Brede class to go on station was named *Ann Ritchie* at Oban by her eponymous donor. This was the third lifeboat given to the RNLI by Mrs. Ritchie: the 37ft Oakley *James Ball Ritchie* and 54ft Arun *The Gough Ritchie* were already on station at Ramsey and Port St Mary respectively.

The Brede class lifeboat was introduced to meet an operational requirement for a boat between the rigid inflatable Atlantic 21 class and the larger lifeboats. Built by Lochin Marine of Rye, the Brede normally carried a crew of four. Twin diesel engines give a maximum speed of more than 19 knots and a range of 125 nautical miles.

8th MAY   LONDON, **1923**

The Prince of Wales (later King Edward VIII) was President of the Institution from 1919 to 1936 and gave great support to the RNLI. The Lifeboat Journal of June 1923 details the events of Prince of Wales Day held throughout Greater London on the 8th May which raised over £5,500. Extracts from the report indicate the help he gave:

"A great factor in the success of the appeal was the personal visits which the Prince of Wales paid to depots in the east and south-east districts, during the afternoon. He drove through the city, and made his first call at the Library Hall in the Whitechapel Road. From here he drove to Rothesay Mansions at Kennington Gate, and thence to Lambeth Town Hall. In both boroughs he was received by the Mayor, Aldermen and Councillors and welcomed by large crowds, and he was entertained to tea by the Mayor of Lambeth. The effect of his visit in rousing public interest in the appeal may be judged from the fact that Stepney raised £163, as compared with £10 in 1921, and Lambeth £311, as compared with £49 in 1921. In fact, nothing was more encouraging than the generosity shown by the people everywhere in the poorer parts of London. In many cases working women were out collecting as early as four in the morning, and in the majority of cases they were at work at 5.30 a.m.

THE PRINCE'S APPEAL

"There is nothing in our long and splendid history as a seafaring people of which we are more proud than the Life-boat Service."

"Most of all we are proud that it is a voluntary service, provided, not by the State, but by the people themselves."

"I appeal to the men and women of our Empire to give generously in support of this great Service. I appeal not only as President of the Institution, but as Master of the Merchant Navy and the Fishing Fleets."

What is the Royal National Life-boat Institution ?

A CHARITABLE SOCIETY which carries on an indispensable NATIONAL SERVICE.

It provides and maintains the Life-boats round the whole of the 5000 miles of coast of Great Britain and Ireland.

It is pledged to place a Life-boat at every spot where one is shown to be necessary and a crew can be obtained.

It gives rewards for every rescue, or attempted rescue, from shipwreck, by whomsoever performed.

It compensates those injured in the Service.

It pensions the widows and orphans of Life-boatmen who give their lives for others, as if they had been Sailors, Soldiers or Airmen killed in action.

Royal National Life-boat Institution,
Life-boat House,
22, Charing Cross Road,
London, W.C. 2.

GEORGE F. SHEE,
Secretary of the Institution.

The 'Prince's Appeal'. The Prince of Wales was President of the Institution from 1919 to 1936 and gave great support to the RNLI.

"In the West End and in the suburbs, although there was not the special stimulus of a personal visit from the Prince, the results were equally satisfactory, and the Institution is deeply grateful to all those ladies who gave many hours of hard and successful work to the lifeboat cause. In making the appeal the Institution was fortunate also in having the cordial help of the Metropolitan and City police, and other public and private bodies.

"In connection with the Day a special wireless appeal was made to all ships, through the generous help of the General Post Office, which sent out the appeal from one of its High-Power Stations. Others, Marconi Company, the Radio Communication Company, and Messrs. Siemens kindly agreed to redistribute it."

9th MAY   LONDON, **1883**

Charles Dibdin was appointed Secretary of the RNLI on the 9th May 1883, following the death in service of Richard Lewis who had held the post from 1850.

From 1870, Charles Dibdin had been Secretary of the Civil Service Lifeboat Fund which over the years has provided many lifeboats for the Institution, the first going to Wexford in 1866. In 1883, he left the Civil Service on his appointment as Secretary of the Institution, the post he held until his death on 7 June 1910.

On his appointment, he started a notebook, now in the RNLI archives, recording background information for his work: a diary of dates of committee meetings: staff details and salaries: site of collecting boxes: moneys received and paid: and much more. He made a note of 'Noblemen and others invited to take part in Annual General Meetings', with appropriate marks. Why was one peer marked with 'not to be asked again' firmly underlined?

For a while he also recorded the daily numbers of letters received and sent alongside, oddly enough, the number of launches. For January 1884, he records a total of 1260 letters received, 922 despatched, and 47 launches. For July 1884, the figures are 610, 477 and 1. In those days the bulk of lifeboat launches took place during winter months with few in the summer - the complete reverse of present trends.

10th MAY   TYNEMOUTH, NORTHUMBERLAND, **1998**

A new lifeboat house at Tynemouth was officially dedicated and opened at a ceremony on Sunday the 10th May 1998.

On the 10th April 1941, two bombs dropped during a German air raid destroyed the then lifeboat-house at Tynemouth, together with the lifeboat *John Pyemont*. She had only been on station since 1939, but even in that short time there had been twenty launches with 59 lives saved.

On the 26th October 1941, the former Tynemouth lifeboat *Frederich Swan* returned on temporary duty from the Reserve Fleet. A new lifeboat-house was completed in November 1947, and the station's new lifeboat arrived on the 29th November. *The Tynesider*, as she was named, was paid for by the Tyneside Lifeboat Appeal set up by the local mayors in February 1943. The cost of the Watson class diesel engined boat was £16,367.

A new lifeboat house was built to provide shore facilities for the Arun class boat which is kept afloat. The 1947 house with slipway was demolished.

11th MAY   LONDON, **1923**

On the 11th May 1923, Sir Godfrey Baring, Bart., was appointed Chairman of the Committee of Management in succession to the Earl Waldegrave who had held the post from 1911. The June 1923 edition of the Lifeboat Journal reported the appointment in fulsome terms:

"Sir Godfrey Baring has been a member of the Committee of Management since 1911, and in 1915 was elected Deputy Chairman in succession to the late Sir John Cameron Lamb, C.B. No reader of the Lifeboat needs to be reminded of the new Chairman's work and indefatigable devotion to the interests of the Lifeboat Service. Not only has he thrown himself into the administration and work of the Institution and organisation of its appeals with all the exceptional energy and ability which have marked all his undertakings, but he has visited every part of the United Kingdom. This was often at the cost of many days' successive travelling, in order to meet the local Committees and present to the public the great claims of the Lifeboat Cause. In all these activities he has brought to the service of the Institution the

ripe experience of affairs obtained in the course of twenty six years of public life and the holding of many public offices including twelve years as Member of Parliament, and many years as Chairman of the Isle of Wight County Council.

"To this experience Sir Godfrey adds a charming personality and an exquisite courtesy as well as exceptional gifts as a speaker, while his ability as a Chairman has been tested and proved by his long tenure of office as Deputy Chairman of Committees."

Sir Godfrey remained Chairman until 1956.

12th MAY   LONDON, **1853**

The July 1853 edition of the Lifeboat Journal reported that, on the 12th May 1853, *"Mr George Palmer, late Deputy Chairman of the Royal Shipwreck Institution, and Inventor of the lifeboats long adopted by the Institution, is no more. The grave has closed over the earthly remains of a firm friend of the shipwrecked; and some notice of his life may therefore be acceptable to our readers."*

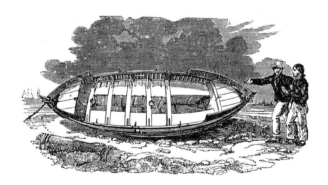

An illustration of George Palmer's boat, 1828, originally reproduced in 'A New Plan for Fitting all boats so that they may be made secure, as Life-boats'.

George Palmer had had an adventurous career as a commander with the East India Company. In the early 1800s he left the sea, became a City merchant, and later a Member of Parliament. He first became connected with the Institution in 1826, and in 1828 his plan of fitting lifeboats was adopted by it and used for quarter of a century until the self-righting lifeboat superseded them.

Palmer's design featured nine air-cases, three on each side, two in the stern and one in the bow, and four tin gunwale cases. There were four scuppers placed on each side just above the air cases. The boat, 26ft 8in in length, could be steered by rudder or by oar and was fitted with two lug sails. They cost £60 each.

13th MAY   ENGLISH CHANNEL, **1971**

A D class inflatable lifeboat was stationed on a wreck-marking vessel near the Varne lightvessel in the Straits of Dover off the Kent coast. Following a request from HM Government, the RNLI supplied one of its inflatable inshore rescue boats on an experimental basis.

Trinity personnel manned the boat - a joint venture by the RNLI and Trinity House. Lieutenant George Cooper, later Chief of Operations, had trained them at the Headquarters in Poole. Although the lifeboat placement was occasioned by shipwrecks near the Varne, no services were recorded, and the boat was withdrawn on the 13th June 1972.

14th MAY   LONDON, **1825**

Apart from the gold, silver and (since 1917) bronze medals awarded for acts of gallantry in saving life from shipwreck, the Institution occasionally awards 'honorary' gold or silver medals in appropriate cases.

On the 14th May 1825, the Committee of Management voted three honorary gold medals. The first medal was awarded to King George IV, the first Patron of the Institution who shortly after its foundation granted it the prefix Royal (see 20th March). The second medal went to Dr. Manners Sutton, Archbishop of Canterbury who had presided at the inaugural meeting on the 4th March 1824. Finally, HRH The Duke of York, a Vice Patron, received a gold medal - he presided at the first anniversary dinner on the 25th May 1825.

Sir William Hillary, Bart., the Founder of the Institution, had been awarded an honorary gold medal on the 10th March 1825. He subsequently won three gold medals for himself saving lives at Douglas, Isle of Man.

From the 13th May 1971through to the 13th June 1972, a temporary lifeboat station was established upon the No.6, Varne, light vessel - shown in this photograph taken in 1971.

15th MAY LONDON, **1984**

Her Majesty Queen Elizabeth the Queen Mother presented awards at the Annual General Meeting held at the Royal Festival Hall in London on the 15th May 1984. Her Majesty has been a Patron of the RNLI since 1937.

At the meeting, Her Majesty presented the RNLI's new colour to Coxswain Leonard Patten of Newhaven. The colour was sponsored by the Clothworkers' Foundation which commissioned the Royal School of Needlework to undertake the work. In her speech the Queen Mother said *"The colour is a most fitting tribute to everyone who has ever been involved with the lifeboat service in the past, and it will carry forward their deeds, to those who will serve in the future."*

At the same meeting Carl Giles, the well known cartoonist, received the certificate making him an Honorary Life Governor of the Institution. Long a supporter, Giles provided each year an appropriate Christmas card for sale in aid of RNLI funds. He had previously been awarded a Public Relations Award in November 1973 for his help.

16th MAY EXMOUTH, DEVON, **1970**

The new Exmouth lifeboat was named *City of Birmingham* at a ceremony at Exmouth Docks on Saturday, the 16th May 1970. The 48ft Solent class lifeboat had cost £72,000 of which £42,000 was provided by a special 'City of Birmingham' Lifeboat Appeal.

The Exmouth lifeboat City of Birmingham that was named on the 16th May 1970 at a ceremony attended by a delegation of supporters from Birmingham.

A special train brought the Deputy Mayor, Alderman Charles Simpson, and 500 supporters from Birmingham. Alderman Simpson had launched the appeal during his term as Lord Mayor, and his wife formally christened the lifeboat at the ceremony.

During its time at Exmouth, the *City of Birmingham* launched on service 58 times and saved 19 lives.

17th MAY   HUNSTANTON, NORFOLK, **1896**

The Hunstanton self-righting lifeboat *Licensed Victualler* put off at noon on the 17th May 1896 in a rough sea and a strong N.N.W. breeze, a vessel having been reported in distress. The vessel proved to be the brig *Amelie*, of Frederickstadt, laden with pit props. She was found water-logged, dismasted, and a total wreck on Heacham beach. Her crew of nine men, who had taken to their boat alongside the ship, were taken into the lifeboat and landed safely at Hunstanton at 2 o'clock.

The lifeboat station at Hunstanton was established in 1867, and the whole cost was defrayed by the Licensed Victuallers of London; the first lifeboat was named *Licensed Victualler*. As the Lifeboat Journal reported in 1888, this boat *'had not long to prove that notwithstanding her name, she could take kindly to water though the retort might be made by one of the trade that she did so with spirit too'.*

The first *Licensed Victualler* served from 1867 to 1887, a second of the same name from 1887 to 1900, and a third 1900 to 1931.

18th MAY   LONDON, **1933**

The Lifeboat Journal of September 1933 reported that:

"Through the kindness of the Underground Railways the Institution held a lifeboat exhibition in the booking hall at the Charing Cross Underground Station, London, which was open to the public for a fortnight, starting on 18 May, and closing after the Whitsuntide holiday, on 5 June. The lifeboat exhibition was the fortieth exhibition to be held in this booking hall. The Underground Railways provided not only the site, but lighting, electric power and policing, without charge to the Institution."

The lifeboat exhibition in the main entrance hall at Charing Cross Underground Station that was held from the 18th May to the 5th June 1933.

"The exhibits were chosen and arranged in such a way as to show the public how the lifeboat service does its work, the changes which have been made in it since the Institution was founded 109 years ago, and the latest developments of mechanical power.

"It includes a series of models of lifeboats, from the first lifeboat, the Original, built in 1789, propelled by oars, made buoyant with cork, and emptied of water by baling, to the modern motor lifeboat with its two water-tight engines, air cases, relieving valves, cabin, searchlight, and line throwing gun. The models also included two launching slipways, a self-righting lifeboat in a tank, which the public were asked to capsize for themselves in order to see the promptness with which a lifeboat will right herself and clear herself of water."

19th MAY   WELLS, NORFOLK, **1963**

Late on the 18th May 1963, Second Coxswain Francis Robert Taylor, D.S.M., launched the Liverpool class lifeboat *Cecil Paine* to go to the assistance of the cabin cruiser *Seamu* which had gone aground at low tide at the entrance to Blakeney harbour. There was a strong W.N.W. breeze and rough seas. The lifeboat reached the casualty at 10.50 p.m. Several attempts had to be made to get alongside *Seamu* as the wind had increased to gale force. Finally, the two men aboard were dragged into the lifeboat which returned to station at 3.25 a.m. on the 19th May.

20th MAY   PORTSBRIDGE, HAMPSHIRE, **1973**

During the Portcreek water fair at Portsbridge on the 20th May 1973, Sir Alec Rose launched the 'Hampshire Rose' appeal in connection with the 150th anniversary of the foundation of the RNLI. Although originally intended to be confined to Hampshire, neighbouring counties also joined in. Some £71,000 was raised.

The Rother class lifeboat *Hampshire Rose was* stationed at Walmer, where she was named by Lady Rose on the 6th September 1975.

21st MAY   PORTHOUSTOCK, CORNWALL, **1899**

About three-quarters of a mile from Porthoustock lifeboat station lie the Manacles rocks. During the early morning of the 21st May 1899 the United States liner *Paris* (10,669 tons), bound from Cherbourg to New York, ran aground on the Lowland point near the Manacles. On board were 370 crew and 386 passengers.

In a report on the stranding, the Lifeboat Journal of August 1899 noted that *"so little cause for alarm for the safety of those on board was there, that, finding his ship fixed, the Captain lowered his gig, and proceeded round the ship to ascertain her precise position. The Porthoustock and Falmouth lifeboats were soon in attendance, but it was at once realised that their services as lifeboats were not required, although use was made of them for*

The American Liner Paris aground on Lowland Point near Coverack on the 21st May 1899. The Falmouth and Porthoustock lifeboats helped by transferring passengers to tugs. The vessel herself was salved after seven weeks of work by a German marine salvage firm.

ferrying many of the passengers from the Paris to the tugs which conveyed them to Falmouth. Shortly after the ship stranded a rocket line was fired over her by the coastguard, so even if the sea had been too rough for boats to work comfortably alongside, she was near enough for the rocket apparatus to have taken people off, if necessary. As there were nearly 800 on board this would have been a slow proceeding."

22nd MAY   BRIDLINGTON, YORKSHIRE, **1965**

In the afternoon of the 22nd May 1965, the Bridlington Liverpool class lifeboat *Tillie Morrison, Sheffield II* safely escorted into harbour nine yachts which had been taking part in a race. A S.S.E. near gale force wind was blowing, and fears had been expressed for the safety of the yachts. The lifeboat was out on service for 5 hours.

The lifeboat ended her service with the RNLI in 1968 but was then sold to the Sumner Lifeboat Institution in New Zealand. Situated near Christchurch on the South Island, this service was

founded in 1898. The lifeboat was renamed *Rescue III* and commenced her service there in 1970.

The first *Tillie Morrison, Sheffield* was at Bridlington from 1947 to 1952. She was the gift of Mr. James Morrison and the late Mr. David Morrison, both of Sheffield, named in memory of their sister. The name was transferred to the new boat in 1953, because when James Morrison died he left £5,000 for the upkeep of the lifeboat named after his sister.

23rd MAY   SWANAGE, DORSET, **1920**

The lifeboat station at Swanage had been closed temporarily on the 9th November 1917 as so many local men were away in the forces. Re-opened twelve months later, a new lifeboat arrived there on the 27th August 1918. This was the self-righting *Herbert Sturmy*. Built at a cost of £2,200 she was provided by a legacy from the late Mrs.H.C. Sturmy in memory of her husband.

The *Herbert Sturmy* was launched for the first time on service at

The Swanage lifeboat Herbert Sturmy and her crew pictured, at the front of her house, in 1924.

6.10 p.m. on the 23rd May 1920, after a rowing boat, with a man and a woman on board, had been reported to be in difficulties, having been carried round Durlston Head by the strong ebb tide.

There was a stiff E.N.E. wind blowing, with choppy seas, as the lifeboat headed out. Coxswain Dyke then saw a small motor boat, with 2 people on board, in distress, the boat's engine having broken down and so he went to their assistance first and took the disabled boat in-tow.

The lifeboat then made for the original casualty, which was found 2½ miles south east of St Adhelm's Head and this boat was also taken in-tow, both boats being towed back to Swanage.

24th MAY   LONDON, **1928**

The Committee of Management passed the following resolution on the 24th May 1928: *'That Lifeboat Stations be presented with a Vellum on completion of a hundred years, this Vellum to be hung in the Town Hall or other public building, that a special Ceremony of Presentation be arranged in each case, and that this Resolution be retrospective.'*

The first Vellum presentations were reported in the November 1928 Lifeboat Journal. This was at Padstow on the 28th May - the station was established in 1827.

The presentations took place on the bridge of the lifeboat tug, the *Helen Peele*, with the station's two lifeboats -*Edmund Harvey* and *Arab* alongside. A large crowd watched from the quay.

25th MAY   CHATHAM, KENT, **1996**

On Bank Holiday Saturday, 25th May 1996, the National Collection of Lifeboats opened its doors to the public in the Historic Dockyard at Chatham.

As the Lifeboat Journal of summer 1996 reported, *"the first steps inside the new National Collection of Lifeboats tell you that this is something very special. Here, for the first time anywhere in the world, the history of a nation's lifeboats and the men who took them to sea is laid out under one roof."*

"The collection runs from pulling and sailing lifeboats of the last century, through high speed inshore lifeboats to the 54ft Arun class, most of which are still in service. The lifeboats range from the virtually 'as-found' state of the 1897 built **St. Paul** *to the apparently still-in-service condition of the modern boats.*

"Here too is the history of the men and women who served aboard them, with hands-on displays of self-righting and of different hull shapes. There are tractors, launching carriages, engines, winches and other equipment of past and more recent times which made the RNLI's lifeboats what they were. Housed in the historic No. 4 Covered Slip, in the centre of the maritime heritage at Chatham's Historic Dockyard in Kent, the collection is not to be missed."

26th MAY   WEYMOUTH, DORSET, **1890**

In a strong easterly breeze and heavy surf, a boat capsized in Weymouth Bay, and two men on board were thrown out. This was seen by two boys, Frank Percy, aged 16, and Frederick Carter, aged 11. They were out in another boat but in smooth water. They rowed into the broken water and were able to save one of the men. Each boy was awarded a silver medal by the Institution.

Frederick Carter is the youngest person to have been awarded a medal during the history of the RNLI.

27th MAY   WALTON AND FRINTON, ESSEX, **1963**

At 10.20 on the evening of the 27th May, 1963, the coastguard informed the Honorary Secretary that the Master of the Galloper lightvessel had reported that a large auxiliary ketch, the *Vandro*, was secured astern of the lightvessel. The report stated that there was a man and a woman on board, and that the woman was in a state of a collapse. The Watson class lifeboat *Elizabeth Elson*, on temporary duty at the station, put out at 10.45 p.m. in a fresh north-north-easterly wind and a rough sea. It was one hour after low water.

The lifeboat reached the lightvessel at 2.45 on the morning of the 28th May and found that the *Vandro's* engine had broken down. She took her in tow, and the bowman and a member of the crew joined the owner and his wife. The woman's condition was such that she couldn't be moved. She therefore remained in the cabin of the ketch whilst the *Vandro* was in tow to Harwich harbour, which was reached about 10.30 a.m. Arrangements had been made for a doctor and an ambulance to be waiting. After the doctor had examined the woman it was decided to leave her aboard the ketch. The lifeboat then took the ketch to a safe mooring near Shotley pier. The lifeboat crew had some breakfast ashore, and then the lifeboat returned to her station, arriving at 1.30 p.m.

28th MAY   NEW BRIGHTON, CHESHIRE, **1975**

Lloyds List of the 23rd July 1975 included the following report, under the title

'STUART IS RNLI'S 100,000TH RESCUE'.

"Although he did not realise it at the time, 13 year old Stuart Nixon of Liverpool who drifted out to sea in a rubber dinghy on 28 May was the 100,000th life to be saved by the Royal National Lifeboat Institution.

"Helmsman Bev Brown and crew member Tony Steen of the RNLI New Brighton inshore lifeboat are to have tea with the Lord Mayor of Liverpool, Mr. O. J. Doyle next Monday to mark the occasion.

"The incident is both a reminder of the long and impressive service rendered to their fellow men by the venerable RNLI, and of the changing and expanding nature of its work. It is just one statistic in its brass bound book of records that are vital to the planning of search and rescue services in the future".

29th MAY   LYME BAY, DORSET, **1991**

The summer 1991 Lifeboat Journal reported the first rescue by the prototype Fast Afloat Boat 3 (FAB 3) whilst it was on trials.

"The prototype of the new Fast Afloat Boat 3 carried out her first service on 29 May while returning from Salcombe to Weymouth, where she is based for some days for familiarisation trials. Staff Officer (Trials and Development) Harry Teare was in command when the coastguard asked the yet un-named lifeboat to locate a

casualty in Lyme Bay, to the west of Portland. Having located the vessel, a yacht called Sualidaz with three people aboard, FAB 3 towed her into Weymouth - a two and a half-hour tow at about 8 knots. FAB 3 was reported to have performed well during service."

FAB 3 was later named the Severn class in keeping with the Institution's practice of naming many lifeboat classes after rivers connected with the service. The first Severn to enter service was stationed at Harwich (see 20th October). Terry Waite CBE performed the naming ceremony, on the 25th May 1997.

30th MAY   DUNKIRK, **1940**

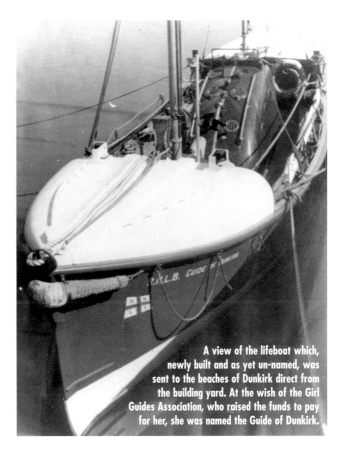

A view of the lifeboat which, newly built and as yet un-named, was sent to the beaches of Dunkirk direct from the building yard. At the wish of the Girl Guides Association, who raised the funds to pay for her, she was named the Guide of Dunkirk.

At 1.15 p.m. on Thursday the 30th May 1940, the Ministry of Shipping telephoned the Institution and asked that as many lifeboats as possible be sent to Dover at once.

In all, nineteen lifeboats went to Dunkirk - eighteen from stations between Gorleston in Norfolk to Shoreham in Sussex plus the Poole lifeboat, and a new un-named boat which had just been completed at Rowhedge Iron Works in Essex.

The Poole lifeboat *Thomas Kirk Wright* is now on display at the old lifeboat house on Poole Quay (see also 21st April).

The un-named boat was later stationed at Cadgwith, and a gift of £5000 from the Girl Guides of the Empire was used to pay for her. Appropriately she was named *Guide of Dunkirk*.

31st MAY   LONDON, 1889

For many years steam tugs had been used to take lifeboats out to near wrecks. The possibility of a steam powered lifeboat presented problems, not least that of keeping the fires going in the conditions in which lifeboats operated. In 1888, however, Messrs. R. H. Green of Blackwall submitted a model of a steam lifeboat which was accepted by the Institution. On the 31st May 1889, the first steam lifeboat, to be named *Duke of Northumberland*, was launched. When completed, she started service at Harwich in September 1890, and subsequently served at Holyhead (1892 - 1893 and 1897 - 1922) and New Brighton (1893 - 1897). Costing approximately £5000, she was 50ft long, with a beam of 14ft 4 inches. The engines developed 170-horse power, the boat was built of steel, and she could carry 30 people in addition to her crew (see also 27th December).

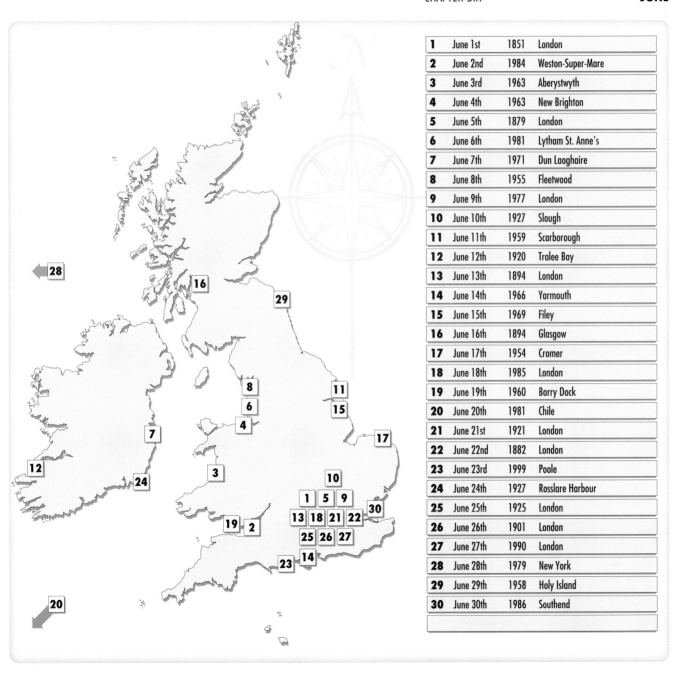

1	June 1st	1851	London
2	June 2nd	1984	Weston-Super-Mare
3	June 3rd	1963	Aberystwyth
4	June 4th	1963	New Brighton
5	June 5th	1879	London
6	June 6th	1981	Lytham St. Anne's
7	June 7th	1971	Dun Laoghaire
8	June 8th	1955	Fleetwood
9	June 9th	1977	London
10	June 10th	1927	Slough
11	June 11th	1959	Scarborough
12	June 12th	1920	Tralee Bay
13	June 13th	1894	London
14	June 14th	1966	Yarmouth
15	June 15th	1969	Filey
16	June 16th	1894	Glasgow
17	June 17th	1954	Cromer
18	June 18th	1985	London
19	June 19th	1960	Barry Dock
20	June 20th	1981	Chile
21	June 21st	1921	London
22	June 22nd	1882	London
23	June 23rd	1999	Poole
24	June 24th	1927	Rosslare Harbour
25	June 25th	1925	London
26	June 26th	1901	London
27	June 27th	1990	London
28	June 28th	1979	New York
29	June 29th	1958	Holy Island
30	June 30th	1986	Southend

1st JUNE LONDON, 1851

Shortly before he became President of the Institution, (see 2nd May), the Duke of Northumberland had himself offered a prize of 100 guineas for the best model of a lifeboat to overcome certain shortcomings in existing boats described in the notice of the competition. The notice had been sent out in October 1850 with a closing date of the 1st February 1851. Two hundred and eighty entries were received, a number coming from abroad. Models would not be retained beyond the 1st April 1851 in case the builder wished to send them to the Great Exhibition to be held in the Crystal Palace in Hyde Park.

The report of the jury appointed to adjudicate on the entries was sent to the Duke on the 1st June 1851. The winning entry came from James Beeching of Great Yarmouth. His plan was used as the basis of the boat built by James Peake, a member of the competition jury, at Woolwich Dockyard, and which was tried out at Brighton (see 3rd February).

To BOATBUILDERS, SHIPWRIGHTS, &c.

GREAT loss of life having occurred from time to time on the coast of Northumberland, and elsewhere, by the upsetting of Life-Boats, and especially in the case of the Shields Life-Boat in December last, whereby 20 Pilots were drowned,

Notice is hereby Given,

That with a view to the improvement of Boats to be employed for such purposes, His Grace the DUKE OF NORTHUMBERLAND offers the Sum of

ONE HUNDRED GUINEAS

For the best MODEL of a LIFE-BOAT, which may be sent to the *Surveyor's Department, Admiralty, Somerset House, London,* by the 1st day of February, 1851.

Captain Sir BALDWIN W. WALKER, K.C.B., Surveyor of the Navy, has consented to act as final referee in adjudging the reward, and has named the following Committee to examine the Models and conduct the requisite experiments.

Captain WASHINGTON, R.N., F.R.S., Inspector of Harbours.
JOHN FINCHAM, Esq., Master Shipwright at Portsmouth Dockyard.
ISAAC WATTS, Esq., Assistant Surveyor, Admiralty, Somerset House.
Commr. JERNINGHAM, R.N., late Inspecting Commr of Coast Guard at Great Yarmouth.
JAMES PEAKE, Esq., Assistant Master Shipwright, Woolwich Dockyard.

And His Grace offers the further Sum of

ONE HUNDRED GUINEAS

For BUILDING a LIFE-BOAT according to the Model which may be approved of.

It is considered that the chief objections to the present Life-Boats, generally speaking, are :—

1. That they do not right themselves in the event of being upset.
2. That they are too heavy to be readily launched, or transported along the coast, in case of need.
3. That they do not free themselves of water fast enough.
4. That they are very expensive.

It is recommended that the Models be made on the scale of one inch to a foot, and that they be accompanied by Plans, Specifications, and Estimates. The Models will not be detained beyond the 1st of April, in case the respective Builders should wish to send them to the GREAT INDUSTRIAL EXHIBITION of 1851.

LONDON, *October,* 1850.

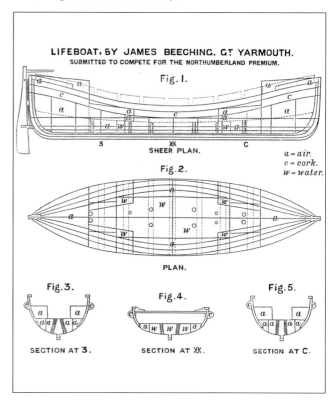

The notice sent out for the Duke of Northumberland Prize, searching for the best design of a new lifeboat.

2nd JUNE   WESTON-SUPER-MARE, SOMERSET, **1984**

A lifeboat alert interrupted the wedding reception of Nick White, a member of the Weston-Super-Mare lifeboat, and Alison Lyall on Saturday the 2nd June 1984.

Nick's best man, brother Tim, and most of the crew were among the guests at the Royal Hotel, close to the lifeboat house. When their warning bleepers went off, they thought it was just a cruel joke - but it was the real thing. All the crew present, including the groom, sprinted from the hotel to the lifeboat station at the end of the Old Pier. Festivities were resumed after a stranded boat had been towed to safety.

3rd JUNE   ABERYSTWYTH, CARDIGANSHIRE, **1963**

Inshore lifeboats were first introduced into service in 1963. The first D class lifeboat was stationed at Aberystwyth on the 23rd May 1963, carrying out its first effective service on the 3rd June. Three persons and a dog cut off by the tide were rescued.

On the 25th May 1964, the ILB was called out to search for a person blown out to sea on an airbed. The airbed was found about two miles from shore, its occupant was rather red in the face and out of breath. He had fallen asleep on the airbed on the beach, with the tide on the flood. When he woke up he was at sea - he then discovered the airbed had a leak and had to keep blowing it up to stay afloat. The wind was too strong for him to paddle back to shore so he had to wait for someone to pick him up.

4th JUNE   NEW BRIGHTON, CHESHIRE, **1963**

The Lifeboat Journal of September 1963 carried the following report:

"At 10.25 p.m. on 4 June 1963, the Formby coastguard informed the Honorary Secretary that four boys were marooned on a marker buoy off Hall Road, Crosby. At 10.40 p.m. the reserve lifeboat White Star, on temporary duty at the station, was launched. There was a light easterly wind and a calm sea, and it was high water. The lifeboat found the boys clinging to a beach mark, but she could not come nearer than 10 yards away from them because of the shallow water.

"The lights of a police car were illuminating the scene, and a member of the lifeboat crew jumped into the sea with a breeches buoy. When he reached the boys he decided that it would be easier to carry them ashore than to the lifeboat. This he did, one by one, landing them on the beach. The lifeboat stood by during the operation, and when the crew member had been re-embarked she returned to her station where she arrived at 12.25 a.m."

5th JUNE   LONDON, **1879**

At a meeting of the Committee of Management on the 5th June 1879, four new Inspectors of Lifeboats were 'elected' to assist the Chief Inspector and his Deputy.

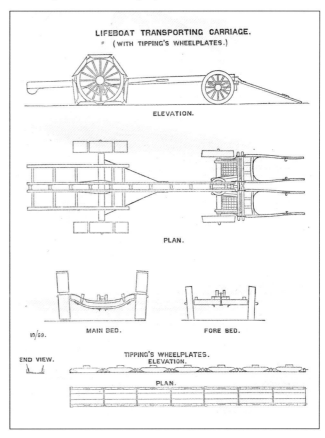

A lifeboat sitting on its carriage. It can be clearly seen how difficult it must have been to move such heavy loads across beaches and foreshores without the use of 'Tippings Wheelplates' to prevent the carriage sinking.

The four included Lieutenant Henry Gartside-Tipping who was appointed to the Irish District where he served for 13 years.

He invented the Tipping's plates that enabled a heavy lifeboat to be transported on her carriage over deep and soft sand. The plates were subsequently adapted to the needs for the artillery. At the outbreak of the 1914-1918 war, and at the age of 66, he volunteered for service in the navy. He was killed in action on the 25th September 1915 whilst in command of the armoured yacht *Sanda*.

6th JUNE   LYTHAM ST. ANNE'S, LANCASHIRE, **1981**

The yacht *Morag*, in a south west by west gale and a very rough sea, was seen heading into more dangerous waters and was rolling heavily off South Shore, Blackpool. The Watson class lifeboat *City of Bradford III* slipped her moorings at 3.20 p.m. The yacht was found a quarter of a mile off shore on the Crusader bank, three-quarters of a mile from St. Anne's Pier, apparently abandoned and towing an inflatable dinghy close behind.

A man could be seen in the water, seemingly clinging to the dinghy's stern. Assistant Mechanic Pearson leapt into the dinghy, then jumped into the sea to drag the man clear as his lifeline had become entangled in some way. He dragged the man round to the port quarter clear of the lifeboat's bow, and climbed on to the yacht to secure a line to the lifeboat. Another crewman jumped

into the yacht, cut the lifeline and pulled the survivor into the casualty. Coxswain Wignall, in spite of having only one engine available, drove straight on to the yacht and took off the survivor and the second lifeboatman. Pearson had already been ordered back on board the lifeboat.

For this service Coxswain Arthur Wignall and Assistant Mechanic Brian Pearson each was awarded the Institution's bronze medal on the 16th September 1981

7th JUNE   DUN LAOGHAIRE, CO. DUBLIN, **1971**

On the 7th June 1971, the Dun Laoghaire lifeboat *John F. Kennedy* attended to two pleasure boats - the motor launch *Maytime* and the sailing boat *Morning Star*, towing them both to safety in Dun Laoghaire Harbour.

The Dun Laoghaire lifeboat John F. Kennedy named on the 12th August 1967 after the late U.S. president.

The *John F. Kennedy*, named on the 12th August 1967 after the late U.S. president, was the first of the new class of Waveney lifeboats to enter service.

The prototype was based on a rescue cutter designed by the United States Coastguard. The RNLI obtained one and numbered it '44-001'. She served in the relief fleet from 1964 until 1997. The only lifeboat not to have a name (nor was she allotted an Operational Number), she is now preserved at Chatham.

8th JUNE
FLEETWOOD, LANCASHIRE, **1955**

In his History of Fleetwood Lifeboats, Jeff Morris records the following service by the Watson class lifeboat Ann Letitia Russell.

"As the Isle of Man's steamer **Mona's Isle** *was leaving Fleetwood at 2.45 a.m on 8 June 1955, she collided with the local fishing vessel* **Ludo** *which sank almost immediately, throwing her crew of three into the water. The steamer searched in the darkness for the missing men, but ran aground on the beach, 100 yards west of the lifeboat house. At 3.30 a.m., the* **Ann Letitia Russell** *was launched and, at the Captain's request, in two trips, landed 153 people from the steamer, being re-housed again at 5.45 a.m. Two of the* **Ludo's** *crew had managed to swim ashore, but the skipper was lost. The* **Mona's Isle** *refloated just after mid-day".*

9th JUNE
LONDON, **1977**

Three lifeboats took part in the Silver Jubilee Pageant on the River Thames on the 9th June 1977. They were the appropriately named *Silver Jubilee (Civil Service No. 38)*, a new Rother class boat destined for Margate; the Sheerness Waveney class boat *Helen Turnbull*; and the former Selsey Watson class boat *Canadian Pacific II*.

The *Helen Turnbull* acted as the Lord Mayor of Westminster's barge, whilst the *Canadian Pacific II* later undertook an extensive tour on the River Thames. On the 28th June, three lifeboats took part in the Fleet Review at Spithead - the Clyde *City of Bristol*, the Arun *Joy and John Wade* and the Oakley *Charles Henry*.

10th JUNE
SLOUGH, BERKSHIRE, **1927**

Prior to the First World War, all carriage-launched lifeboats had to be launched either by human effort or with the help of horses. In 1920 trials began to see if it would be possible to use tractors. Early trials proved successful, but it was found that the first tractors were not powerful enough at some stations for launching over the shingle or soft mud.

In 1926, the RNLI approached the 'Four Wheel Drive' Lorry Company to see if it could provide a more powerful tractor and one that was capable of working in the worst conditions. This the FWD did and on the 9th May 1927, initial trials took place at the maker's works, which proved most encouraging. The tractor and the special carriage, weighed a total of 11½ tons. The tractor was powered by a 60 h.p. petrol engine and, with 4 forward and 2 reverse gears, it had a top speed of 12 m.p.h., the engine being made completely watertight. At a ceremony at the Slough works of the FWD Company on the 10th June 1927, H.R.H. The Princess Victoria formally christened the first of these tractors, (T23), *Princess Victoria*, this being the only RNLI tractor to be named. Only 4 of these large tractors were built, each one costing nearly £4,000.

After extensive trials at a number of locations, modifications were made to this tractor, to strengthen the frame and to provide increased pulling power, eventually giving a draw-bar pull of 15,000 lbs. In 1928, the *Princess Victoria* was placed 'on service' at Hoylake, serving there for 12 months, before being transferred to Clogher Head, in Eire, where she served until 1951.

11th JUNE
SCARBOROUGH, YORKSHIRE, **1959**

The first lifeboat of the Oakley class was named *J.G.Graves of Sheffield* at a ceremony at the Scarborough lifeboathouse on the 11th June 1959. The Lifeboat Journal of September 1959 reported on the naming ceremony:

"The lifeboat was a gift of the J. G. Graves Charitable Trust, and Mrs. R. J. Drummond-Jackson, daughter of the founder of the trust and herself one of the trustees, presented the boat to the Institution. Admiral Sir William Slayter, a member of the Committee of Management, accepted the lifeboat and handed her over to the branch, Mr. D. B. Atkinson, Honorary Secretary of the branch accepting her. The Mayor of Scarborough, Councillor J. A. Kennedy, opened the proceedings, and the Vicar of Scarborough, the Rev. Canon D. Oxby Parker, assisted by the President of the Scarborough Free Church Council, the Rev. R. B. Hyde, dedicated the lifeboat. Commander L. F. Hill, the Central District Inspector, described the boat. After a vote of thanks had been proposed by Captain J. E. Cooper, Chairman of the branch and seconded by Mrs. E. C. Nicholson, Chairman of the Scarborough Ladies Lifeboat Guild, Lady Georgiana Starkey named the boat. The Falsgrave County Modern School choir conducted by Miss. Miriam Dowson led the singing."

12th JUNE   TRALEE BAY, CO. DERRY, **1920**

On the 12th June 1920, two boys were bathing at Lighthouse Point, Tralee Bay, Co. Kerry. John F. O'Mahoney, son of the Chief of Customs at Fenit, and his friend Bernard Kelly, were both 12 years old, and neither could swim more than a few strokes. It was a cold day, and a moderate gale was blowing off shore. Kelly got into difficulties.

Unable to reach him, O'Mahoney, with the help of some little girls, managed to launch a canvas canoe. The tide was ebbing and a strong off shore current swept him past the drowning boy. O'Mahoney was himself finally rescued by HMS *Heather* - the canoe was eight miles out, and the boy was lying naked and wet in the bottom.

Although it was not strictly an attempt at rescue from shipwreck, the Committee of Management felt it to be a case of so exceptional character as to justify them in giving a generous interpretation to the rule governing the bestowal of the Institution's medals. O'Mahoney was awarded the Institution's bronze medal and also received two War Savings Certificates.

13th JUNE   CITY OF LONDON, **1894**

The August 1894 Lifeboat Journal reported that *"a public meeting in furtherance of the objects of the RNLI was held on Wednesday afternoon, 13 June 1894, in the Egyptian Hall at the Mansion House, by the special invitation of the Lord Mayor of London.*

"His Royal Highness the Duke of Saxe-Coburg and Gotha attended and proposed the motion - 'That this meeting of Citizens of London is of the opinion that the Royal National Lifeboat Institution, which is maintained entirely by voluntary contributions, deserves the most earnest and hearty support of the people of this first maritime port in the world, and pledges itself to do its utmost to promote its objects and welfare.

"This was duly carried, and Captain Lord Charles Beresford then proposed 'that steps be taken to form a branch of the Institution in the City of London' together with a powerful committee headed by the Lord Mayor and Sheriffs. The resolution was agreed to with acclamation."

14th JUNE   YARMOUTH, ISLE OF WIGHT, **1966**

At 3.37 p.m. on the 14th June 1966, there was an alert that a helicopter had crashed in the Solent near West Lepe buoy. The lifeboat *The Earl and Countess Howe* left her moorings together with the IRB at 3.55 p.m. There was a light westerly wind and a smooth sea. The tide was flooding.

A search was carried out between the East and West Lepe buoys, and the helicopter was eventually found about half a mile to the south of the entrance to Beaulieu river. Its tail was projecting above the water but there was no sign of the crew. The lifeboat attached a buoy to the tail of the helicopter. This was recovered later, when a Royal Navy helicopter attached another buoy to the machine. The IRB and lifeboat returned to their station at 5.35 p.m. and 6.20 p.m. respectively.

15th JUNE   FILEY, YORKSHIRE, **1969**

From the January 1970 Lifeboat Journal comes the following report.

"At 9.43 p.m. on 15 June 1969, the coastguard reported that a man and two small children were cut off by the tide under the cliffs one mile north west of Filey Brigg. When the IRB was launched at 9.55 p.m, the weather was misty with poor visibility. After a two mile passage around Filey Brigg in failing light the IRB approached the reported scene of the incident. It was just possible to see the party huddled against the crumbling cliff face.

"The northerly swell had built up in the locality and was breaking over rocks at the foot of the cliff, making it very difficult to work into a position where the party could be reached. Eventually the man and children were safely brought across the weed-covered rocks, but care was needed to avoid the deep rock pools in the area. The IRB returned at 10.30 p.m."

16th JUNE   GLASGOW, **1894**

A report on the naming of the new steam lifeboat *City of Glasgow* appeared in the August 1894 Lifeboat Journal:

"This lifeboat was sufficiently far advanced to attend the highly

successful *'Lifeboat Saturday'* demonstration which took place in Glasgow on Saturday, 16 June, 1894, when she was publicly named, in the presence of at least 30,000 people, by Mrs Bell, the wife of the Lord Provost. It will be remembered that the citizens in connection with the *'Lifeboat Saturday'* demonstrations of 1893 and 1894 have raised the cost of the boat for the Institution.

"The Lord Provost, in making the presentation of the boat on behalf of the subscribers, referred in terms of praise to the great work which had been accomplished in the past by the Royal National Lifeboat Institution. He said that up to the close of last year it had granted rewards for saving 37,855 persons from shipwrecks on our coast. Further, when they looked round and considered that on their side of the River Clyde there were then in view about that number of people, they had brought home to their minds how great a work that was. Again, there was not only the saving of the lives of all those people from a watery grave, but they had also the many thousands interested in them to whom the Institution had brought joy and gladness.

"The lifeboat, on her return from Glasgow, was handed over to the builders, Messrs. R. and H. Green, of Blackwall Yard, for completion and bringing up in all points to the specification, prior to being finally taken over by the Institution for duty. Harwich has been selected as the station at which the boat is to be placed."

The *City of Glasgow* served at Harwich from 1894 to 1901, except for a short period from the 24th November 1897 to the 1st February 1998 when she was at Gorleston. At Harwich she launched 23 times and saved 32 lives; at Gorleston 3 launches with no lives saved.

17th JUNE   CROMER, NORFOLK, **1954**

Henry Blogg first joined the crew of the Cromer lifeboat in January 1894 at the age of 18. He was appointed Second Coxswain in 1902 and Coxswain in 1909. He retired in 1947 at the age of 71. During his service in the Cromer lifeboats 873 lives were saved. He won the Institution's gold medal three times and the silver medal four times. He was decorated with the George Cross and the British Empire Medal. He died on 13 June 1954.

At the funeral service held in Cromer Parish Church on 17 June 1954, more than 1,400 people crowded into the church and many more stood on the pavements outside. The President of Cromer branch of the Institution said *"we are here to pay the last tribute to a very gallant man of simple tastes, great courage and strong character. His exploits are known to the whole nation."*

18th JUNE   LONDON, **1985**

On the 18th June 1985, the Post Office issued a set of stamps to commemorate Britain's contribution to the international safety network. The 17p stamp of a lifeboat launching marked the 200th anniversary of Lional Lukin's patent (see 25th February). Other watersheds for 1985 were Britain's hosting the eleventh conference of the International Association of Lighthouse Authorities and also the 50th anniversary of radar.

The 22p stamp featured Beachy Head lighthouse with a section of an Admiralty chart; the 31p showed a communications satellite over the Atlantic and the 34p depicted a buoy warning shipping to keep south of a marked hazard.

19th JUNE   BARRY DOCK, GLAMORGAN, **1960**

Just before midnight, the coastguard informed the Honorary Secretary of Barry Dock lifeboat station that the sand dredger *Ron Woolaway* had capsized near Flatholm Island. The message also stated that her crew of seven were safely ashore on the island.

A request was made for the lifeboat to take dry clothing to the men and return with them to Barry. Enquiries were made at the offices of the British Sailors' Society. No clothing was immediately available, but the motor lifeboat *Rachel and Mary Evans* put out at 12.20 a.m. on the 19th June 1960 in foggy weather, when the tide was in half flood. The lifeboat picked up the seven men and landed them at Barry at 2.10 a.m. where they were provided with dry clothing, which the British Sailors' Society had by then obtained for them.

20th JUNE   VALPARAISO, CHILE, **1981**

The former Barnett class lifeboat *Southern Africa* was sold to the

Chiliean Lifeboat Society in 1981. At a ceremony at Valparaiso on the 20th June 1981 she was re-named *Valparaiso III* when the bonds between the Botes Salvavidas de Valparaiso and the RNLI, described by the Chilean organisation as *'our spiritual mother'*, were stressed.

Built in 1949 the lifeboat was stationed at Dover until 1967 where she launched 263 times and saved 186 lives. In the relief fleet from 1967 to 1981 she launched a further 39 times, saving 10 lives.

21st JUNE   LONDON, **1921**

The November 1921 Lifeboat Journal reported on the founding of the Ladies Lifeboat Guild.

The Inaugural Meeting of the Guild was held in London on the 21st June 1921 at Claridge's Hotel, at the invitation of the President, the Duchess of Portland, who took the chair, and who delivered an address on the aims of the Guild. The other speakers were Sir Godfrey Baring, Bt., the Deputy-Chairman of the Institution, Lady Baring, Lady Cynthia Colville, and Mr. George F. Shee, M.A., the Secretary of the Institution. This inaugural meeting was immediately followed by two others in and near London, one at Hampstead Garden Suburb and the other at St. Albans. Meetings followed at towns throughout the country.

The Duchess explained that the purpose of the Guild was 'to bring all women workers into closer touch will each other and with the Honorary Secretaries and Committees of the Branches in virtue of the fact that they will be reorganised as members of a Guild.'

22nd JUNE   LONDON, **1882**

A circular letter from Headquarters to Honorary Secretaries on the 22nd June 1882 stated that the Institution had decided *"to supply Owners or Masters of Fishing Vessels with an Aneroid Barometer of a superior and reliable character, at a small cost, which must make this useful instrument a welcome addition to every decked fishing-boat's equipment."*

In the November 1883 Lifeboat Journal, it was reported that

applications had been received for more than 1,200 barometers. The Committee had decided to extend "to poor Masters and Owners of Coasters, under 100 tons burden, the privilege of purchasing for eleven shillings and sixpence, one third of the retail cost, a first class Aneroid barometer."

23rd JUNE   POOLE, DORSET, **1999**

As part of the 175th anniversary celebrations, the 18th International Lifeboat Conference was held in Poole in June. Over 100 representatives from 40 countries attended, from as far afield as China, New Zealand, South Africa and Estonia.

On the 23rd June, an international flotilla of lifeboats - old and new - sailed through Poole Harbour and past the review stand on

Poole Quay. Led by the pulling and sailing lifeboat *Queen Victoria* (Bembridge 1887-1902), the flotilla had lifeboats from ten countries, including Norway, France, Canada and the United States. There were also historic British and foreign lifeboats, as well as examples of every RNLI operational lifeboat serving in the current fleet. After the flotilla, the Mayor of Poole, Admiral of the Port, honoured the RNLI by granting it the honour of the Freedom of the Borough of Poole.

24th JUNE   ROSSLARE HARBOUR, CO. WEXFORD, **1927**

The new Rosslare Harbour lifeboat *K.E.C.F.* carried out its first service on the 24th June 1927 when she went out to the lugger *Mona* and saved four persons. This lifeboat was the first Institution boat to be fitted with wireless. A description of the equipment can be found in the May 1927 Lifeboat Journal.

P.N. 48.

ROYAL NATIONAL LIFEBOAT INSTITUTION
WIRELESS TELEGRAPHY INSTRUCTIONS.
ROSSLARE HARBOUR LIFEBOAT.

1. The Wireless Operator will be held responsible for the proper working of his set and for the efficient and economical maintenance of the apparatus. He will be expected to make any necessary adjustments and, as far as possible, to remedy any faults which may develop.

2. The Operator is not to alter the arrangements of, or to take apart any portion of the apparatus except for the purpose of effecting necessary repairs. No additional apparatus shall be connected to the Installation without authority. The apparatus as installed is licensed by the Government, and any alterations would be a breach of the licence.

3. The Wireless Telegraphy apparatus is not to be used whilst the Lifeboat is in harbour unless the message to be sent is of such urgency as to warrant its use in preference to the telegraph. Only messages directly referring to life-saving should normally be sent under these conditions.

4. The Operator is to inspect the apparatus and all parts of the rigging for the same daily. Particular attention is to be paid to the condition of the accumulators.

5. All messages other than those addressed to vessels will be transmitted or received through Fishguard Radio. Procedure in dealing with traffic will be in accordance with the Rules contained in the Postmaster-General's Handbook.

6. Whilst the Lifeboat is at sea every opportunity is to be taken by the Operator to familiarise himself with his installation by receiving messages. All such messages are to be logged in the Wireless Log provided for that purpose. The Head Office may be communicated with for exercise purposes, but in such event any message transmitted is to be preceded by the word " Exercise."

7. It is of the utmost importance that full details of all signals sent and received, as well as particulars of all occurrences, such as change of watch, breakdowns or adjustment of apparatus, etc., be entered in the Log Book at the time of the occurrence.

8. The following instructions are to be carried out when the Lifeboat proceeds to sea on Service :—

   (a) A brief Message is to be sent via Fishguard Radio to the Head Office (telegraphic address " Lifeboat Institution, London ") reporting the fact of the Lifeboat proceeding to sea, outlining very briefly the reason for so doing. For example :—
   " Lifeboat Institution London
   Rosslare Lifeboat proceeding to assistance fishing vessel ashore Haven Point S.E. gale
   Rosslare Lifeboat."

   (b) When the service is completed a further Message reporting the result is to be sent. For example :—
   (1) " Lifeboat Institution London
   Rosslare Lifeboat returning stop Rescued crew 3 stop Vessel total wreck
   Rosslare Lifeboat."

   (2) " Lifeboat Institution London
   Rosslare Lifeboat returning stop Vessel refloated unaided
   Rosslare Lifeboat."

   Messages of this nature serve the double purpose of notifying both Fishguard Radio and the Head Office of the movements of the Lifeboat. Fishguard Radio will then be on the look-out for any messages from or to her.

9. The original copy of any message sent or received on life-saving service is to be handed to the Honorary Secretary, who will attach the same to the Return of Service. The message is also to be logged in accordance with Paragraph 7 of these Instructions.

10. A continuous Wireless Telegraphy watch, subject, however, to the provisions of Paragraph 13, is to be kept whilst the Lifeboat is at sea. If, however, the circumstances of the case require the Lifeboat to be at sea for a period exceeding four hours and if after maintaining watch for this period the operator finds it necessary to relinquish watch for a length of time, he should inform Fishguard Radio when he will resume watch.

11. When the Certificated Operator is not on watch, a " Watcher " will listen for Distress Calls (SOS) or the Safety Signal (TTT).

12. Every opportunity should be afforded to members of the Crew showing an aptitude for wireless work to be given facilities in receiving actual signals and for practice on a dummy morse key with a view to attaining a standard of qualification for the Postmaster-General's Certificate. No member of the Crew will, however, be allowed to operate the installation until such time as he is in possession of the Postmaster-General's Certificate.

13. Whilst actually engaged in life-saving, i.e., alongside a wreck or other occasions of emergency, it is probable that the services of every man will be required, and in such event the Operator will be authorised on the Coxswain's instructions to leave his instrument and assist the remainder of the Crew. He should, however, advise Fishguard Radio that he is about to leave his instrument, stating the probable duration of his absence, and resume his wireless duties at the earliest possible moment.

14. Whilst the Lifeboat is in harbour the Operator will carry out such orders as may be issued by the Coxswain for visual look-out duties or such other work connected with the lifeboat Station as may be required.

15. The Radio Communication Company's Inspector will periodically inspect the installation, and the operator must render all possible assistance to him in the performance of this duty.

16. Requisitions for stationery and any other supplies are to be made to the Head Office on the usual Demand Forms and submitted through the Honorary Secretary.

By order of the Committee of Management,
GEORGE F. SHEE,
Secretary.

28th April, 1927.

The instructions, dated the 28th April 1927, that were issued to the Rosslare lifeboat regarding the operation of their wireless unit.

The Rosslare Harbour Motor lifeboat at sea with the wireless aerial fitted and ready for operation.

The wireless transmitter and receiver unit as fitted to the Rosslare Harbour lifeboat (inset).

"The wireless installation, which has been placed in the cabin, is the ¹/₄ kilowatt installation designed by the Radio Communication Company for ships' lifeboats. The whole of the transmitting and receiving apparatus is enclosed in a watertight case. The operator works through a hole in the case fitted with a waterproof sleeve, and in the front of the case there is a window, lighted by a small lamp, through which he can see the controls, receiver valves, and writing tablet.

"The boat went from the building yard at Cowes to Ireland at the end of April, and the wireless was tested during the trip, getting communication with Niton Wireless Station at a distance of 85 miles. Since then it has communicated with Portpatrick, a distance of 185 miles".

In his report of the trip the District Inspector wrote, *"I do not think there is anything of interest to record except perhaps that fried sausages and tea were enjoyed on the passage. The former were cooked in the lid of a biscuit tin slung over the funnel, and a kettle was boiled in eight minutes by the same method."*

25th JUNE   LONDON, **1925**

The Lifeboat Journal of November 1925 recorded the awards to the Institution made by foreign societies on the occasion of the 100th anniversary in 1924 and in particular one from the USA.

"The Institution has been awarded the 'Gold Life-saving Medal of Honor" of the United States of America, which was personally presented on 25 June 1925 by Commander C. D. Hinckley, of the U.S. Coastguard. With the medal was the following letter from Rear-Admiral T. C. Billard, Commandant of the U.S. Coastguard:

"The Honorable the Secretary of the Treasury authorizes me to present to the Royal National Lifeboat Institution of Great Britain the Gold Life-saving Medal of Honor of the United States Government in commemoration of the one-hundreth anniversary of the Institution, and in recognition of the renowned service the Institution has rendered humanity in saving lives from the perils of the sea ...I desire to renew my expressions of profound admiration for your Institution. The record of its achievements in the cause of humanity have brought enduring distinction and honor to the life saving annals of the world. The United States

Coastguard is happy to join hands with its sister Service across the sea in hearty felicitation and good will."

In addition to the American Medal the Institution received the Gold Medals of both Dutch Lifeboat Societies and of the Spanish and Norwegian Societies. There was the Silver Medal of the Greek Fund for Naval Pensions, which is awarded for saving life at sea, and Illuminated Addresses from the Swedish Government, the Swedish Lifeboat Society and the French Lifeboat Society.

26th JUNE   LONDON, **1901**

A very elaborate Fête was organised at Stafford House, home of the Duke and Duchess of Sutherland, on the 26th June 1901 by the West End of London Ladies' Auxiliary. The General Committee for the event included five Duchesses and eleven other titled ladies.

A grand concert and variety entertainment was given in the Picture Gallery. The Ben Greet Co. performed the 'Comedy of Errors' in the open air, and the band of the Royal Artillery played in the garden.

As the August 1901 Lifeboat Journal indicated, this *'was one of the most successful and remarkable undertakings ever carried out in connection with a charity'.*

27th JUNE

The RNLI was closely involved with the 90th birthday celebrations of Her Majesty Queen Elizabeth the Queen Mother. Her Majesty has been a Patron of the Institution since 1937.

On the 27th June 1990, Horse Guards Parade was the scene of a pageant staged by charities and institutions connected with Her Majesty. An Atlantic rigid inflatable, towed by a Land Rover, represented the RNLI at Horse Guards Parade, with 15 lifeboatmen, two staff, and two voluntary fund-raisers making up the tableau.

Steven Simmons and Philip Howard of the RNLI's Cowes base drove the Land Rover, whilst the Atlantic 21 was manned by lifeboatmen Martin Ellison, Joe Breen and Billy Ellison from Portaferry. Tony Bebbington, David Knowles and Geoff Barfoot of Poole escorted the RNLI colour that was born by Teesmouth Coxswain Peter Race.

Flanking them were Norman Urquhart and Colin McCaffrey of Thurso (whose Arun class lifeboat is named *Queen Mother*), Barry Roberts and Richard McLaughlin of Trearddur Bay, Tony Hawkins and Peter Killick of Dover and Ian Vincent and Ron Latcham of Hartlepool. Mrs. Dru Dennis of the Godstone branch and John Cox of the St. Albans branch represented the fund-raisers at this auspicious occasion.

A few weeks later the RNLI took part in the Queen Mother's review of yachts at Spithead on the Solent, when the Yarmouth and Bembridge lifeboats led the huge escort which accompanied the Royal Yacht *Britannia* on her passage through massed ranks of yachts anchored in her honour. Yarmouth's Arun class *Joy and John Wade* took the westbound leg and Bembridge's Tyne class *Max Aitken III* the eastbound - the two lifeboats executing an impressive switch from a very hemmed-in position as *Britannia* turned through 180 degrees. Portsmouth and Lymington's Atlantics and Calshot's Brede class lifeboat were also at sea as part of the safety arrangements for the huge fleet of yachts.

28th JUNE

Nine men from The Mumbles lifeboat station flew to New York on the 28th June 1979 to take part in International Lifeboat races there, competing against teams from the US Army and Navy and ships' crews.

The races were held in 28-foot wooden boats, over a course of one mile in New York harbour. The team from The Mumbles reached the finals, and there they came second, whilst a crew from the Queen Elizabeth II came third. The trophy was won by a team from Hartlepool, Teesmouth and Crimdon Dene in 1980 and retained by Newquay, Cornwall in 1981.

29th JUNE

During the visit of H. M. the Queen and H. R. H. the Duke of Edinburgh to Holy Island on the 29th June 1958, the North Sunderland Liverpool class lifeboat *Grace Darling* was given the task of escorting the royal barge.

During this duty the Coxswain saw a small motor boat in difficulties a mile and a half east of Holy Island. The lifeboat made for the position and found the motor boat *Lady Francis* of Holy Island with her engine broken down. The *Lady Francis* had fourteen passengers and crew on board. The lifeboat took her in tow to Holy Island harbour and then continued escorting the royal barge.

30th JUNE

As reported in the autumn 1986 Lifeboat Journal, the 645-tonne coaster *Kingsabbey* ploughed into Southend Pier on the evening of Monday, 30th June 1986. She came to rest athwart the lifeboat slipway destroying piles supporting the front of the boathouse. More damage was done while the coaster extricated herself from this position but fortunately the station's Atlantic 21 rigid inflatable lifeboat *Percy Garon II*, named only two months earlier by Princess Anne, although trapped inside the boathouse was unharmed.

The lifeboat was salvaged from the boathouse the next day together with all the equipment needed to allow her to operate again from a temporary base and, just 48 hours after the accident, she was back in service. The boathouse, however, was structurally so badly damaged that it was decided that it would have to be demolished. The severed walkway has been repaired and a temporary boathouse has been built on the very end of the pier where the lifeboat is launched by davits.

The severed pier at Southend with the isolated lifeboat station on the left. The lifeboat, thankfully, survived the incident intact and was able to go straight back into service.

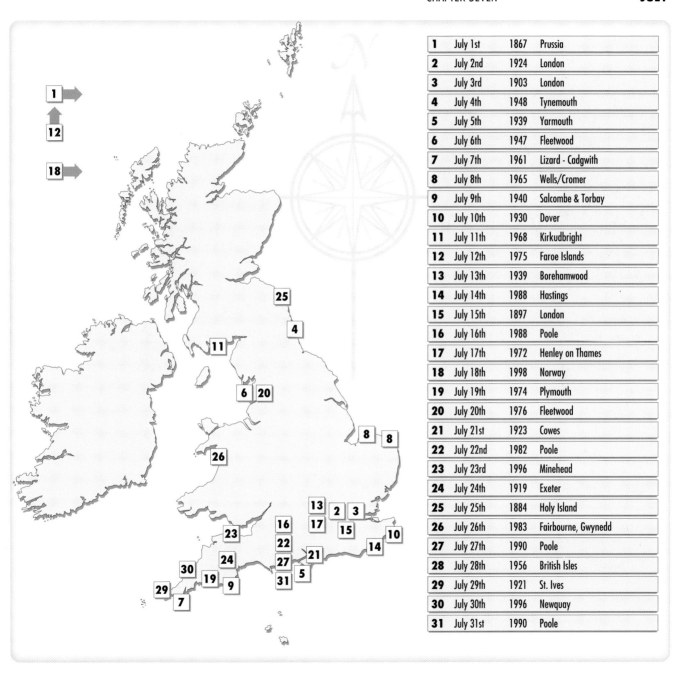

1	July 1st	1867	Prussia
2	July 2nd	1924	London
3	July 3rd	1903	London
4	July 4th	1948	Tynemouth
5	July 5th	1939	Yarmouth
6	July 6th	1947	Fleetwood
7	July 7th	1961	Lizard - Cadgwith
8	July 8th	1965	Wells/Cromer
9	July 9th	1940	Salcombe & Torbay
10	July 10th	1930	Dover
11	July 11th	1968	Kirkudbright
12	July 12th	1975	Faroe Islands
13	July 13th	1939	Borehamwood
14	July 14th	1988	Hastings
15	July 15th	1897	London
16	July 16th	1988	Poole
17	July 17th	1972	Henley on Thames
18	July 18th	1998	Norway
19	July 19th	1974	Plymouth
20	July 20th	1976	Fleetwood
21	July 21st	1923	Cowes
22	July 22nd	1982	Poole
23	July 23rd	1996	Minehead
24	July 24th	1919	Exeter
25	July 25th	1884	Holy Island
26	July 26th	1983	Fairbourne, Gwynedd
27	July 27th	1990	Poole
28	July 28th	1956	British Isles
29	July 29th	1921	St. Ives
30	July 30th	1996	Newquay
31	July 31st	1990	Poole

1st JULY   PILAU, PRUSSIA, **1867**

The Lifeboat Journal of the 1st July 1867 carried the following description of 'A Prussian Grace Darling':

"At Pilau, in Prussia, now lives a woman who has for some years consecrated her life to the noble and dangerous task of rescuing persons from drowning. Whenever a tempest comes on, day or night, Catherine Kleinfeldt, who is the widow of a sailor, is ready with a boat, in which she puts out to sea, and frequently goes farther than any other, in order to give help to those who may be shipwrecked. More than 300 individuals have been saved by her efforts; and, accustomed for 20 years to make voyages with her husband, she possesses a skill and hardihood that render these efforts unusually successful.

"When she is seen, the greatest respect is paid to her, and the sailors regard her as their guardian angel; the very children of the fishermen go upon their knees to her, and kiss the skirt of her dress.

"The Prussian and other Governments have decreed her medals, and the Principality of Pilau has made her an honorary citizen for life. She is about sixty years of age, with an athletic figure of great strength (a Grace Darling enlarged into gigantic proportions); she has a masculine countenance, which, however, is softened by the benevolent expression that it constantly wears".

2nd JULY   LONDON, **1924**

As part of the celebrations of the centenary of the Institution, an International Lifeboat Conference was held in London on the 1st and 2nd July 1924. This was attended by representatives from many countries around the world.

One of the decisions made at this first such conference was *'that an international lifeboat organisation be formed on the lines of the Red Cross Society, with all National Lifeboat Societies as its members'.* The RNLI is the Headquarters and Secretariat for the International Lifeboat Federation, as it is now called. Conferences are held every four years when matters of mutual interest are discussed. As part of the 175th anniversary celebrations of the RNLI, the 18th conference was held at Poole (see 23rd June).

3rd JULY   LONDON, **1903**

The following description of a royal event at Marlborough House comes from the November 1903 Lifeboat Journal.

"The Lifeboat Saturday workers throughout the country, and more especially those connected with the Ladies Auxiliaries, have been greatly encouraged and stimulated in their self denying efforts during the past summer by the gracious and very important personal interest taken in their work by the Princess of Wales. She is not only the Vice-Patron of the Royal National Lifeboat Institution, but also the President of the Ladies Auxiliaries.

"The 3rd July 1903 will long be remembered by the same 125 ladies, who, gathered from all parts of the United Kingdom - England, Scotland and Ireland - met at Marlborough House on that day by the kind invitation of their Royal President. These ladies were either Presidents or local Ladies Auxiliaries, or had, for other reasons, been specially selected by the various Ladies' Committees of the Lifeboat Saturday Fund, to represent them at this pleasant function. Each lady on being presented to the Princess, handed her a purse representing the financial results of the most recent collection made by their respective committees. It was generally felt that, thanks to this mark of favour to, and interest in, the kind work shown by Her Royal Highness, even better results would be obtained by them in the near future".

4th JULY   TYNEMOUTH, NORTHUMBERLAND, **1948**

Late in the afternoon of the 4th July, 1948, a sudden freak squall broke from the north and at 4.59 p.m. the coastguard telephoned that three small sailing yachts had capsized in the haven. Within fifteen minutes the motor lifeboat *Tynesider* had put out. Mr E Selby Davidson, the Honorary Secretary of the station, was on board her. The sea was rough, and a strong northerly breeze was blowing, with torrential rain. When she reached the harbour entance the lifeboat saw the tug *Wearmouth* had gone to the help of the yachts. She then saw a motor fishing boat, the *Girl Carole*, of South Shields, in difficulties near the rocks of the south pier. Her engines had broken down. The lifeboat went to her help, rescued the crew of two and took the boat herself in tow, but she quickly filled with water and had to be abandoned.

The lifeboat then left the harbour and there she saw two other boats in distress two miles to the south of the south pier. She found that they were the motor yawl *Vigilant*, of Sunderland, and the motor fishing boat *May*, of Newcastle. The *Vigilant* had gone to the help of *May* and had taken her in tow, but seas broke over her, flooding her engine room, and she too was helpless. With some difficulty, in the heavy seas, the lifeboat got a rope to the *Vigilant*, rescued her two men and rescued the two men from the *May*. All four were exhausted and the lifeboatmen gave them rum. The lifeboat took the two boats back to North Shields and arrived back at her station at 7.45 that evening.

5 JULY   YARMOUTH, ISLE OF WIGHT, **1939**

At 7.20 p.m. on the 5th July 1939, the coastguard reported two men were in danger on a pile driver at Milford-on-Sea. A moderate squally S. S. W. gale was blowing, with a rough breaking sea. The motor lifeboat *S.G.E.* was launched at 7.32 a.m. and went to the pile driver, which was then two hundred yards from the shore. The lifeboat anchored to windward, veered down and with some difficulty rescued the two men. They were given stimulants and taken to Yarmouth.

The lifeboat was the second to be named *S.G.E.* The first boat, on station from August 1936, had been destroyed by fire on the 8th June 1937 whilst at the boatyard of Groves and Gutteridge. The new boat, on station from April 1938, served until 1963. In April 1964 she was sold to the Government of St. Helena and became a workboat named *John Dutton*.

6 JULY   FLEETWOOD, LANCASHIRE, **1947**

Attempts to attract attention by vessels in distress can sometimes go wrong as the following report from the September 1947 Lifeboat Journal illustrates:

"At 3.00 in the afternoon of 6 July, 1947, a message was received from the Wyre Lighthouse that a motor fishing vessel, the Wyvern, of Ramsgate, bound for Fleetwood, was making distress signals in the shallows of Pilling Sands. The motor lifeboat Ann Letitia Russell was having her engines overhauled, but she was launched at 3.25 p.m. on one engine, in a moderate west-north-west gale, with a heavy sea. The Wyvern's engine had broken down, so she had rapidly drifted into the shallows. There her crew set fire to

fishing nets as a distress signal, and in doing so set fire also to their own vessel.

"When the lifeboat arrived she found the flames spreading rapidly in the gale, and the three people on board - one of them the owner's wife - were exhausted. The lifeboatmen attempted, without success, to put out the fire, so she rescued the three people and brought them to Fleetwood, arriving at 4.05 that afternoon".

7 JULY   LIZARD–CADGWITH, CORNWALL, **1961**

The new lifeboat station at the Lizard-Cadgwith was formally opened by H. R. H. the Duke of Edinburgh, who is himself a member of the Committee of Management of the Institution, on the 7th July 1961. His Royal Highness also named the new lifeboat *The Duke of Cornwall (Civil Service No.33)*. A large crowd assembled in fine weather to watch the ceremony, and they were highly entertained when the Duke said of the lifeboat: *"I feel a certain parental interest in her. It is the second time I have had a hand in launching the Duke of Cornwall."*

Launching at Polpeor was always difficult in certain states of wind and tide. In the winter of 1957-58 wave tests were carried out a little further down the coast at Kilcobben. The tests proved successful, and two years later work started on a new lifeboat station. This photograph was taken during construction on the 19th June 1960.

The Chief Inspector of Lifeboats, Lt.Commander W. L. G. Dutton, described the new boat, which is one of the new 52-feet Barnett

The new Kilcobben house, which was operational from June 1961 and was formally opened the following month by the Duke of Edinburgh. There are 200 steps for the station personnel, and an inclined railway for stores and stretcher cases.

class. Sir Eric Seal, Chairman of the Civil Service Lifeboat Fund, then presented the boat to the Institution. As its name implies, this is the thirty-third lifeboat which the Civil Service Lifeboat Fund has provided. In accepting the boat and handing her over to the branch, Earl Howe, Chairman of the Committee of Management, pointed out that the new lifeboat station had been built at a cost of more than £90,000.

The lifeboathouse is built at the base of the cliffs at Kilcobben. There are 200 steps for personnel and an inclined railway for stores and stretcher cases.

The first lifeboat presented by the Civil Service Lifeboat Fund was, appropriately enough, the *Civil Service No.1* which went into service at Wexford in 1866.

8th JULY   NORFOLK, **1965**

Princess Marina, Duchess of Kent, named two new lifeboats in Norfolk on the 8th July 1965. They were the *Ernest Tom Nethercoat*, a 37-foot Oakley class for Wells, and the *William Henry and Mary King*, also an Oakley, for Cromer.

Princess Marina became President of the RNLI following the death of H. R. H. Prince George, Duke of Kent, in an aircraft crash in 1942. On the 11th July 1967, Princess Marina was awarded an honorary gold medal on completion of 25 years as President. Her son, the present Duke of Kent, was similarly awarded an honorary gold medal when he completed 25 years as President in 1994.

9th JULY   SALCOMBE and TORBAY, DEVON, **1940**

The potential dangers faced by lifeboatmen during the Second World War are well illustrated by the following rescue.

At 7.10 p.m. on the 9th July 1940, the Prawle Point Signal Station reported that a vessel was being bombed by enemy aeroplanes three or four miles away. A fresh S W wind was blowing, but the sea was smooth. At 7.30 p.m. the Salcombe motor lifeboat *Samuel and Marie Parkhouse* was launched. A motor boat, manned by three men, was also sent out from Lannercombe, as the vessel was sinking fast. The motor boat reached the vessel first, and found her to be the steamer *Talvaldis*, of Riga. She had not only been bombed, but had been repeatedly machine-gunned, and one of her crew had been killed. The remainder had abandoned ship. The motor boat rescued six of them from a raft and then stood by the steamer's boat, with six more men on board, which was waterlogged. When the lifeboat arrived at 8.45 p.m., she rescued the six men from the waterlogged boat; took on board all men from the motor boat; and then towed the motor boat to Lannercombe. She arrived back at her station at 10 p.m.

News of the attack on the steamer was also sent to Torbay, and the motor lifeboat *George Shee* put out at 7.39 p.m. On her way she passed the Dutch motor vessel *Jola*, which had also been attacked. She was making for Dartmouth with three of her crew wounded by machine gun bullets. The *George Shee* arrived at the scene of the attack on the *Talvaldis* to find that the men had been rescued, and returned to her station, arriving at midnight.

10th JULY   DOVER, KENT, **1930**

The 10th July 1930 saw the first of three royal naming ceremonies carried out in that month. The Prince of Wales (later King Edward VIII), President of the RNLI, named the lifeboat *Sir*

William Hillary at Dover. A special one-off design built especially for use in the English Channel, she was requisitioned in October 1940 and used as an RAF Air Sea Rescue vessel.

The Dover lifeboat Sir William Hillary powering out to sea.

On the 21st July, the Duke of Gloucester named the new Barnett class lifeboat *Princess Mary* for Padstow. She served there until 1962. Four days later, on the 25th July, Prince George (later Duke of Kent and President of the RNLI) named the new Ramsgate lifeboat *E.M.E.D.* for Walton and Frinton, and the Watson class *Edward Z Dresden* for Clacton-on-Sea.

11th JULY   KIRKCUDBRIGHT, DUMFRIES AND GALLOWAY, **1968**

The RNLI receives assistance from many sources, as illustrated by this report of help given by the Army.

During July 1968, a squadron of Royal Engineers repaired the track to the lifeboat station at Kirkcudbright, Scotland. The stations is four miles from the town and about a mile from the public road, access being by a private track which is also a pedestrian right of way.

A year earlier the track had been severely damaged by a combination of an extremely high tide, storm force winds from an unusual direction, and a much flooded river. Over a distance

of more than 100 yards and to a depth of 25 feet the track was breached and made completely impassable to traffic. Temporary repairs were, however, effected by Coxswain George Davidson, the crew and volunteer helpers.

Coastal erosion experts estimated that the cost of repairs would amount to £2,700 or more. Through HQ Scottish Command help was given under OPMAC (Operations with Military Assistance to the Civil Community). The 117 Field Support Squadron, R.E. reconnoitered the location, and plans were drawn up for the work to be carried out during the squadron's annual training that summer. Work began in earnest on the 1st July, and by the 13th the track was fully repaired.

12th JULY   FAROE ISLANDS, **1975**

At the invitation of the Faroese Lifesaving Society, the Kirkwall 70ft Clyde class lifeboat *Grace Paterson Ritchie* visited the Islands from the 12th July 1975. The Society was keen to develop a lifeboat service as an extension to the coast rescue equipment companies already established in the islands. The Faroese Government met all expenses for the trip.

During the four-day visit, demonstrations of the lifeboat's capabilities were keenly appreciated. The lifeboat was in command of Lt. Cdr. Brian Miles, who was appointed Director of the RNLI in 1988, a post from which he retired at the end of 1998.

13th JULY   BOREHAMWOOD, HERTS, **1939**

Since 1882, the Institution had maintained a store-yard at Poplar on the Thames where lifeboats were fitted out. By 1937, when the majority of the fleet were motor lifeboats, larger and more modern workshops were needed. A site was chosen outside London where there were excellent facilities for road transport. The new Depot was officially opened on the 13th July 1939. The October 1939 Lifeboat Journal described the new facilities in some detail:

"The depot has been designed and equipped on most modern lines, with ample space, air and light. It has workshops and stores covering a floor area of nearly an acre and a quarter. One of the

storerooms is for the Institution's supplies for appealing to the public. In it are stored the 40,000 collecting boxes, in the form of lifeboats, and the nine million paper flags which the Institution uses every year on lifeboat flag days.

"There are canteens and recreation rooms for staff, and three cottages for the depot foreman, the storehouseman, the deputy storehouseman and their families".

The front façade of the new depot of the Institution that was officially opened at Borehamwood, Hertfordshire, on the 13th July 1939.

During the Second World War, RNLI Headquarters moved to Borehamwood from the centre of London. From the middle of 1941 until the end of the war, the depot machinery shop was engaged in making light metal parts for Mosquito aeroplanes. In total the site made and assembled some 100,000 parts for the British war effort.

14th JULY   HASTINGS, SUSSEX, **1988**

A brand new class of lifeboat made her first official public appearance on Thursday, 14th July 1988 when she was launched from Hastings beach. This was the 12 metre (38 ft) Mersey class lifeboat, capable of $17^1/_2$ knots and specially designed to enter the water from a carriage. In announcing the new class name of 'Mersey', the Institution's Director Lt. Cdr. Brian Miles, said:

"This is a historic day for the RNLI. We now have a carriage launched lifeboat which has twice the speed of those she is designed to replace. The new class represents the final piece of jigsaw in our plan to complete the introduction of fast lifeboats by the year 1993."

He went on to say that the name of the 'Mersey' class was particularly appropriate. "There are stations on the approaches to the Mersey which are in line to receive this new class. We also used to operate a Liverpool class lifeboat so it is pleasant to be able to reaffirm our links with the area and its great maritime traditions in this way."

The £350,000 aluminium hulled Mersey class was designed and developed entirely by RNLI staff. She is self-righting, has twin 285 h.p. Caterpillar 3208T turbo-charged diesel engines, carries a crew of six and is fitted with the latest communication and navigational equipment.

15th JULY   LONDON, **1897**

Following charges of extravagance in the methods used for raising money, the Institution pressed for the appointment of a select committee of the House of Commons to investigate the way in which it discharged its responsibilities.

Appointed on the 17th March 1897, the Committee held nearly thirty meetings as well as sending questionnaires out to Coxswains, Honorary Secretaries and other interested parties. On the 15th July 1897, the Committee issued its report completely exonerating the Institution from the charges made against it.

The Report ended with the following words:

"Your Committee cannot conclude their Report without recording their opinion that the thanks of the whole community are due to the committee of the Royal National Lifeboat Institution for the energy and good management (often in very difficult circumstances) with which they have for so many years successfully carried out the national work of life-saving, and this without reward or payment of any sort. And your Committee regret it is not in their power to suggest some further protection for charitable institutions against attacks of irresponsible persons, which attacks may, as in the present case, turn out unfounded and untrue".

16th JULY   POOLE, DORSET, **1988**

On the 16th July 1988 the then British Prime Minister, Mrs. Margaret Thatcher, visited the headquarters of the RNLI in Poole to open the new fund-raising centre which was provided entirely by Mr. William Knott, a retired Poole business man. Mr. Knott had approached the Institution with the offer of constructing the building on the depot site to allow expansion of fund raising activities and to enable staff previously accommodated in outside portable buildings to move into the main depot.

The new Bill Knott Building provides office and storage space for many publicity and fund raising aids, including flag day supplies, souvenirs, the printing department and design studio.

On their arrival the Duke of Atholl, Chairman of the Institution, received Mrs. Thatcher and her husband. They were shown over the prototype 47ft Tyne class lifeboat and a new 52 ft Arun, lying alongside the depot quay, before inspecting the Bill Knott Building. Then came the opening ceremony. In her speech Mrs. Thatcher thanked the RNLI for 158 years of selfless service, remembering both the lifeboat crews and the fund-raisers, with their complementary views of courage and generosity. The crews, she said, possessed the lonely virtue of courage, which each man had to find for himself. No one could give it to him. The fund-raisers and those who, like Mr. and Mrs. Knott, gave back to society something of what life had given to them displayed the lonely virtue of generosity.

Following her visit, Mrs. Thatcher wrote: *"To be able to open the Bill Knott Building was a real privilege and to meet so many of the people involved in keeping the lifeboat service operational was a real pleasure. My admiration for your work is unbounded: you hold an unparalleled place in the hearts of the people of our country."*

17th JULY   HENLEY-ON-THAMES, OXFORDSHIRE, **1972**

For the first time ever, a reigning monarch named a lifeboat when H. M. Queen Elizabeth II christened the Solent class reserve lifeboat *The Royal British Legion Jubilee* on the 17th July 1972 at Henley-on-Thames.

In her speech the Queen said that it was an imaginative decision

A view of the lifeboat The Royal British Legion Jubilee afloat on the River Thames beneath the imposing backdrop of Windsor Castle.

to bring the lifeboat up the Thames and that this was *'in recognition of the wonderful support which the Royal National Lifeboat Institution receives from its inland branches as well as from coastal towns and villages'.*

On the 14th July 1977, Her Majesty named the new Waveney class lifeboat *The Scout* at her station, Hartlepool.

The Waveney Class lifeboat The Scout that was named on the 14th July 1977 by Her Majesty Queen Elizabeth II.

18th JULY   NORWAY, **1998**

Fund-raising with a difference! Many forms of sponsored events take place every year, but on the 18th July twenty-seven cyclists set out on the RNLI Arctic Cycle Challenge. Starting from Tromso, the cyclists covered 482 km along the Arctic Highway all the way to the North Cape, the northernmost point in Europe. They also visited the northernmost lifeboat station in Europe - at Honningsvag.

Crew members from several lifeboat stations joined the challenge - from Porthcawl, Bude, Newquay, Padstow, Rock, Staithes and Runswick, Harwich, as well as staff from Headquarters.

19th JULY   PLYMOUTH, DEVON, **1974**

As part of the celebrations commemorating the 150th anniversary of the founding of the RNLI, an International Lifeboat Exhibition was held at Plymouth from the 19th July to the 17th August 1974.

The opening ceremony took place on a brilliant day with the sun beating down on a cluster of white marquees in West Hoe Park, close by the sea. There was an atmosphere of cheerful expectancy; flags were flying; the Royal Marine Band breaking into the gaiety of 'Celebration'. Then 'The Year of the Lifeboat' reached its climax as, at noon, H. R. H. the Duke of Kent, President of the RNLI, accompanied by the Lord Mayor of Plymouth, Councillor F. Johnson, disembarked from Plymouth's new 44ft Waveney lifeboat at the Royal Western Yacht Club of England. They then walked through cheering crowds to join the guests assembled for the opening ceremony of the first ever International Lifeboat Exhibition.

The Duke had already met British and overseas lifeboat officials and crews in Millbay Docks. There he had embarked in Plymouth's new boat, *Thomas Forehead and Mary Rowse II*, and he had been escorted into Plymouth Sound by the whole fleet of 11 visiting lifeboats, dressed overall, with Plymouth's 18ft McLachlan and an Atlantic 21 as well.

20th JULY   FLEETWOOD, LANCASHIRE, **1976**

The first lifeboat naming at Fleetwood since 1939 was carried out by H R H the Duke of Kent, President of the RNLI, on the 20th July 1976. Present at the ceremony was Jeffrey Wright, Coxswain in 1939, awarded the Institution's silver medal in 1941, and David Scott, at 27 then the youngest Coxswain in the fleet.

The 44ft Waveney class lifeboat was named *Lady of Lancashire.* An anonymous donor, believed to be a Lancashire businessman, had met the cost of the boat.

21st JULY   COWES, ISLE OF WIGHT, **1923**

Another lifeboat 'first' occurred on the 21st July 1923, when the first 60ft Barnett class lifeboat was taken over from her builders, J. Samuel White & Co., at Cowes on the Isle of Wight.

Billed in the June 1923 Lifeboat Journal as 'the most powerful lifeboat in the world', the twin-screw Barnett had two six cylinder light petrol engines of 90 h.p. each. An interesting feature of this lifeboat was a net which could be stretched amidships for people to jump into from a wrecked ship.

The class was named after its designer, Mr. J. R. Barnett, OBE, MINA, of the Glasgow firm of G. L. Watson. He had been the Institution's Naval Architect since 1904, succeeding Mr. G. L. Watson (see 7th April). He retired at the end of July 1947. Some thirty-seven Barnett Class lifeboats were constructed, being supplied in one of three different lengths.

22nd JULY   POOLE, DORSET, **1982**

From the 22nd-24th July 1982, and for the first time in its history, the Institution opened its head office and depot at Poole to the public. It was an entirely new departure that provided a unique opportunity for all those on whose support and generosity the RNLI depends. It would enable them to see behind the scenes of the lifeboat service and to visit the offices, works and stores which provide the essential back-up for both lifeboat stations and fund-raising branches and guilds.

There were guided tours of the head office building: lifeboats to be visited: helicopter and lifeboat rescue exercises: displays to illustrate the work of the depot: fund raising efforts and much more. Some 10,000 people visited the Institution's headquarters during the open days. These are now a regular feature normally held every two years.

23rd JULY   MINEHEAD, SOMERSET, **1996**

Minehead's D class lifeboat carried out a service on the 23rd July 1996 which saved two people and their yacht in difficult conditions, but which was somewhat overshadowed in press reports by the interruption of their cricket match and the subsequent destination of the survivors!

The crew were indeed in the middle of a cricket match when their pagers went off and they were called to the aid of *Tumbleweed*, a 21 ft yacht aground on nearby Warren Point, in an onshore wind up to Force 5.

After the first attempt to tow her off failed, the inflatable went in again. With waves breaking over both *Tumbleweed* and the lifeboat, two of the lifeboat's crew members went into the water and managed to get the yacht's head into the wind and reconnect the tow. For about ten minutes they held this position, with the lifeboat's prop occasionally hitting the stony bottom and the yacht bumping heavily. But at last a bigger wave lifted her and she began to move, with the two lifeboat crew scrambling aboard.

There was not enough water in Minehead harbour, and with the female yacht crew member looking very pale she was taken ashore while the yacht was anchored, with a lifeboatman aboard, to wait for enough water. It was only after landing that the lifeboat crew realised that they had three stumps instead of blades on the prop! It was changed immediately, and as soon as there was enough water in the harbour *Tumbleweed* started her engine and came in, escorted by the lifeboat and just as darkness fell.

The yacht's skipper was re-united with his wife in the boathouse, to find she'd booked a room ashore - in the 'Old Ship Aground'!

24th JULY   EXETER, DEVON, **1919**

Many lifeboat supporters give years of dedicated service to the cause. An example of this is described in the September 1919 Lifeboat Journal.

"A very pleasant ceremony took place in the Guild Hall, Exeter, on 24 July 1919, when Mr. Courtenay H. Edmonds, the Honorary Secretary of the Exeter Branch, and Mrs. Ferris Tozer, the Honorary Secretary of the Ladies Auxiliary, received presentations in recognition of their long and valuable services.

"In the case of Mr Courtenay Edmonds, this gentleman has been Honorary Secretary of the Exeter branch for over half a century. The Committee of Management have marked their appreciation of this wonderful length of service, which has seldom been exceeded in the case of Honorary Secretaries, by the presentation of a handsome silver rose bowl, suitably inscribed. The Mayor of Exeter, Sir James Owen presented this, and Mr. Edmonds, in replying, expressed his great pleasure at the fact that the collection in Exeter in the last completed year (1918) was the largest on record".

The Mayor also presented Mrs. Ferris Tozer with the gold brooch of the Institution, and expressed his warm appreciation of the immense amount of invaluable work she had done in furthering the lifeboat cause in Exeter. Mrs. Tozer, in acknowledging the gift, suggested that women could hardly do better work than to further the efforts of the Institution in the saving of life - the lives mostly of strong, capable, skilful men.

25th JULY   HOLY ISLAND, NORTHUMBERLAND, **1884**

A new lifeboat, the self-righting *'Grace Darling'* was placed on station at Holy Island on the 25th July 1884. Later, this was the first lifeboat to be given an official number, or O.N. as it is referred to.

The official numbering system was introduced as part of the technical reorganisation that followed the appointment of G. L.

Watson as Consulting Naval Architect in 1887 (see 7th April). At the end of 1886 there were 290 lifeboats at stations plus reserve lifeboats. All these had to be surveyed before they were passed as having the qualities necessary in a lifeboat, and only then were they allocated an O.N.

26th JULY   FAIRBOURNE, GWYNEDD, **1983**

Quick thinking by 14 year old Mark Lacey saved a man from drowning at Fairbourne on the 26th July 1983. Mark and a friend had just returned to the beach after a trip in Mark's 10ft Achilles inflatable when he noticed what appeared to be 'a covered inflatable' about three quarters of a mile off shore, apparently with someone in difficulties.

Shouting to a woman on the beach to telephone the rescue services, Mark headed his own inflatable for the casualty. There he found a man floundering in the water whom, with difficulty, he managed to drag into his own boat. Returning to the beach at full speed, Mark was able to deliver the man into the hands of the doctor who arrived shortly after.

The Institution awarded Mark Lacey the Thanks of the Institution inscribed on Vellum and an inscribed wristwatch.

27th JULY   POOLE, DORSET, **1990**

The Institution is continually updating or renewing shore facilities at many stations around the coast. New lifeboat houses may be required to house larger boats: developments in ports may necessitate a move to a new berth: better crew facilities are needed.

At Poole, the lifeboat station had for many years been located in a yacht marina at Lilliput. In 1989, the lifeboats moved to new berths next to the lifting bridge at Poole Quay. The new lifeboathouse provides storage for equipment, stores and protective clothing, as well as washing facilities and a crew room for the volunteers who man the two lifeboats.

On the 27th July 1990, the Mayor of Poole, Councillor Mrs Anne Stribley, officially opened the new lifeboat house. The Mayor of Poole is also Admiral of the Port.

28th JULY   BRITISH ISLES, **1956**

The December 1956 Lifeboat Journal contained a table giving details of lifeboats involved in services during a period of twenty four hours on the 28th-29th July 1956.

This table clearly indicated the difference between the number of services carried out in the summer months compared with the very few such services in the early years of the Institution. The great growth in pleasure sailing, and now surf boarding and wind surfing is mainly responsible for this.

The table shows there were 52 launches from 38 stations. 243 hours were spent at sea; 107 lives were rescued; 14 vessels saved and another 7 helped.

29th JULY   ST. IVES, CORNWALL, **1921**

Headlined in the Lifeboat Journal of November 1921 as *"Ten Crews Rescued in Seven Hours"*, the work of the St. Ives lifeboat *James Stevens No. 10*, was fully described.

On the 29th July 1921 the St. Ives lifeboat performed a series of arduous services, going out five times to the rescue of no fewer than ten vessels, and saving forty men in the course of seven hours. On the 28th July a strong gale was blowing S. S. W, which, early on the following morning, suddenly veered to N. N. W.. This threw a very heavy sea into St. Ives Bay, where a fleet of over 30 Breton crabbers had taken shelter - as well as a number of other vessels.

The first signal of distress was shown at about 6.00 a.m., when a Bideford ketch, the *F. H. Bolt*, was seen to be dragging her anchors and driving towards Porthminster Point. The lifeboat was immediately launched and took off the crew of three men. Shortly afterwards another ketch, the *Anne*, of Gloucester, signaled for help, and her crew of four men were brought safely ashore. The next signal came at 10 a.m. from one of the Breton fishing boats, the *St. Eloi*, of Camaret, and her five men were taken off. Immediately afterwards, three other crabbers asked for help, the *Susanne Yvonne*, the *St. Mauday*, and the *Eclair*, and from these twelve men were rescued. The final call came just after noon, and the lifeboat put out for the fifth time, bringing in the crews, sixteen men in all, of four more crabbers, the *Anne*

Marie, the *En Avant*, the *Turquoise*, and the *Providence*. Altogether she saved, during the services, seven Englishmen and thirty-three Frenchmen.

In view of the prolonged and arduous nature of the service, and the skill in which the Coxswain, Robert Wedge, handled the lifeboat, the Committee of Management awarded him the Thanks of the Institution inscribed on Vellum, and gave extra monetary rewards to the crew. A Letter of Thanks was also sent to the Honorary Secretary of the Station, Mr. C. J. A. French, who remained on duty the whole time and kept the lifeboat afloat until the gale began to moderate and the remaining craft in the Bay were out of danger.

30th JULY   NEWQUAY, CORNWALL, **1996**

Both of Newquay's inshore lifeboats were involved in a rescue on the 30th July 1996. Two adults, a baby and two dogs were stuck at the base of cliffs after they had been cut off by the tide at Bedruthan Steps. The service, in a breaking 6ft swell, was described by the Honorary Secretary as 'one of the most dangerous undertaken' by the station and was recognised by letters of congratulation from the RNLI's Director.

The Atlantic 75 *Phyllis* and the D class *Lord Daresbury* had launched at 4.23 p.m., following a report that a family had been cut off and were some 9m up a steep cliff face backing the cove at Bedruthan Steps about three miles away. When the Atlantic reached the scene about 20 minutes later a rescue helicopter had already arrived, but could not winch the families to safety because of the high, steep cliff. A Force 4 breeze was kicking up a swell more than 6ft high which was breaking heavily against the base of the cliff. Worse, there was still an hour to go before spring high water.

Conditions inside the little cove were also too dangerous for the 7.5m Atlantic. When the smaller, more manoeuvrable D class arrived a few minutes later it was decided to use her to run in through the surf and pick casualties off the cliff face one at a time - transferring them to the Atlantic which would stay outside the surf line. Jeremy Griffiths moved across from the Atlantic to the D, which then went in through the breaking seas to put him and D class crew member Ian Jepson ashore with lifejackets for the trapped family.

RNLI National Lottery

As a result of the new Lotteries and Amusements Act 1976 (which does not extend to Northern Ireland) we are now able to have a National Lottery to raise funds for the Life-boats and also give realistic prizes. If successful we hope to be able to increase the prize list for subsequent lotteries.

Each card consists of four tickets, each at 25p. Of course you do not need to take all of these but just fill in the one you would like entered in the draw. Retain the left hand portion for your own records and put the remainder into the business reply paid envelope together with your remittance.

No receipt will be sent but the centre portion will be retained in our office so that a check can be made at any time on request.

The entire administration of this lottery will be carried out by the Appeals Office at Life-boat House and no extra staff will be employed. Our aim is to keep the overheads as low as possible.

The actual draw will be supervised by a member of our Committee of Management and will take place at Life-boat House on 30th September 1977.

If you inadvertently forget to include your remittance then your ticket will be void.

We will keep you informed through the Life-boat Journal of the results of each lottery which initially we will organise every six months.

No ticket may be sold to any person under the age of 16 or to employees of the Life-boat Institution.

WIN £1,000 and other PRIZES

Take a chance and help the LIFE-BOATS

The D moved back out into the safety of deeper water while the lifejackets were put on and then went back to take the mother aboard, taking her back to the Atlantic. The next trip was aborted when the inflatable was completely filled by a breaker, but the next three runs were accomplished safely - bringing out a baby, then the father and two large dogs, and finally the two lifeboatmen.

With everyone safely aboard the larger Atlantic both lifeboats headed for home, arriving at Newquay at 5.50 p.m.

31st JULY   POOLE, DORSET, **1990**

The draw of the 50th RNLI Lottery was held at Poole headquarters at 12.30 p.m. on Tuesday 31st July 1990. Jean Boht, who played Nellie Boswell in the popular BBC TV series 'Bread', made the draw.

The cast were appearing in the stage version at the Pavilion Theatre, Bournemouth.

By this time, lotteries had been run for over 12 years and had raised well over £2 million. The first prize, on this occasion, was £2,000. The first lottery draw had been made on 30th September 1977 with the main prize of £1,000.

The publicity pamphlet for the first ever RNLI lottery.

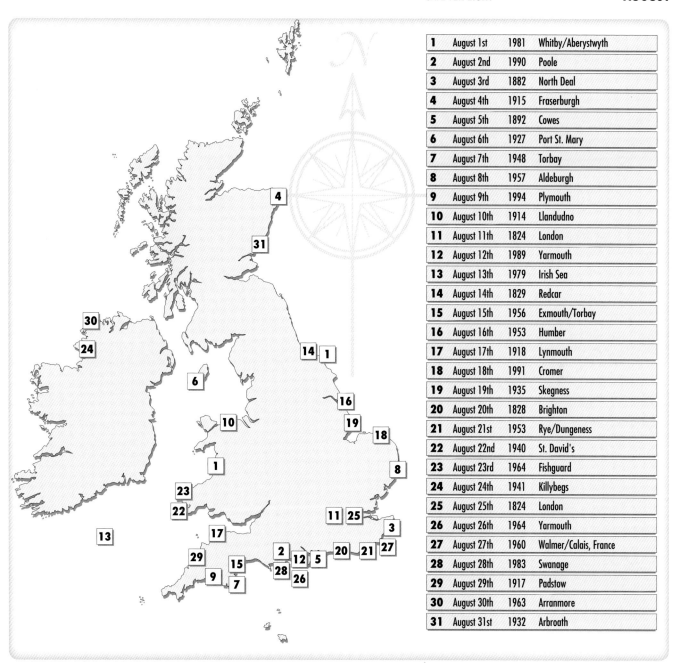

1	August 1st	1981	Whitby/Aberystwyth
2	August 2nd	1990	Poole
3	August 3rd	1882	North Deal
4	August 4th	1915	Fraserburgh
5	August 5th	1892	Cowes
6	August 6th	1927	Port St. Mary
7	August 7th	1948	Torbay
8	August 8th	1957	Aldeburgh
9	August 9th	1994	Plymouth
10	August 10th	1914	Llandudno
11	August 11th	1824	London
12	August 12th	1989	Yarmouth
13	August 13th	1979	Irish Sea
14	August 14th	1829	Redcar
15	August 15th	1956	Exmouth/Torbay
16	August 16th	1953	Humber
17	August 17th	1918	Lynmouth
18	August 18th	1991	Cromer
19	August 19th	1935	Skegness
20	August 20th	1828	Brighton
21	August 21st	1953	Rye/Dungeness
22	August 22nd	1940	St. David's
23	August 23rd	1964	Fishguard
24	August 24th	1941	Killybegs
25	August 25th	1824	London
26	August 26th	1964	Yarmouth
27	August 27th	1960	Walmer/Calais, France
28	August 28th	1983	Swanage
29	August 29th	1917	Padstow
30	August 30th	1963	Arranmore
31	August 31st	1932	Arbroath

1st AUGUST   WHITBY, YORKSHIRE AND ABERYSTWYTH, CARDIGANSHIRE, **1981**

The autumn 1981 Lifeboat Journal contained the following notes on old pulling lifeboats being used for fund raising.

"Former crew members of the last pulling lifeboat in service with the RNLI, Robert and Ellen Robson of Whitby, relived the days of oar power on the 1st August 1981, when they rowed the lifeboat in Whitby Harbour as part of the lifeboat day demonstrations. The combined ages of the twelve-man crew came to 742 years and former lifeboat inspector Cdr. Leslie Hill went out with them. The following day the present Whitby lifeboat crew rowed the lifeboat from Whitby to Robin Hood's Bay, and sponsorship money already collected has passed the four figure mark."

The *Robert and Ellen Robson* had served at three stations during its career between 1918 and 1957 - Aberdeen, Tramore and, finally, Whitby. During this time she had launched 21 times and saved 14 lives.

The crew of the Aberystwyth lifeboat rescued the occupants of a broken down motorboat on the 12th August when they were out in a replica of an old fashioned pulling lifeboat. The replica had been built to raise money for the RNLI and the crew were at sea practising for a sponsored row when they found the motor boat in trouble. They towed her safely back to Aberystwyth.

2nd AUGUST   POOLE, DORSET, **1990**

In a statement to the press, Lt. Cdr. Brian Miles, Director of the RNLI, said on this day:

"I am delighted to announce that we can now promise a lifeboat on scene in all weathers quicker than ever before and at virtually any point 50 miles off the coast within four hours of launching. That represents a 20 mile extension to our previous declared cover."

The press release also commented on response times:

"As further indication of the current speed of reaction, in fair weather lifeboats can now reach virtually any point 30 miles off the coast within two hours and remain on scene for at least four hours.

"A recent survey has also shown that over the last ten years the average time taken to alert the crew and launch an all-weather lifeboat has fallen from 16$\frac{1}{2}$ minutes to under 14 minutes. Inshore lifeboats on average take less than eight minutes from the first alert to launch. The increased use of pagers has helped to speed up launch times".

3rd AUGUST   NORTH DEAL, KENT, **1882**

On the 3rd August 1882, the Committee of Management voted a silver medal to Assistant Coxswain Richard Roberts of North Deal. It was stated that he had been out on every service, except one, a total of 78 times in 17 years, helping to save 202 lives.

It was the practice of the RNLI, for many years, to award silver medals to Coxswains on retirement or resignation in recognition of their gallant services over many years. The last such medal was awarded in 1907 only shortly after the first motor lifeboats came into service. One gold medal only was awarded to a Coxswain on retirement - to Charles Fish of Ramsgate in 1891 (see 8th October).

4 AUGUST   FRASERBURGH, ABERDEENSHIRE, **1915**

The new self-righting motor lifeboat *Lady Rothes* was named at Fraserburgh on the 4th August 1915. The event was reported in the November 1915 Lifeboat Journal:

"A very interesting ceremony took place at Fraserburgh on 4 August, when the new motor lifeboat, the Lady Rothes, presented to the Institution by Mr. T. Dyer Edwardes, was named and launched in the presence of some thousands of people.

"The boat was generously presented by Mr. Dyer Edwardes, to quote his own words at the naming ceremony, "As a thank-offering to Almighty God for preserving the life of my only child from a great peril, in the foundering of the White Star liner Titanic" in May, 1912. Mr. Dyer Edwardes' daughter, the Countess of Rothes, was one of the comparatively few people who were saved from that terrible disaster. On that occasion she gave an example of coolness and courage which materially contributed to calm and comfort the boatful of terrified women and children with whom she found herself. There were only three sailors in

charge and, in order to assist, Lady Rothes took the helm and held it for eight to ten hours, in spite of the cold and fatigue from which she suffered".

The report went on to conclude:

"It is a matter of great satisfaction to the Institution and the donor that the Lady Rothes should have been able to render valuable service a few days after her arrival at the station. She saved the crew of fourteen of the s.s Glenravel, of Belfast, which had been sunk by an enemy submarine about fifteen miles from Fraserburgh".

5th AUGUST   COWES, ISLE OF WIGHT, **1892**

After successful trials at Harwich, it was decided that the steam lifeboat *Duke of Northumberland* should be transferred to Holyhead for fuller experiments. En route she arrived in Cowes in time for 'Cowes Week'. There, on the 5th August 1892, the Emperor of Germany and his suite inspected her. The Kaiser went for a short run in her, and on leaving His Majesty expressed his high approval of her design and capabilities.

The previous day, the Prince of Wales had also inspected the boat and expressed *"his warmest approval of her and what he had seen of her working".*

6th AUGUST   PORT ST. MARY, ISLE OF MAN, **1927**

The November 1927 Lifeboat Journal carried the following sad report.

"A most unfortunate accident, resulting in the death of the Coxswain, occurred at Port St. Mary, Isle of Man, on the 6th August 1927, on which day Lifeboat Day and Road Practice of the lifeboat were to be held. Coxswain Kneen, in firing the maroon to call out the crew, was struck by it on the forehead and died shortly afterwards.

"Coxswain Kneen, who was 58 years old, was a specially good Coxswain, taking the greatest pride in the lifeboat and boathouse. He had been appointed Bowman in 1896, Second Coxswain in 1902, and Coxswain in 1916. He left a widow and

an unmarried grown-up daughter. The Institution, following its custom of pensioning the widows and dependant children of all lifeboatmen who lose their lives at service, have given Mrs. Kneen a pension.

"A careful inquiry was held into the accident, and it was suggested that it would not have occurred had the mortar been placed on a post above the level of the firer's head. The advisability of doing this was considered before the mortars and maroons were introduced, in place of the rocket distress signal, two years ago. It was then decided that it was better to adhere to the practice, approved by the Home Office, of burying the mortar, the reason being that if the mortar were to explode there would be no risk to those standing round being struck by pieces of flying metal.

"At some stations, however, it is not possible to bury the mortar, and at these it is mounted on a portable base, strict instructions being given that no one shall be allowed to stand near when the maroon is fired. The Institution has issued sandbags to all stations which use the portable base with instructions that these are to be filled and packed round the mortar. Meanwhile the Board of Trade is carrying out further experiments".

7th AUGUST   TORBAY, DEVON, **1948**

Assistance was rendered by the Torbay lifeboat *George Shee* during the yachting events of the 1948 Olympic Games, help which was subsequently reported that year in the October Lifeboat Journal.

On the evening of the 7th August 1948, a sudden gale got up from the south-east, and anxiety was felt for the crews of the two Swedish training ships *Falken* and *Gladan*, anchored off Paignton for the yacht racing in Torbay in the games of the XIV Olympiad. They were on an exposed dead lee shore in shallow water.

The motor lifeboat *George Shee* was launched at 9.45 p.m. in rough seas with heavy rain. Before she reached the training ships the lifeboat saw signals from the outer harbour and found the motor yacht *Jinty* on fire, following an explosion in the pantry. It had done considerable damage, but fortunately the crew of nine were all on deck at the time. The lifeboat stood by while they were all taken off by other boats and then went to the Swedish ships to see if there was need for her to stand by or to guide them to a safer anchorage. She found that the officer commanding was ashore, so she went to Torquay and there embarked him, another officer and nine cadets. With them she returned to the *Falken*. The officers got aboard despite the heavy seas, but it was too rough for the cadets to attempt it, so the lifeboat brought them back to Brixham, where they were accommodated on H.M.S. *Barbastel* for the night. Meanwhile the lifeboat kept watch on the Swedish ships until the storm abated just after midnight.

8th AUGUST   ALDEBURGH, SUFFOLK, **1957**

It is not always the weather that causes problems for fishing boats, as the following illustrates.

At 12.35 early on the morning of the 8th August 1957, the coastguard telephoned that the Norwegian fishing vessel *Jenco II* was adrift near the Shipwash Sands. The skipper was apparently intoxicated. At 1.58 a.m. the No. 1 lifeboat *Abdy Beauclerk* was launched with three policemen on board. There was a slight swell, a light south-easterly breeze blowing, and the tide was ebbing. The lifeboat came up with the fishing vessel one mile north-east of Shipwash lightvessel. They found that she had a crew of three.

The three policemen and two members of the lifeboat crew were put aboard, and then the *Jenco II* was piloted to Harwich with the lifeboat in attendance. Harwich was reached at 6.30 a.m.,and for the next three and a quarter hours the lifeboat was used to ferry police to and from the fishing vessel. She left for her station at 9.45 a.m. arriving at 12.30 p.m.

9th AUGUST   PLYMOUTH, DEVON, **1994**

Plymouth's Arun class lifeboat *City of Plymouth* was kept particularly busy on the 9th August 1994, answering six calls in the one day.

The first call came shortly before 1.00 a.m. to the yacht *Blue Star* some 25 miles south east of the station. In gale force conditions the yacht was reached at 1.55 a.m. A very slow tow got the casualty back at Plymouth at 7.35 a.m. Two hours later, in quick succession the lifeboat launched to bring a French yacht into

port, then towed in a small motor boat with a damaged rudder, and finally helped to berth a yacht on which there had been a fire.

At 4.30 p.m. only minutes after completing the above services, the *City of Plymouth* was called out to a casualty on a yacht in nearby Jennycliffe Bay. A man with a head injury was brought ashore to a waiting ambulance. The final service of the day was to a motor cruiser which had run out of fuel for her main engine.

The crew had been out almost continuously for eighteen hours. The Honorary Secretary reported that 'the skill and endurance of the crew were well tested and worthy of note'.

10th AUGUST   LLANDUDNO, CAERNARVONSHIRE, **1914**

Lifeboats go out regularly on practice launches, and sometimes the practice became reality. On the 10th August 1914, while the lifeboat *Theodore Price* was out for practice, in a strong breeze and choppy sea, two pleasure rowing boats were seen drifting out to sea. There were three women and one man in one boat, and three women and three men in the other boat.

Owing to the condition of the sea, which was rapidly increasing, the men were unable to make any progress and they soon became exhausted. Becoming terrified they made frantic signals for help, and the lifeboat proceeded to them. Having taken the endangered people into the lifeboat, Coxswain Griffiths towed the boats ashore.

11th AUGUST   LONDON, **1824**

Mr. Pellew Plenty, of Newbury, attended a meeting of the Committee of Management on the 11th August 1824 and exhibited a model of a lifeboat he had designed. In his book 'The Lifeboat Story', (1957), Patrick Howarth describes the boat, saying that *"in appearance Plenty's boats suggested a small type of Norfolk wherry.*

"Their most evident characteristic was the broadness of their beams amidships, they had straight keels, and a thick lining of cork on the bottom gave protection on stony beaches. Pellew Plenty's type of boat was not a self-righter, but she had six

scuppers or draining valves which to a limited extent served to free her from water".

The Committee agreed to order two boats to be delivered in October. Mr. Plenty confirmed the order on the 18th August at a cost not to exceed £100 per boat. Each boat was to be 18ft long, 6ft 3inches wide, 2ft 6 inches deep, and weigh 8 hundredweight (4cwt of wood, 4cwt of cork).

12th AUGUST   YARMOUTH, ISLE OF WIGHT, **1989**

The Yarmouth Arun class lifeboat *John and Joy Wade* left her moorings at 11.30 p.m. on the 12th August 1989, to the assistance of the coaster *Llanishen* which had caught fire some six miles S.S.W. of the Needles. Before the lifeboat reached the scene, an explosion rocked the casualty, and fire enveloped the aft end of the ship.

A helicopter lifted the five man crew to safety from the fo'c'sle, leaving the vessel unmanned, drifting and ablaze. Whilst waiting for a fire fighting team and tug, the lifeboat stood by and then put a line aboard the coaster. It was four hours before the tug arrived with the fire crew. The lifeboat's pump with a crew member in charge was put aboard the casualty to help remove the water being used on the fire.

The tug took over the tow, but only when the fire was considered to be out did the lifeboat recover her crew member and pump and return to station at 9.30 a.m.

13th AUGUST   IRISH SEA, **1979**

With the swift approach of a rapidly deepening area of low pressure, the winds were rising dramatically. The worst of the weather was building up in the south Irish Sea. Across the 150 mile stretch of sea between Land's End and the Fastnet Rock was strung out the International Fastnet Race fleet of 303 yachts.

The first indications of trouble came when the Baltimore lifeboat *The Robert* was the first to launch at 10.15 p.m. on the 13th August 1979, to go to help the yacht *Regardless*. The casualty, with a crew of nine, was towed to Baltimore. Altogether over the next three days, thirteen lifeboats, coming from both sides of the

Irish Sea, took part in the operation, towing in or escorting 20 yachts and rescuing 60 lives.

14th AUGUST   REDCAR, YORKSHIRE, **1829**

The Institution's gold medal was awarded to Lieutenant Richard Elworthy Pym, R.N., who, on the 14th August 1829, launched the Redcar lifeboat *Zetland* to go to the aid of the brig *Aurora*. Ten lives were saved in frightful conditions.

The lifeboat Zetland, from an original drawing. This lifeboat can now be seen in the Zetland Museum at Redcar, and is the oldest surviving lifeboat in the world.

The *Zetland* lifeboat is the oldest existing lifeboat in the world. Built by Henry Greathead (see 30th January) in 1802, at a cost of £200, the lifeboat was on service for 78 years and saved over 500 lives. *Zetland* is now preserved in a museum at Redcar.

15th AUGUST   EXMOUTH and TORBAY, DEVON, **1956**

Children out in small boats can get into difficulties as the incident described in the December 1956 Lifeboat Journal describes. Fortunately there was a happy ending.

"At 4.40 on the afternoon of the 15th August 1956, the Brixham coastguard rang up to say that the Devon County Constabulary had reported that two children who had gone out from Dawlish in a small boat had been missing since the day before. The Torbay lifeboat George Shee put out at 5.10 p.m. There was a moderate sea, with a gentle south-westerly breeze blowing and an ebb tide. At 5.30 p.m. the Exmouth lifeboat Maria Noble was launched to help the Torbay lifeboat in her search.

"Both lifeboats searched in co-operation with aircraft over a wide area. Finally the aircraft located the boat off Hopes Nose. The lifeboats both made for the position, with the aircraft indicating the direction by green flares. The lifeboats were in constant communication with each other. The Torbay lifeboat came up with the dinghy and took off the two children, a fourteen-year-old boy and his nine-year-old sister. They had been afloat for thirty-three hours and were very tired and cold. They were wrapped in blankets and given hot drinks, and were landed at Exmouth where their anxious parents had waited for their return. The Exmouth lifeboat arrived back at her station at eleven o'clock and the Torbay lifeboat at 12.45 early on the 16th".

16th AUGUST   HUMBER, YORKSHIRE, **1953**

The only permanent lifeboat station maintained by the RNLI with resident full time crew members is at Humber on Spurn Head.

Hull Trinity House had originally established the station at the end of October 1810. In 1908 control passed to the Humber Conservancy Board, before, in February 1911, coming within the auspices of the RNLI. There is a full time crew at this station by virtue of its location. The fact is that Spurn Head is extremely isolated, with no village, town or habitation nearby, and that the site suffers frequently from the effects of bad weather.

There have been occasions when storms have severed links with the mainland - for example, during the east coast storms of early 1953 the roadway was breached, sections being washed away.

Not all services there are to ships in distress in the North Sea or the River Humber as the following report shows. At 5.50 on the evening of the 16th August 1953, the Mablethorpe coastguard rang up to say the Superintendent of Trinity House at Great Yarmouth had asked if the lifeboat would land an injured man from the Humber lightvessel. At six o'clock the lifeboat *City of Bradford II* was launched in a smooth sea with a light south-westerly breeze blowing.

She took the injured man, who had crushed a finger, to Grimsby and reached her station again at 11.30pm. The paid permanent crew saw all their expenses refunded to the Institution by Trinity House.

ROYAL NATIONAL LIFE-BOAT INSTITUTION.

INSTRUCTIONS TO THE
Coxswain Superintendent and Crew of the Life-Boat
STATIONED AT SPURN.

22, Charing Cross Road,
LONDON, W.C.

1st *May*, 1911.

For the purpose of ensuring good order and proper conduct on the part of the Coxswain and Crew of the Life-Boat at Spurn during their continuance in the Service, the Committee of Management do hereby direct the strict observance of the following Instructions:—

1. The Coxswain Superintendent of the Boat, hereinafter called "the Coxswain," is required to be sober and watchful and at all times ready and diligent in the performance of his duty; he must keep with regularity a daily journal of the wind and weather, and of any other circumstances and occurrences connected with his office; and make his report thereof to the District Inspector on his visits of Inspection or whenever called on to do so. He must report to the Secretary all occasions on which assistance is rendered by the Crew of the Boat and in all urgent cases must as soon as possible make a special report by telegraph.

2. The Coxswain is invested with the full command of the Boat's Crew.

3. The Coxswain is to see that a regular watch is kept by night as well as by day.

4. The Coxswain and Crew of the Boat are on all occasions to use their utmost endeavours to save the lives of the Crews of such ships and vessels as may unfortunately be driven on the Outer or Inner Binks, or on shore or be in distress elsewhere at Spurn or in the vicinity thereof.

5. The regulations under which the Life Boat may be used for salvage purposes which are laid down in the General Regulations of the Institution, are strictly to apply to this station. Should the service rendered by the Life Boat result in the salvage of property, the Coxswain and Crew must, in order to make themselves eligible to participate in any remuneration received from the owners of the vessel salved, forego their pay for the day or days they are engaged in the salvage work.

6. Whenever the Boat is made use of, the Coxswain is to see that she is afterwards properly moored and taken care of.

7. Once in every year at the least the Boat is to be drawn on shore and her bottom carefully examined as she lies on the beach, and any defect that may be found must be at once reported. And whenever she may have touched the ground, or be suspected of having done so, or whenever from any other reason it may be requisite, she must undergo the same examination.

8. Not less frequently than once a quarter the riding bridle of the moorings is to be carefully examined and seen to be in proper condition and reported upon.

9. The Coxswain and 2nd Coxswain of the Boat shall never be both absent from Spurn at the same time. No member of the Crew of the Boat shall leave Spurn without the consent of the Coxswain.

10. Every member of the Crew of the Boat who shall proceed to Grimsby to sell crabs or fish shall return by the next ebb tide.

11. The Coxswain is to enforce strict compliance with these Instructions, and to cause a copy thereof to be placed in each cottage, as well as in some conspicuous part of his own house.

By order,

A. D. BURNETT BROWN
Secretary.

The regulations for the Humber, (Spurn), lifeboat station that were issued in 1911.

An aerial photograph that clearly illustrates the isolated position of the Humber (Spurn) lifeboat station at the mouth of the Humber. The access road, frequently breached by storms, can be seen in the background. (By kind permission of Hunting Aerofilms).

17th AUGUST   LYNMOUTH, DEVON, **1918**

On the 17th August 1918, the steamer Oiz was run ashore after being badly holed in a collision in the Bristol Channel. The Lynmouth self-righting lifeboat *Prichard Frederick Gainer* was launched at 7.25 a.m. and found the vessel under the North Walk.

The 24 crew of the *Oiz* had taken to their boats and were landed by the lifeboat at 9 a.m.

Payment for the service is recorded as:

13 men at 10/-	£ 6	10	-
26 helpers at 2/-	£ 2	12	-
Signalman	£ -	2	-
Telegraph Messenger	£ -	2	-
Head Launcher extra	£ -	2	-
2 steering pole men @ 6d	£ -	1	-
	£ 9	9	-

The total of £9.9s.- was paid on the 26th August, but 6 shillings were later returned on the 7th October with no reason given. It is worth noting that the *Prichard Frederick Gainer* served at Lynmouth from 1906 to 1944, launched 17 times, saving 41 people.

18th AUGUST   CROMER, NORFOLK, **1991**

The winter 1991/1992 Lifeboat Journal recorded the return home of a famous lifeboat to her station. The 18th August 1991 saw the handover of Cromer's famous wartime lifeboat *H. F. Bailey* by Peter Cadbury to the town's lifeboat museum.

Once commanded by legendary Coxswain Henry Blogg, *H. F. Bailey* served at Cromer from 1935-1945, saving 518 lives. She left the RNLI fleet in 1974 and was on display in a Surrey theme park until 1989 when she was sold to a London surveyor. In April 1991, Peter Cadbury, grandson of the founder of the chocolate empire, bought the boat at auction for Cromer as a memorial to his late father Major Egbert Cadbury, who commanded the Royal Naval Air Station, Great Yarmouth, during World War I.

In May she returned to Cromer promenade for restoration, a task willingly undertaken by former lifeboat mechanic Danny Abbs, his wife Jenny, former crewman Lewis 'Tuner' Harrison and university student Rob Webster. The day was memorable for another reason, too, as Cromer RNLI welcomed several survivors rescued by *H. F. Bailey* during the war from s.s *Meriones*, s.s *English Trader* and *Convoy 559*. It was an emotional moment as the visitors met up with the three surviving crew members from 50 years ago.

19th AUGUST   SKEGNESS, LINCOLNSHIRE, **1935**

'Old lifeboats never die' may well have been one heading for a report in the March 1936 Lifeboat Journal.

*"Shortly before eleven on the morning of the 19th August 1935, the motor pleasure cruiser, **Elizabeth Allen**, of Skegness, set out for a trip with over a hundred passengers on board. The weather was fine, but hazy; the sea was calm, and there was no wind. The **Elizabeth Allen** was about a quarter of a mile from the shore, when she was seen to be going slow, and then dense volumes of smoke were seen pouring out from her, amidships.*

"The lifeboat crew were immediately assembled, but as the sea was smooth and several boats were out at sea, the lifeboat was not launched. Of the boats at sea, three were old lifeboats of the Institution, converted to pleasure boats, and all three went at once at full speed to the Elizabeth Allen's help. The first to reach her was the motor boat Grace Darling II (which, as a lifeboat, had been stationed at Coverack, Cornwall) with Coxswain George Perrin of the Skegness motor lifeboat in command. Dense smoke was enveloping the Elizabeth Allen, her master and engineer were busy with fire extinguishers, and some of the passengers were screaming. Coxswain Perrin got alongside. By his firmness and coolness he prevented any panic, and took off 68 of the passengers, most of them women and children.

"Two other motor pleasure boats, the Shamrock and the Skylark, converted lifeboats and both in command of members of the crew of the Skegness lifeboat, had now come up on the other side of the Elizabeth Allen and took off the remainder of the passengers. By the time they had been landed the fire was extinguished, and the Elizabeth Allen was towed back."

The Institution awarded Coxswain George Perrin an aneroid barometer, inscribed, and sent letters of thanks to Mr. Wilfred Grunnill and Mr. Hedley Grunnill, who were in command respectively of the *Shamrock* and *Skylark.*

20th AUGUST   BRIGHTON, SUSSEX, **1828**

On the 20th August 1828, the Committee of Management were read a letter from Captain Saumarez R.N. of Brighton about the lifeboat station there. He made certain recommendations that the Committee accepted. These included:

1) that Lieutenant Williams should be Honorary Secretary and receive subscriptions

2) that over the doors of the lifeboathouse should be painted

> "Supported by Voluntary Subscription
> Ship'k Institution
> Boat House"

3) that the boat should be tried 2 or 3 times in the season under the direction of Lt. Williams.

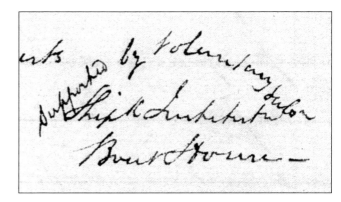

The original hand written minute of the Committee of Management suggesting how the wording should appear over the front of the Institution's lifeboat stations.

21st AUGUST   RYE, SUSSEX, **1953**

The Dungeness Watson class lifeboat *Charles Cooper Henderson* was called out at 6.15 p.m. on the 21st August 1953 to the auxiliary ketch *Moya*. The Fairlight coastguard had reported that the yacht was making distress signals some distance from Rye harbour.

Launched at 6.30 p.m., she found the *Moya*, with a crew of eight, three quarters of a mile south-east of Rye. The sea was rough and a strong westerly breeze was blowing. The yacht had fouled her propeller and her crew asked to be towed to Rye harbour. The lifeboat took her in tow, but on entering the harbour the *Moya* took a heavy sheer and struck a pier. She was badly holed, and the lifeboat rescued her crew, abandoned her and landed the crew at Rye harbour. She then returned to her station, arriving at 10.20 p.m.

22nd AUGUST   ST. DAVID'S, PEMBROKESHIRE, **1940**

The record of war-time services includes the following one from St. David's.

*"At 11.35 a.m. the coastguard reported a vessel in distress two miles westward of the Smalls Lighthouse. Permission to launch was got from the naval authorities, and the motor lifeboat **Civil Service No. 6** put out at 12.40 p.m. Dr. Joseph Soar, Mus. Doc.,*

the Honorary Secretary of the station, went with the boat. The sea was rough, with a fresh N. W. breeze blowing. The lifeboat kept in communication with the Smalls Lighthouse by wireless, and the lighthouse gave her a course, as the vessel in distress, which had sent out an SOS, had by now completely disappeared. After going some three miles the lifeboat saw a jacket on a pole, and found that it was a signal from survivors on a raft. They were from the s.s. **Thorold**, of Montreal, a Canadian Lake boat, now owned in Newcastle. She was bound with coal from Cardiff to London, and had been attacked by three German bombers, which after they had wrecked her, circled round machine gunning her crew.

"The lifeboat made straight for the raft, but before she reached it she found the master of the **Thorold** clinging to a plank. He was badly hurt and in a state of collapse. Two of the lifeboatmen, D. Lewis and G. Davies, jumped into the sea and helped the master into the lifeboat. Then the lifeboat found the second engineer on a piece of wreckage, and finally reached the raft from which the thirteen remaining survivors of the **Thorold's** crew of 24 were rescued. The lifeboat made straight for home and on the way asked, by wireless through the Smalls Lighthouse, that doctors and ambulances should be ready when she arrived. Two of the rescued men, however, had died before the lifeboat reached shore."

It is worth noting that the Honorary Secretary, Dr. Soar, was awarded the Institution's bronze medal three years later in 1943 for his part in helping rescue a man trapped on cliffs near Llanunwas, Solva.

23rd AUGUST   FISHGUARD, PEMBROKESHIRE, 1964

The news of accidents to boats at sea can sometimes take some time to reach the authorities. This was certainly the case in this report of a service in Fishguard in the December 1964 Lifeboat Journal.

"At 4.55 a.m. on the 23rd August 1964, the coastguard told the Honorary Secretary that a boat was reported to have sunk off Cardigan Island and her occupants had reached the island. The sea was rough, with a strong south-westerly breeze and a flood tide. At 5.25 the lifeboat **Howard Marryat** was launched. Soon afterwards she heard from the coastguard that while three people

had landed on Cardigan Island two others were still clinging to their overturned boat.

"The lifeboat found the motor boat about three miles north east of the island. One man was found clinging to the hull but the other had been washed away several hours previously. A member of the lifeboat crew, who had swum over to him, dressed the survivor in a breeches buoy. He was hoisted aboard the lifeboat where the bowman, who is also the station's honorary medical advisor, treated him. The other member of the motor boat's crew could not be found. At 11.45 a.m. the lifeboat entered Fishguard where the exhausted man was taken to hospital by ambulance. One of the three survivors who reached the island climbed a 50 foot rocky cliff face, walked about 330 hundred yards across the island and then swam 100 yards to raise the alarm. This man was taken back to the position at his request by one of two local boats which put out to assist, and was later transferred to the lifeboat for medical treatment. Local boats rescued the other two survivors".

24th AUGUST   KILLYBEGS, CO. DONEGAL, 1941

In 1941, the Air Ministry asked the Institution if it could open more stations on the west coast of Ireland for the help of aeroplanes forced down by bad weather, lack of fuel, or as a result of enemy action, as they flew in from the Atlantic. Since Eire was a neutral country, the RAF could not place its own rescue launches on their coasts, but the lifeboats were part of a single fleet of the British Isles. With the consent of the Eirean government, the RNLI was able to do as the Air Ministry requested.

On the 24th August 1941, an auxiliary station was opened at Killybegs in Co. Donegal with the Barnett class lifeboat Queen Victoria. This lifeboat had been at St. Peter Port, Guernsey, but when Germany occupied the island in June 1940, she was at a builders yard at Cowes for overhaul and so escaped capture, (although a reserve boat taking her place had fallen into German hands), being placed on the reserve list.

By the spring of 1944 some forty auxiliary lifeboat stations had been opened in Britain and Ireland. Thirteen of them in Eire; three in England (such as Millom, Cumberland); nineteen in Scotland (for example Staffin on the Isle of Skye) and four in Wales (such as Aberdovey in Merionethshire). The station of

Killybegs closed at the end of the war, though the last to close was Valentia, (Eire), in November 1946.

Lifeboats from the reserve fleet could not be spared for these stations, except at Killybegs as already mentioned, and it was not possible to have new boats built. As a result the RNLI equipped motor fishing boats, paid their skippers retaining fees and rewarded them and their crews for any rescues that they made - to ship and aircraft alike. These boats became known as auxiliary rescue-boats.

25th AUGUST   LONDON, **1824**

On the 25th August 1824, the Committee was read a letter from Mr. Secretary Robert Peel signifying 'that His Majesty (King George IV) was graciously pleased to comply with the Committee's request to have His Majesty's Head borne on the medals of the Institution as Patron thereof.'

At the same meeting, Mr. William Wyon of the Royal Mint was recommended 'as the Artist being the best Engraver of Human Figures and also of the Head of His Majesty, which he had executed for the coins'. The first medals were not completed until June 1825 when the minutes record letters of thanks from those to whom they had been awarded.

26th AUGUST   YARMOUTH, ISLE OF WIGHT, **1964**

Over a year after she was first introduced experimentally into the lifeboat service, the 48 foot 6 inch Oakley prototype lifeboat, *The Earl and Countess Howe*, was named and dedicated at Yarmouth, Isle of Wight, on the 26th August 1964. The lifeboat was named after the late Earl Howe, former Chairman of the Committee of Management, and his widow, Sybil, Countess Howe, in recognition of their valuable services to the Institution. Earl Howe died only two months before the ceremony and his daughter-in-law, Countess Howe, named the new lifeboat. Earl Howe had been Chairman of the Committee of Management from 1956 to 1964. This lifeboat, now on display in the Depot in Poole, was the first to be fitted with radar.

The original medals of the Institution carried the head of King George IV, the first Patron of the Institution.

27th AUGUST   WALMER, KENT AND CALAIS, FRANCE, **1960**

On the 27th August 1960, the Walmer lifeboat *Charles Dibdin (Civil Service No.32)* paid a courtesy visit to the Calais lifeboat station - the Calais lifeboat having been present at its naming in 1959. The Mayor of Calais presented Coxswain Frederick Upton with a plaque in recognition of past services to the crews of French vessels in the Channel.

Two other ex-lifeboats with their owners aboard accompanied the Walmer boat. One was the former Walmer lifeboat *Charles Dibdin (Civil Service No.2)*, which was owned by Mr. H. Schermuly, President of the Walmer branch; the other was the former Poolbeg boat *Helen Blake*, owned then by the Secretary of the Institution, Lieut. Colonel Charles Earle. The *Helen Blake* is now on display at Chatham.

28th AUGUST   SWANAGE, DORSET, **1983**

Three grandsons of Victor Marsh, the Coxswain/Mechanic of the

Swanage Lifeboat were christened on board the vessel on Sunday the 28th August 1983. She was the 37ft 6-inch Rother class lifeboat *J. Reginald Corah*.

The babies were Gary Marsh, whose three-year-old brother Alan was also christened on board the lifeboat and whose father was another member of the crew; and James Chadwick, whose parents were home on two weeks holiday from Germany. Belinda, James's mother, no doubt remembered her wedding in October 1980 when the lifeboat was called out twice, once during the ceremony and again during the reception.

29th AUGUST   PADSTOW, CORNWALL, **1917**

On the 29th August 1917, the Admiralty commandeered the RNLI steam tug *Helen Peele* from Padstow for service in Portland harbour and the naval base. There she remained until the 17th April 1919 when, after repairs at Swansea, she returned to Padstow.

The *Helen Peele* was the only steam tug in the RNLI fleet

The steam lifeboat Helen Peele pictured in Padstow Harbour and taken from a post card in the Gordon Campbell Collection.

(although there had been steam lifeboats). She was designed by Mr. G. L. Watson and built by Ramage & Ferguson, Leith, for a total cost of £9,784. She was 95 ft long, and beam of 19ft 6ins.

Apart from the war service Helen Peele was on station from the 11th September 1901 until 1929. During that time she was used to tow out the self-righting lifeboat Edmund Harvey. She also went out on service on her own on 19 occasions saving 10 lives. Whilst with the Admiralty she saved 11 lives in 1917.

30th AUGUST   ARRANMORE, CO. DONEGAL, **1963**

On occasions, a lifeboat is the only means of communication with islands off the coast when rough weather prevents conventional craft from going out. This report from December 1963 is an example of help given by the RNLI to the local community.

"At 5.30 on the afternoon of Friday, 30 August 1963, the Honorary Secretary received a call from the priest of Tory Island, who was stormbound on the mainland, that a woman was dangerously ill on the island and had asked for a priest. The lifeboat Edward Z

Dresden, on temporary duty at the station, put out at 7.30 p.m. for Burtonport, but the priest was involved in a car accident and did not arrive at Burtonport until 9.30 p.m. He embarked in the lifeboat, but about half way across the Tory Island lighthouse reported that, owing to heavy seas, landing on the island was impossible. It was low water with a strong breeze from the south-west. The lifeboat then returned to her station. At ten o'clock the following morning the lifeboat again put to sea and arrived at the island at 1.30 p.m. and landed the priest. The lifeboat returned to her moorings at four o'clock."

31st AUGUST   ARBROATH, ANGUS, **1932**

On the 31st August 1932, H.R.H. The Duchess of York named the new motor lifeboat at Arbroath. *The John and William Mudie* was paid for from a legacy from the late Misses Isabella and Elizabeth Mudie of Dundee. She was named after their brothers, one of whom had spent many years in the Far East, the other a town councillor in Dundee. Nearly 57 years later, on the 9th August 1989, Queen Elizabeth The Queen Mother (formerly the Duchess of York) named the new Arun lifeboat *The Queen Mother* at Thurso.

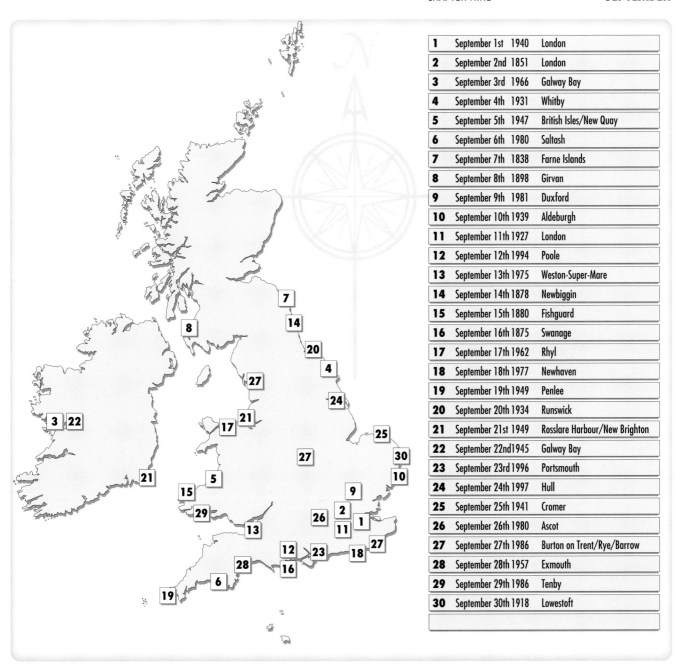

1	September 1st	1940	London
2	September 2nd	1851	London
3	September 3rd	1966	Galway Bay
4	September 4th	1931	Whitby
5	September 5th	1947	British Isles/New Quay
6	September 6th	1980	Saltash
7	September 7th	1838	Farne Islands
8	September 8th	1898	Girvan
9	September 9th	1981	Duxford
10	September 10th	1939	Aldeburgh
11	September 11th	1927	London
12	September 12th	1994	Poole
13	September 13th	1975	Weston-Super-Mare
14	September 14th	1878	Newbiggin
15	September 15th	1880	Fishguard
16	September 16th	1875	Swanage
17	September 17th	1962	Rhyl
18	September 18th	1977	Newhaven
19	September 19th	1949	Penlee
20	September 20th	1934	Runswick
21	September 21st	1949	Rosslare Harbour/New Brighton
22	September 22nd	1945	Galway Bay
23	September 23rd	1996	Portsmouth
24	September 24th	1997	Hull
25	September 25th	1941	Cromer
26	September 26th	1980	Ascot
27	September 27th	1986	Burton on Trent/Rye/Barrow
28	September 28th	1957	Exmouth
29	September 29th	1986	Tenby
30	September 30th	1918	Lowestoft

1st SEPTEMBER   LONDON, **1940**

During the Second World War, publication of the Lifeboat Journal had to be suspended because of the need to economise in the use of paper. The last full edition was April 1940. In place, single sheet bulletins were issued. In all 26 such bulletins were circulated, the last in December 1946. The first one, September 1940, included the following information of lifeboat work during the first year of the war:

"A YEAR OF WAR: In the first year of war lifeboats were launched to the rescue 1108 times and rescued 2302 lives. They rescued more lives in this one-year of war than in the last five years of peace. They rescued on the average 44 lives a week. In the last war the weekly average was 21. 64 MEDALS: Sixty-four gold, silver and bronze medals were awarded for gallantry. As many medals have been won in this one year of war as in the last six years of peace."

2nd SEPTEMBER   LONDON, **1851**

In the archives in the library at Poole is the Petty Cash Book covering the years 1824-1852. Accounting in those pre-computer days was much simpler! An entry in the book for the 2nd September 1851 reads: *"moving chairs, books etc. from 8 Great Winchester Street to John Street - porter and horse and cart 3/6d".*

Until 1851, the Institution had been based in the City of London. The Headquarters has, over the years, been at the following sites:

1824	12 Austin Friars
1826	18 Austin Friars
1832	20 Austin Friars
1846	8 Great Winchester Street
1851	20 John Street, Adelphi
1855	14 John Street, Adelphi
1904	22 Charing Cross Road WC2
1931	42 Grosvenor Gardens, Victoria
1974	Poole

3rd SEPTEMBER   GALWAY BAY, CO. GALWAY, **1966**

The December 1966 Lifeboat Journal reported the arrival of the two men who had rowed across the Atlantic.

When *English Rose III*, rowed by Capt. John Ridgway (20) and Sergeant Chay Blyth (20), was sighted off the North Aran lighthouse on the 3rd September 1966, at the end of its epic 92 day 3,000 mile voyage from Boston, Massachusetts USA, the Galway Bay reserve lifeboat *John R. Webb* was the first vessel to greet the rowers as they prepared to make landfall.

The two rowers, whose approach had alerted the lifeboat service along the southern part of Ireland, were not expected, however, to make landfall in the Galway Bay area.

English Rose III was first sighted just before 4.15 p.m. by the North Aran lighthouse who reported that a rowing boat containing two men was about 150 yards off the small island on which the lighthouse stands. Heavy rain and thick mist prevented the three lighthouse keepers from keeping the boat in view. The boat therefore was in grave danger owing to the extremely bad weather conditions (the wind was force 7-8) and the rocky coast without any landing space on the north side of the island. At 4.45 p.m. the Galway Bay reserve lifeboat set out, and at 6 o'clock she came up with the rowing boat - the internationally famous *English Rose III* carrying the two intrepid Atlantic travellers.

Father Joseph McNamara, Honorary Secretary of the Galway Bay lifeboat, who was the first to greet the Atlantic rowers when they stepped ashore at Kilronan, reports: 'Apparently they had been blown off their intended course to England. They came aboard the lifeboat which took in tow their 22 foot boat. The journey to Kilronan pier was difficult because of the heavy seas but they arrived there at 7.40 p.m. and stepped joyously ashore where they were greeted by a large crowd who had gathered despite a heavy rainstorm blowing at the time.'

4th SEPTEMBER   WHITBY, YORKSHIRE, **1931**

Even before the more aptly named Inshore Lifeboats were thought of, lifeboats had been called in to help when floods made their help invaluable. Flooding by the River Esk on the 4th September 1931 presented a particular danger at Ruswarp, one and a half miles up the valley from Whitby. Road and rail bridges were impassable, so help from the RNLI was sought.

The Whitby 34 feet No. 2 rowing lifeboat *Jacob and Rachel*

Valentine was got out at 5.40 p.m. She was dragged the mile and a half to Ruswarp by road, seventy people giving their help. An hour after leaving Whitby she was launched on the flooded road at the riverside, just below the church. The current was so strong that it was impossible for her crew to row against it, but with the crew at the oars and helpers bearing on a rope, she was, with great difficulty, got half a mile upstream. At one point she grounded on the road and had to be dragged some way before she would refloat. Then she was rowed out into mid-stream, anchored, and dropped down to a house where two women, one of them about 90 years old and bed-ridden, were marooned in the upper storey with 10 feet of raging water around them.

Owing to a submerged stone wall, it was impossible for the lifeboat to get alongside the house by about 4 feet, but fortunately a small boat, with three Whitby fishermen onboard, had, half an hour before, been veered down the river by a rope from the shore. These men were cheering the women by telling them that the lifeboat was on the way. Their boat was useless to bring the women ashore, but it was used as a bridge, and the women were carried across it into the lifeboat. The three fishermen then got onboard her; their boat was taken in tow and the lifeboat was hauled upstream again. During this operation she got athwart a telegraph pole; the small boat was swamped and the lifeboat had to leave her cable and anchor in the river.

The lifeboat then dropped down the river to the Mill House and rescued two more women and a man from a bedroom window. Here, again, she could not get alongside the house but a ladder was placed from the boat to the window, and the three people crawled across it. The five rescued people were then landed in a garden, and the lifeboat fastened up at the roadside. It was now dark, for the work of the rescue had taken over two hours. It had been carried out under great difficulties - the strong current, floating trees and other obstacles, and submerged walls, fences, and hedges. The lifeboat was lucky to have passed through these unaccustomed dangers with no more damage than two small rents in the outside planking on the starboard bow. One of the crew, however, was injured, being struck and knocked over by the hauling rope.

5th SEPTEMBER   BRITISH ISLES, **1969**

A successful fund-raising campaign by Birds Eye Food Ltd ran from the 18th July to the 5th September 1969. During that

Preparing for the inaugural ceremony of the new lifeboat Birds Eye at New Quay. She was a 37ft Oakley Class lifeboat, with the service number ON.996.

period, more than 8½ million specially printed packs of Birds Eye fish fingers were on sale. Every one of these carried a message about the lifeboat campaign and all had a special token on the back. The tokens were valued at 4d., 8d., and 1s. according to the size of the pack. Birds Eye Foods undertook to pay the money equivalent of all the tokens returned towards the cost of a new lifeboat for the RNLI.

Immediate support for the campaign came from Tesco, whose Chairman, Sir John Cohen, announced that every token left in a Tesco store would be worth double its face value, and they would provide the protective clothing and life jackets for the crew of the new boat. The campaign was successful, and a new 37foot Oakley class lifeboat was duly named *Birds Eye* at New Quay, Cardiganshire on the 9th September 1970.

6th SEPTEMBER   SALTASH, CORNWALL, **1980**

Trevor England, Coxswain of the Padstow lifeboat, received the London Cornish Association Shield, awarded annually by the Cornish Gorsedd for outstanding community service to the county. The presentation took place on the 6th September 1980 at the Saltash Comprehensive School. The Grand Bard of Cornwall, Richard Jenkin, presented the shield after citations read in Cornish and English.

Coxswain England was awarded the Institution's silver medal in 1977 for a rescue in which two people, their dog and yacht were saved in a gale and heavy seas. The lifeboat had to be taken between the yacht and rocks, some of which were submerged, in order to pass a tow. He was awarded a bar to his silver medal for a service in 1979 when the Padstow lifeboat launched into a force 12 gale and conditions which were described as *"the worst in living memory"* to stand by a disabled Greek freighter. The lifeboat kept close to the freighter for nine hours in such huge waves that she frequently disappeared from view. The Coxswain afterwards said that he and his crew felt like *"an insect in a ploughed field".*

7th SEPTEMBER   FARNE ISLANDS, **1838**

For their efforts in saving nine survivors from the *Forfarshire* on the 7th September 1838, William Darling and his daughter were

A picture of the famous rescue of William and Grace Darling. The original caption reads 'Through this passage Grace Darling and her Father .... reached their goal'.

each awarded the Institution's silver medal on the 24th October the same year.

The medal voted to Grace Darling was the first awarded to a woman. Since then, only 19 other medals - all silver - have been awarded to women. The last of these were to Mrs. Wallace and Miss Ellen Blyth of the Point of Ayre lighthouse on the Isle of Man when, on the 11th March 1888, they helped save four men from a schooner.

All the medals awarded were for shore boat services - i.e. no lifeboats involved. Now that there are over 200 women lifeboat crew members, surely the day will come when we have the first medal awarded to a lifeboat woman?

8th SEPTEMBER — GIRVAN, AYRSHIRE, **1898**

Problems of communication in the earlier days produced some enterprising exploits as the report of the Committee Meeting held on the 8th September 1898 well illustrated.

The Thanks of the Institution on Vellum were voted *"to Mr. McKenna, Postmaster of Girvan, and to Mr. Chas. Lawson, for riding a tandem-cycle from Girvan to Ballantrae, a distance of 13 miles, and giving information that a vessel was in distress on the 28th August. An interruption in the telegraph system prevented a message being sent by wire. The cyclists arrived about 3 o' clock in the morning, covered with mud and thoroughly soaked by rain."*

The vessel in distress was the barque *Firth of Cromarty* of Glasgow. The Girvan lifeboat *Sir Home Popham* launched at 2.15 a.m., returning to station at 6.15 a.m on the 28th August 1898. The Ballantrae lifeboat *William and Harriet* was towed 11 miles along the coast to Cairn Ryan, where she was launched at 7 a.m. Twenty three helpers, including drivers, and seven horses were paid for this service.

9 SEPTEMBER — DUXFORD, CAMBRIDGE, **1981**

On the 9th September 1981, the lifeboat *Jesse Lumb*, which had just finished 42 years service with the Institution, became a permanent exhibit at the Imperial War Museum's collection at Duxford Air Field, Cambridgeshire. The *Jesse Lumb*, which was built in 1939, was stationed at Bembridge on the Isle of Wight and was busy throughout World War Two rescuing ditched aircraft crews and other war-time casualties.

The *Jesse Lumb* is a 46 foot Watson class lifeboat and was stationed at Bembridge from 1939 to 1970 when she entered the RNLI's reserve fleet. During her time on the Isle of Wight she launched 294 times, saving 280 lives. Fifteen of these services were during the War.

A local publican at Duxford, Bill Sawkins, was delighted to see the *Jesse Lumb* ending her days so near to him. He was once rescued by this lifeboat and has been a keen supporter of the RNLI ever since. The lifeboat is still on display at Duxford.

10th SEPTEMBER — ALDEBURGH, SUFFOLK, **1939**

As Charles Vince wrote in his book 'Storm on the Waters', the Aldeburgh No. 1 motor-lifeboat Abdy Beauclerk was involved in the first war time service after what had been a period of calm.

*"The hush was broken for the lifeboat service on the 8th day. In the afternoon of the 10th September - a still summer afternoon when there seemed no perils at sea - the steamer **Magdapur**, of Liverpool, struck a mine 2 miles off the Suffolk coast. It broke her back and she began to sink. Five of her crew had disappeared in the explosion. The Aldeburgh lifeboat brought the rest ashore. There were 74. Some dozen of them were wounded and all were smothered in black oil. When they had been landed, carried to the waiting ambulances or helped up the beach, it took two and a half hours to clean the lifeboat of the oil and blood."*

The *Magdapur* was the first ship to be sunk by a mine. Those 74 men were the first of that long procession from the sea, from mined, torpedoed and bombed ships. Men found broken and dazed on rafts and wreckage, burnt by explosions, weak from long hours in the water, clogged and helpless with oil - whom the lifeboats were to bring ashore in the succeeding months.

11th SEPTEMBER — LONDON, **1927**

The BBC's *'The Week's Good Cause'* featured the broadcast of

'SOS'. This was a Lifeboat Dialogue written by Commander Stopford C. Douglas RN, Deputy Chief Inspector of Lifeboats. Sir Gerald du Maurier and Mrs Mabel Terry-Lewis played the two parts.

Responses to this appeal continued to come in for the following three weeks. Altogether 420 were received, the total sum contributed being £376 17s 2d. The contributions varied from ten guineas to sixpence. They came from all over Great Britain, from Inverness to Exeter, and four came from Antwerp. Among those who responded were *"An old soldier in his eighty-fifth year," "An old soldier living in Belgium," "A sailor's wife," "A sailors widow,"* and *"A poor woman".*

On the 16th September, Mr. Edgar Johnson, the District Organising Secretary for the North of England, gave a talk from the Newcastle-on-Tyne Station called *"The Sea-Fighters of Northumbria".* On the 1st October, Captain A. S. Balfour, OBE, late of the Royal Indian Marines and a member of the Edinburgh Committee, gave a talk from Edinburgh, on *"Shipwrecks on the Scottish Coasts".*

12th SEPTEMBER   POOLE, DORSET, **1994**

For the first time, the RNLI had 100 serving female crew members when 24 year old Holly Phillips joined the Poole inshore lifeboat crew on the 12th September 1994.

The first ever lifeboat woman joined the crew of the Atlantic College inshore lifeboat in South Wales in 1969. Since then numbers have fluctuated, but this was the first time triple figures had been reached. Female crew members are now active on inshore and all weather lifeboats.

13th SEPTEMBER   WESTON-SUPER-MARE, SOMERSET, **1975**

The Weston-Super-Mare McLachlan lifeboat launched at 10.31 p.m. on the 13th September 1975. The night was very dark and an easterly gale was blowing over a rough sea with squally rain showers.

A motor boat had been reported wrecked at the base of a sheer cliff in a small cove, midway along the north side of the Brean Down peninsula, south-west of Weston-super-Mare. The five men on board were by then standing on a rocky ledge and were in danger of drowning in the rising tide. After making one run in through rough and confused seas, frequently grounding on submerged rocks, Helmsman Morris approached again and heaved a line ashore so that four men were hauled out to the lifeboat. The fifth man waded out, and all were landed at Ferry Stage, Uphill, at 11.20 p.m.

For this service Helmsman Julian Morris received the Institution's bronze medal.

14th SEPTEMBER   NEWBIGGIN, NORTHUMBERLAND, **1878**

Normally lifeboats launch to save crews from ships. Just occasionally there is a reversal of direction, as witnessed by this report of service by the Newbiggin lifeboat *William Hopkinson* of Brighouse on the 14th September 1878 and recalled in the November Lifeboat Journal of that year.

"On 15 September several of the large herring boats belonging to this place were lying at anchor in the bay when a very violent gale suddenly sprang up, and they were in great danger of sinking at their moorings or being driven on the rocks. Their crews, who were ashore, were totally unable to go out to them in small boats or cobles generally used by them.

"The lifeboat was accordingly brought into requisition, and the fishermen taken out to their boats, which were then safely got out of the bay or into shelter, with the exception of one, which was stove on the rocks."

The *William Hopkinson* of Brighouse was at Newbiggin from 1865 to 1885. A Miss Hopkinson 'in memory of her brother' paid for it. In all the boat launched 40 times, saving 103 lives.

15th SEPTEMBER   FISHGUARD, ANGLESEY, **1880**

On the 15th September 1880, Fishguard was visited by a very strong gale from the N.N.E., accompanied by a heavy sea. The smack *Catherine*, of Cardigan, bound thence to Swansea, in ballast, and the brigantine *Osnabrick*, of Papenberg, Hanover, bound from Sundsvall, Sweden, to Cardigan, with timber, were at anchor in the roadstead. As both were riding very heavily, a sharp look-out was kept on them during the day.

"At about 5.45 p.m. a signal of distress was hoisted by the smack, and the No. 1 lifeboat Sir Edward Perrott, was at once launched, and went out splendidly through the broken sea. She took off the smack's crew of two men, and then proceeded to the brigantine to ascertain whether any aid was required. The Master, however, declined any help as he was in hopes the gale was breaking up, and he thought that his vessel would be able to ride it out, as she had three anchors ahead. The boat then returned ashore and landed the smack's crew in safety. At 10 p.m. just as the lifeboat had been placed in her house, the brigantine burnt signal lights, having parted her principal chain.

"The lifeboat was immediately taken out again and proceeded to the Osnabrick. But before she could reach her the two remaining chains had given way and she rapidly drifted on the sands, where a fearful sea was washing over her. As she had stranded in the midst of the broken water, considerable difficulty was experienced by the lifeboatmen in taking off her crew. Several times the boat completely filled. However, this was eventually accomplished in safety, and the crew, consisting of six men, and the Captain's wife, were brought ashore in safety."

16th SEPTEMBER   SWANAGE, DORSET, **1875**

The February 1876 Lifeboat Journal describes the reason for the establishment of a lifeboat station at Swanage.

"In the month of January, 1875, a shipwreck took place on the Peveril Ledge, off this place. It was only with difficulty, and by incurring much risk, that the crew were saved through the exertions of the Coastguardmen in their boats - it being impracticable to convey the intelligence of the wreck to Poole, the nearest lifeboat station, until some time had elapsed. Thereupon the National Lifeboat Institution offered to form a lifeboat station at Swanage, in the event of the local residents being prepared to extend their co-operation to the undertaking.

"The gift was readily accepted, and a large lifeboat, 35 feet long, 9 feet wide, and rowing 10 oars double banked, was accordingly provided for this station. A substantial and commodious house has been erected for the lifeboat on a convenient site, kindly

granted for that purpose by the Earl of Eldon. A stone launching slipway, in front of the house, has also been constructed for the use of the boat. The lifeboat and its equipment was presented to the Institution by S. J. Wilde, Esq., of London, on behalf of his aunt, the late Miss M. R. Wilde; that lady, having requested Mr. Wilde as her residuary legatee, to make the gift of the lifeboat to the Society. The boat, in accordance with the desire of the deceased lady, is named the **Charlotte Mary**, after two sisters who had pre-deceased her, and with whom she had lived in close affection for more than sixty years. The public inauguration of the new lifeboat took place on 16 September 1875 under the superintendence of Captain Ward, R.N., Inspector of Lifeboats to the Institution, Richard Lewis Esq., Secretary to the Institution, also being present."*

17th SEPTEMBER   RHYL, FLINTSHIRE, **1962**

On the 17th September 1962, a rescue was effected by a lifeboat to a hovercraft for the first time. Hovercraft *VA3-001* had been in use during the summer operating between Rhyl and Hoylake.

At the end of the season, the craft was on moorings at Rhyl to await a tug to tow her to Liverpool.

In a gale that night the hovercraft broke loose. The Rhyl Liverpool class lifeboat *Anthony Robert Marshall* was launched at 1.17 a.m. and finally, with great difficulty, got alongside the hovercraft so that the three crew on board jumped into the lifeboat. Shortly afterwards the hovercraft hit the promenade. For this service Coxswain Harold Campini was awarded the Institution's silver medal. The hovercraft was saved and subsequently went back into service.

18th SEPTEMBER   NEWHAVEN, SUSSEX, **1977**

Sunday the 18th September 1977 marked the culmination of a year of concerted effort by Round Tablers throughout the country in one of the biggest fund-raising efforts of its kind ever organised. It was a day when two organisations covering the same geographical areas and both dedicated to the service of others, the Round Table and the RNLI, came together in mutual celebration.

The occasion was the naming ceremony of the Newhaven 44-foot

Waveney lifeboat *Louis Marchesi of Round Table*. The National Association of Round Tables (Great Britain and Ireland) had decided at their Blackpool annual conference in 1976 that they would commemorate their golden jubilee by providing a memorial to their founder, Louis Marchesi, in the form of a lifeboat.

It was a historic decision for it was the first time in the movement's 50 years that all Round Tables banded together in one project. The strength of the Round Table movement has always been in the autonomy of its 1200 Tables. Each is fiercely independent and with a membership of young men under 40, dedicated to 'adopt, adapt and improve', local Tables have raised hundreds of thousands of pounds for charities over the years. The RNLI has frequently benefited from such collections in the past and inshore lifeboats and pieces of equipment have been typical targets.

As a result of the appeal, over £215,000 was raised. £150,000 was used for the Newhaven lifeboat. The balance was used on capital projects in Scotland, Wales and Ireland.

19th SEPTEMBER   PENLEE, CORNWALL, **1949**

A service by the Penlee lifeboat was given the headline *'On two different planes'* by the December 1949 Lifeboat Journal.

About 3.18 in the afternoon of the 19th September 1949, the Penzer Point coastguard phoned, saying that the Culdrose Air Station had reported a crashed Firefly aeroplane, three miles south of Penzer Point. Worse, a Sea Otter rescue seaplane had landed near her and could not take off again. The lifeboat *W. and S.* was launched at 3.40 p.m. in a choppy sea, with a light southeasterly breeze blowing, and stood by the seaplane as she taxied across Mount's Bay. Five miles west of the Lizard a RAF rescue launch took her in tow and headed for Helford River. The services of the lifeboat were therefore no longer required. She was recalled to her station, arriving at 6 o'clock in the evening. A trawler rescued the pilot of the Firefly.

20th SEPTEMBER   RUNSWICK, YORKSHIRE, **1934**

H.R.H. The Princess Royal (Princess Mary) named the new motor lifeboat at Runswick Bay, Yorkshire, on the 20th September 1934. The new boat was built out of a legacy from the late Mrs. E Boldren Brown, of Scarborough, and the name intended for her was *The Always Ready*. The name was changed to *Robert Patton - The Always Ready*, in honour of Coxswain Robert Patton. He had sadly died of injuries received in the rescue of a lame man when the new lifeboat went out to the help of the steamer *Disperser*, of West Hartlepool, which was sinking in a gale on the 8th February 1934.

Whilst trying to get the man into the lifeboat, Coxswain Patton was dragged out of the boat. Still holding the man, knowing him to be disabled, the Coxswain fell into the sea and when the lifeboat was swept back, was crushed between it and the steamer. He was crushed twice more after the seaman had been dragged inboard. Returning to Runswick at 6.15 a.m. the Coxswain was admitted to hospital, gravely injured. He died nine days later at the age of 46. In his own words *"I could not have let the poor lad go, as he might have drowned"*.

The Princess Royal presented Patton's widow with the posthumous gold medal awarded to him by the Institution on the 8th March 1934.

21st SEPTEMBER   ROSSLARE HARBOUR, CO. WICKLOW; NEW BRIGHTON, CHESHIRE, **1949**

It is not often that the same boat required assistance twice in one month from lifeboats at stations some way apart. On the 21st September 1949, the Rosslare Harbour lifeboat *Mabel Marion Thompson* went out at night to bring ashore the Master and crew of the *Susan Vittery*. This ninety years old motor schooner was rolling badly, making very heavy weather and leaking.

Earlier in the month the New Brighton lifeboat *William and Kate Johnston* had gone out to the schooner when she grounded in the River Mersey. The lifeboat stood by while the *Susan Vittery* was re-floated and then taken in tow by a tug to a safe anchorage.

22nd SEPTEMBER   GALWAY BAY, CO. GALWAY, **1945**

When a gale blew up in the night, two steam trawlers dragged their anchors and went on to the rocks about a mile from Galway

Bay lifeboat station. At 12.35 a.m. on the 22nd September 1945 the motor lifeboat *K.E.C.F.* was launched. She found the trawler *Trumpeter*, of Milford Haven, on a reef, with seas washing right over her. With great difficulty she rescued her crew of twelve. The lifeboat then made for the other trawler, the *Ilfracombe*, also of Milford Haven, and rescued her crew of thirteen. She landed both crews and reached her station again at 2.45 that morning. At 4.45 a.m., in moderating weather, at the request of the *Trumpeter's* skipper, she took him and four of his crew out to the trawler again, but another trawler was found to have taken charge of the *Trumpeter*, and the lifeboat brought the five men back at 6 o'clock.

At 9.45 a.m. another trawler sent a small boat ashore with the message that she had picked up a wireless report from the *Ilfracombe*. It stated that her skipper and seven members of the crew had reboarded her in a shore boat, and were in difficulties once more as she had filled with water and was now listing dangerously. The lifeboat again put out at 9.55 a.m. took off the eight men and landed them. She arrived back at her station at 11.15 a.m.

23rd SEPTEMBER PORTSMOUTH, HAMPSHIRE, **1996**

The spring 1997 Lifeboat Journal included a report on the result of fund raising when a cheque for £64,350 was presented to the RNLI.

"Representatives from the Civil Service Motoring Association (CSMA) and Frizzell Financial Services jointly presented a cheque to the RNLI on 23 September 1996 for the purchase of an Atlantic 75 lifeboat at Portsmouth lifeboat station.

"The money was raised by donations from CSMA members taking part in competitions and other functions and is the continuation of the support they have given the RNLI since 1984 - within which time they have contributed nearly £250,000."

The new Atlantic 75 lifeboat was named *CSMA Frizzell* on the 26th April 1997.

24th SEPTEMBER HULL, YORKSHIRE, **1997**

Humber's new £1.3m Severn class lifeboat, *Pride of the Humber*,

sailed into Hull Marina in brilliant sunshine for her royal naming ceremony on the 24th September 1997. All members of the RNLI's only full time lifeboat crew were present. The men live in the RNLI houses at the tip of the remote Spurn Point, and each member of the crew normally works six days a week. The entire team turned out to hear H.R.H. The Duke of Kent name the lifeboat which had been funded thanks to the supreme fund-raising efforts of individuals and companies throughout the North East of England.

More than 1,000 guests witnessed the naming ceremony as they basked in the Indian Summer sunshine. Divisional Inspector Kieran Nash accepted the lifeboat on the station's behalf, and the crowd roared its approval as Kieran announced that he would check with Superintendent Coxswain Brian Bevan and crew if they would care to accept the boat, and they replied that they would!

Brian Bevan is such a well-known and respected character in the region that a bear, named Bevan Bear, in his honour, was sold to raise funds for the new lifeboat. Sales of the bear put £38,000 in the appeal's coffers. Thousands of fund-raising events

Superintendent Coxswain Brian Bevan of the Humber lifeboat. He is the only lifeboatman to have received at the same annual Presentation of Awards, the gold, silver and bronze medals.

throughout the 1994/95 Humber Lifeboat Appeal, boosted by bequests from Miss Lucy Chandley, Miss Margery Hooton and Mrs. Self of Cleethorpes, provided the funding for the lifeboat.

Brian Bevan is the only lifeboatman to have received at the same annual Presentation of Awards the gold, silver and bronze medals. This was in 1979, for services in December 1978 and two in February 1979.

25th SEPTEMBER CROMER, NORFOLK, **1941**

Between the 17th September and the 6th November 1941, the Cromer lifeboats were engaged by the Admiralty to help salvage what was described only as 'a valuable cargo' from the s.s. *Teddington* of London. She had been attacked by German aeroplanes and set on fire. Her crew were taken off by a naval vessel, leaving the steamer stranded about 3 miles from Cromer.

On the 17th September the Admiralty salvage officer asked for the services of the No. 1 motor lifeboat *H. F. Bailey* to take firemen and motor pumps to the vessel. Later in the day she took out acetylene plant, and on subsequent days carried the salvage men and stevedores between Cromer and the wreck. Working in relays the lifeboatmen gave much help with the work of salving cargo, and it was not until the 6th November that the last lifeboat trip was made.

On several occasions the No. 2 motor lifeboat *Harriot Dixon* went out in place of the *H. F. Bailey* and between them these two boats were engaged on twenty eight days as follows: The No. 1 lifeboat, September 17, 18, 20, 21, 22, 23, 24, 25, 29 and 30; October 2, 3, 5, 6, 7, 8, 9, 14, 15, 17 and 18; and November 6; the No. 2 lifeboat, September 19; October 1, 19, 21 and 22; and November 4. The Admiralty paid the expenses of the lifeboats.

26th SEPTEMBER ASCOT, BERKSHIRE, **1980**

A very successful fund raising day was held at Ascot Races when over £63,000 was raised. The tide was high for the RNLI on the 26th September, bringing lifeboat people from round the coast, and many inland cities, towns and villages as well, to join with race goers for this year's Ascot Charity Race Day. The six

'maroons' between 2.15 and 4.50 were for horses on a beautiful autumnal afternoon, with a slight haze to soften the sun, little wind and visibility of - well, quite enough furlongs to see the runners approaching right round the course.

By mid morning people were beginning to gather and already members of the Ascot branch were at the entrance gates with collecting boxes, while the souvenir caravans manned by Ascot and Central London Committee branches were doing brisk business. In the area just behind the Grand Stand, where an Atlantic 21 was on display, Southern District branch members scarcely paused all day in the sale of tickets for their district raffle for a Mini car. An auction luncheon, for which the Duke of Atholl, Chairman of the Institution, was host, was held in one of the Royal Enclosure restaurants. Most of the lots were stallion nominations from leading studs, and the auction, conducted by racing commentators Peter O'Sullevan and Lord Oaksey, raised a wonderful £35,000.

27th SEPTEMBER BURTON-ON-TRENT, STAFFORDSHIRE; BARROW, CUMBRIA; AND RYE, SUSSEX, **1986**

Three inshore lifeboats, each of a different class, were handed over to their stations on the 27th September 1986.

At Burton-on-Trent, specially brewed commemorative beer was the unusual souvenir on sale when Hartlepool's new Atlantic 21 lifeboat *Burton Brewer*, was handed over to the station in Burton-on-Trent. The Midlands town, famous for its brewery, had raised the money to provide the lifeboat. At the start of the proceedings cadets from s.s. *Modwena* paraded the lifeboat through the town before she was placed on display in front of the Bass Museum.

At Barrow, model lifeboat rallies organised by Des Newton since 1979 helped provide funds to pay for their new D class inflatable lifeboat. Appropriately, the boat was named *Modeller I*. Meanwhile, at Rye Harbour, their new C class inflatable lifeboat was dedicated. The Lewes Lifeboat Appeal provided the funds for this.

28th SEPTEMBER EXMOUTH, DEVON, **1957**

'Never give up' might well be the heading for this service described in the December 1957 Lifeboat Journal.

"At 9.30 on the night of the 28th September 1957, the coastguard telephoned that three red flares had been seen eight to ten miles south of Lyme Regis, and that an RAF rescue launch was putting out to search. At 9.48 p.m. the lifeboat **Maria Noble** *was launched in a slight swell. There was a gentle breeze and the tide was flooding.*

"The lifeboat searched the area for over four hours but found nothing and began to put back to her station. Near the Exmouth fairway buoy the Coxswain saw red flares being fired from Orcombe Ledges. The lifeboat made for the position and found the sloop **West Wind**, *of Lyme Regis, aground. Her engine had broken down and she had been driven on to the ledges when her anchor*

had failed to hold. She had a crew of four. The lifeboat took the sloop in tow and reached her station at 7.40 a.m."

29th SEPTEMBER
TENBY, PEMBROKESHIRE, 1986

H. R. H. Princess Alexandra named a new lifeboat the *RFA Sir Galahad* at Tenby on the 29th September 1986. The 47ft Tyne class lifeboat was largely funded through a successful appeal by the Royal Fleet Auxiliary to help provide a lifeboat in memory of officers and men who were casualties in the Falklands conflict. Representatives of the R.F.A. and the Falklands were among the guests at the lifeboat's naming. It was poignant that the music

The 47ft Tyne Class lifeboat RFA Sir Galahad that is stationed at Tenby in Pembrokeshire.

was played by the Band of the Welsh Guards, since it was while disembarking Welsh Guards in Bluff Cove that *R.F.A. Sir Galahad* came under severe attack.

In her speech, Princess Alexandra said: *"Your new lifeboat will open a fresh chapter in the station's history - her crew will carry on the proud traditions. She is named in the memory of the men who lost their lives serving others in the Royal Fleet Auxiliary. It seems a most fitting tribute, as this boat will also serve - in saving lives. Those who worked so hard in raising the money to provide the lifeboat must be proud to see her today and to think ahead to the work she will do in future years."*

30th SEPTEMBER   LOWESTOFT, SUFFOLK, **1918**

During the wars, despite the absence of young men in the forces, lifeboats were still crewed by volunteers of all ages.

At Lowestoft, on the 30th September 1918, eighteen men turned out to go to the aid of the sloop H.M.S. *Pomona.*

Two men were over 70, 12 in their sixties and the other four in their fifties. The wreck was 17 miles from Lowestoft, a gale was blowing with continuous heavy rain. The rescue was successful - nine men being saved, although the Captain had drowned.

Coxswain John Swan was awarded the Institution's silver medal and Second Coxswain George Ayers the bronze medal. Reporting the service at the Annual General Meeting, it was stated that it had been a most impressive sight to see these old men grey haired and bent, and the majority afflicted with the attendant ills of old age, struggling in the darkness against the wind and rain.

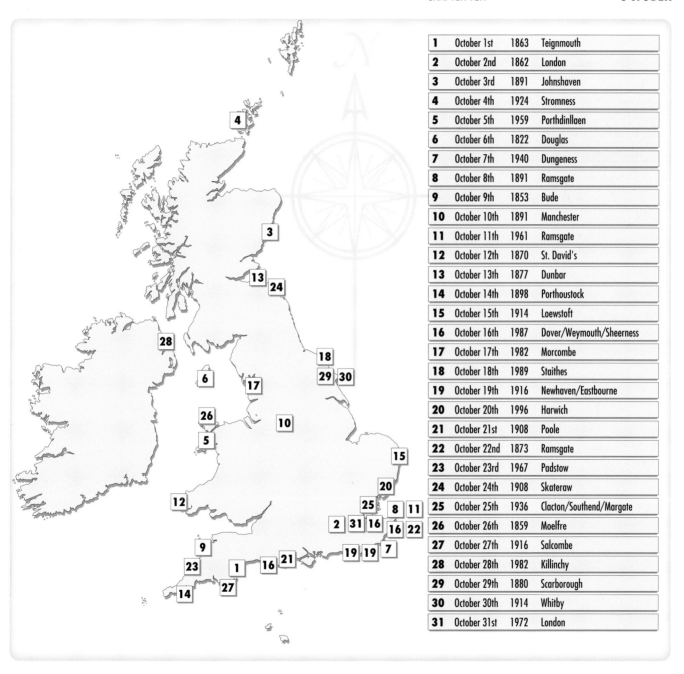

1	October 1st	1863	Teignmouth
2	October 2nd	1862	London
3	October 3rd	1891	Johnshaven
4	October 4th	1924	Stromness
5	October 5th	1959	Porthdinllaen
6	October 6th	1822	Douglas
7	October 7th	1940	Dungeness
8	October 8th	1891	Ramsgate
9	October 9th	1853	Bude
10	October 10th	1891	Manchester
11	October 11th	1961	Ramsgate
12	October 12th	1870	St. David's
13	October 13th	1877	Dunbar
14	October 14th	1898	Porthoustock
15	October 15th	1914	Loewstoft
16	October 16th	1987	Dover/Weymouth/Sheerness
17	October 17th	1982	Morcombe
18	October 18th	1989	Staithes
19	October 19th	1916	Newhaven/Eastbourne
20	October 20th	1996	Harwich
21	October 21st	1908	Poole
22	October 22nd	1873	Ramsgate
23	October 23rd	1967	Padstow
24	October 24th	1908	Skateraw
25	October 25th	1936	Clacton/Southend/Margate
26	October 26th	1859	Moelfre
27	October 27th	1916	Salcombe
28	October 28th	1982	Killinchy
29	October 29th	1880	Scarborough
30	October 30th	1914	Whitby
31	October 31st	1972	London

1st OCTOBER   TEIGNMOUTH, DEVON, **1863**

The Lifeboat Journal of the 1st October 1863 reported the stationing at Teignmouth of a new lifeboat.

"A new 33 feet lifeboat, rowing ten oars, has been stationed at Teignmouth. This boat is an experimental one, being built of iron, and being the first lifeboat on the self-righting principle which has been made of that material. She was built by Mr. Hepworth, the iron ship-builder, at Millwall, London, and under the immediate superintendence of Mr. Joseph Prowse, of H. M. Dockyard, Woolwich, Surveyor to the Institution. She has been remarkably well built, and in the strongest manner possible, being made of the best charcoal iron. Her cost was raised at the British settlements at Hong Kong and Shanghai, in 1862, by W. H. Harton Esq., member of the General Committee of the Institution, in conjunction with Messrs. Gilman and Co., of Hong Kong, for the express purpose of presenting a lifeboat to the Institution, to be stationed on the English coast. In compliment to the subscribers, who thus remembered an important work in their own country when far away from it, she has been named China".

Experience showed, however, that this iron lifeboat was not suitable for this particular station, it proving difficult to launch the heavy boat over the sandy fore-shore. She was therefore replaced by a conventional wooden lifeboat. The iron lifeboat, which was never launched on service at Teignmouth, was re-allocated to the New Brighton Lifeboat Station, where she was kept afloat at moorings on the River Mersey.

The name *China* was transferred to the new boat at Teignmouth, whilst the iron boat became the *Willie and Arthur* at New Brighton (1864 - 1867), and then the *Eleanora* at Buddon Ness (1867 - 1870).

2nd OCTOBER   LONDON, **1862**

Since the design of the first medals in 1824, the obverse had carried the head of King George IV, the first Patron. On the 24th April 1860, the RNLI was granted a Charter of Incorporation by Queen Victoria. Consideration was then given to replacing the head of George IV. Advice was sought from Leonard Charles Wyon, Engraver at the Mint, who was the son of William Wyon who had designed the first medal. He wrote on the 14th February

1862 that 'the Royal Academy of Arts had changed the obverse of its medal with each different reigning monarch'. On the 6th March, the Committee of Management agreed to adopt the same procedure. The new design by Leonard Wyon was approved on the 2nd October 1862.

The obverse was changed again for Edward VII and George V. Shortly after his succession, however, King George VI decreed that his likeness should appear only on medals for which he had given his sanction. The obverse was therefore changed to the head of Sir William Hillary, the Institution's founder.

3rd OCTOBER   JOHNSHAVEN, KINCARDINESHIRE, **1891**

A new lifeboat station was established at Johnshaven in 1891 for the service of fishing boats which were often in danger when making for the harbour there. The new lifeboat, a 31ft self-righter, was paid for from the legacy of Mr. Alexander Davidson of Hampstead and named, as he wished, *Meanwell of Glenbervie.*

The public inauguration was held on the 3rd October 1891, and this was described at length in the November 1891 Lifeboat Journal of which the following are extracts:

The house that served as the base of the Johnshaven lifeboat station throughout its life from 1891 to 1928. Built on a site granted by Hercules Scott of Brotherton Castle, the building work cost £627.10s.10d.

"In honour of the event the day was observed as a holiday in the village, and numbers of farmers in the neighbourhood gave their servants a half day holiday to allow them to be present at the ceremony. Various public bodies, Volunteers and Masonic and other lodges in Johnshaven were invited by the Committee to be present and take part in the procession, and a hearty response was made.

"The Volunteers assembled in the Drill Hall, while the other bodies assembled at the shore. There was a fair muster of men belonging to the 9th (Johnshaven) and 10th (St. Cyrus) Batteries 1st AVR under the command of Major Beattie. Mr. George, Chief Constable of the County, and a staff of men were on duty, and Mr. George, who was mounted, acted as Grand Marshal. It was calculated there were more than a thousand persons in all the procession, which was the largest ever seen in the village. The lifeboat with crew on board, wearing their cork lifebelts and red caps, was drawn by six powerful horses from Brotherton Home Farm and, needless to say, was the feature of the display.

"After the ceremony, the boat was then, amidst loud cheering, launched into the outer harbour, the Montrose Band striking up "Weel may the boatie row". It was then pulled to the inner harbour, where the crew got on to the quay and capsized it, when it self-righted in the exceptionally short time of a couple of seconds. The crew then went on board and pulled out to sea, where the boat was tested both under oars and sails. The sea was comparatively calm, but it behaved admirably. After remaining out for some time it was again headed for the harbour and placed in the boathouse."

4th OCTOBER   STROMNESS, ORKNEY, **1924**

The Minutes of the Committee of Management of the 16th October 1924 record the details of a remarkable rescue at Stromness.

*"Directed that a Letter of Appreciation be addressed to Coxswain William Johnston, in recognition of the meritorious manner in which he navigated the Stromness motor lifeboat **John A. Hay**, on 4 October, when she rescued from shipwreck the crew, ten in number, of the steam trawler **Hesonite**, of Hull. The vessel was wrecked on the North Crags, Birsay, Orkneys, during a dense fog, and the lifeboat was launched to go to her aid at 4.30 a.m.*

"So dense was the fog that the only guide that the Coxswain had to steer by was the broken water on the rocks and crags along the coast. Under these very difficult conditions he safely brought the lifeboat to the wreck, a distance of twenty miles. Through the local press the rescued men expressed their thanks to the lifeboatmen for their services."

5th OCTOBER   PORTHDINLLAEN, CAERNARVONSHIRE, **1959**

Just occasionally, a lifeboatman has himself to be rescued, as was the case on the 5th October 1959. At 3.32 in the afternoon, the coastguard informed the Honorary Secretary that the fishing boat *Arfon* was in difficulties two miles north east of Trevor. She had a crew of four including her owner, who was the Second Coxswain of the lifeboat.

At 4.30 p.m. the lifeboat *Charles Henry Ashley* was launched into a slight sea. There was a fresh south-south-easterly wind and it was half an hour before low water. The lifeboat made for the position given, as did a helicopter from the RAF station at Valley. The helicopter rescued the fishing boat's crew, and the lifeboat, which reached the scene shortly afterwards, took the fishing boat, that was submerged on a sandbank with only her mast showing, in tow. The lifeboat reached her station at 9.10 p.m. The Second Coxswain made a donation to the funds of the Institution.

6th OCTOBER   DOUGLAS, ISLE OF MAN, **1822**

Sir William Hillary, founder of the RNLI, was himself often involved in helping save lives from shipwrecks. The first time he did so was on Monday the 6th October 1822, when the RN cutter *Vigilant* wrecked on St. Mary's Isle during a gale. Sir William took an oar in one of the small boats that went out to pull the cutter off the rocks. Despite the very difficult conditions, hawsers were got aboard *Vigilant*. Strenuous efforts by the oarsmen in the small boats were successful and the cutter was pulled from the rocks and across the bay to safety. Other ships were also in difficulties, and Sir William organised further help, himself offering cash rewards to volunteers.

It was shortly after these experiences that Sir William's '*Appeal*' for the establishment of a '*national institution for the*

123

preservation of lives from shipwreck' was published on the 28th February 1823.

7th OCTOBER   DUNGENESS, KENT, **1940**

During the Battle of Britain, RNLI lifeboats rescued eight German airmen. One such service took place at Dungeness on the 7th October 1940. At 2.10 p.m. information was received by telephone that a fighter aeroplane had crashed in the sea. A few minutes later one of the lifeboatmen reported that he could see a small object on the water. A light westerly breeze was blowing, with a moderate sea.

The motor lifeboat *Charles Cooper Henderson* was launched at 2.25 p.m. and three miles to the N. E. by E. of the lifeboat station they found a German pilot in a small rubber boat. He was taken into the lifeboat, disarmed, his head injuries dressed, and landed at the station at 3.25 p.m. where a military escort awaited him.

In his book 'Storm on the Water' Charles Vince stated that such actions caused resentment in certain quarters, and the Institution *'was condemned for rescuing men who should have been left to perish'*. As he rightly pointed out: *'when it was founded it had pledged itself to go to the help of all in peril at sea round the shores of the British Isles without distinction of race, in war and in peace. That promise had been scrupulously kept for 116 years. It had been kept in the last war (i.e. 1914- 1918) with universal approval'.*

8th OCTOBER   RAMSGATE, KENT, **1891**

One of the most famous Coxswains in the lifeboat service was Charles Edward Fish of Ramsgate. Indeed, he was the only Coxswain to be awarded a gold medal on his retirement.

In the Committee minutes of the 8th October 1891 it was recorded that *'he had been out three hundred and fifty three times and helped save eight hundred and seventy seven lives'.* He had been awarded a first gold medal for the service to the *Indian Chief* (see 6th January).

When he died on the 5th July 1915, the August 1915 Lifeboat Journal started his obituary with the following words:

One of the most famous Coxswains in the history of the RNLI - Charles Edward Fish of Ramsgate.

"In spite of the diatribes of pacifists against war as a relic of barbarism and the embodiment of all evil, the present stupendous struggle has once again proved that, not withstanding the horrors, the misery and the grief that war brings in its train, it is also the fruitful soil on which spring the noblest and most selfless deeds of which mankind is capable. And so it is on all the battlefields which have been drenched with noble blood and on all the seas on which the British flag has flown, there have been countless instances of heroism, endurance and self sacrifice, so that the test and standard of heroism has become unconsciously brightened and strengthened. There has been in many ways, a revaluation of values in this as in other aspects of human life.

"In ex-Coxswain Charles Fish, whose death occurred on the 5th

July, there died a man who would have stood the severest test which might have been applied even by a jury of naval and military VCs. No man embodied more fully the spirit of heroic endurance, splendid seamanship and kindly humanity which have characterised the lifeboatmen of Britain for over a century, and he was himself intimately connected with the history of the lifeboat service for nearly fifty years."

9th OCTOBER   BUDE, CORNWALL, **1853**

The lifeboat station at Bude was revived by the Institution in 1853, and a new Peake designed lifeboat had only recently arrived there when called out on service on the 9th October 1853.

The Bideford sloop *Margaret* ran on to the Chapel Rocks at the entrance to the harbour. The lifeboat launched with a mixed crew of coastguardsmen and volunteers. The two crew of the sloop were rescued just before she sank. This was a new lifeboat, and the January 1854 Lifeboat Journal included the following comment on the service: *"The silver medal of the Society was, on this occasion voted to W. H. Tregidgo, the Coxswain (who had before distinguished himself by saving life). Double the usual scale of pay was also voted to the boat's crew, in consideration of their having so readily placed confidence in an untried boat, when the salvation of life was their object."*

10th OCTOBER   MANCHESTER, LANCASHIRE, **1891**

The Winter 1991/92 Lifeboat Journal carried the following article on the centenary of the first of what became known as 'flag days':

"100 years ago on 10 October 1891, the first ever street collection for a national charity was held in Manchester on behalf of the RNLI. The important historical landmark was celebrated by a gathering on the 8th October 1991 in Albert Square, Manchester when a modern inshore lifeboat was drawn by Webster's Brewery shire horses, echoing the original lifeboat parade all those years ago."

A special lifeboat day collection took place in Manchester on Saturday the 12th October, and a five day exhibition highlighting

An illustration showing the image of Charles Macara who instigated the first ever 'flag day' in Manchester on the 10th October 1891.

the anniversary was displayed at two branches of the National Westminster Bank.

The first lifeboat Saturday followed the worst lifeboat disaster in RNLI history when 27 lifeboatmen from St Anne's and Southport stations perished attempting to rescue the crew of the German barque *Mexico*. As well as setting up a disaster fund for the widows and orphans, Manchester businessman Charles Macara introduced 'Lifeboat Saturday', featuring a grand cavalcade, to make the public at large aware of the service provided by the brave volunteer lifeboatmen and the need for widespread financial support. Soon similar Lifeboat Saturdays were being held in other towns and cities throughout the British Isles.

Macara's wife Charlotte formed the 'Ladies Ancillaries' who helped with the collections and began to hold other fund raising events and to collect from houses. It heralded the growth of the RNLI local branch system and house-to-house collections which remain a basis for the Institution's raised income today.

In 1990, RNLI flag days and house to house collections exceeded £2 million. The debt which the RNLI and indeed all charities - owe to Charles Macara is considerable for, as his biographer W. Haslam Mills declared *"he brought charity into the streets and streets into charity".*

11th OCTOBER   RAMSGATE, KENT, **1961**

Lifeboats at some stations regularly carry out exercises with helicopters, although they do not usually end as did this exercise reported in the March 1962 Lifeboat Journal!

At 6.07 on the evening of the 11th October 1961, the lifeboat *Michael and Lily Davies* had just completed an exercise with a Royal Air Force helicopter at Ramsgate. There was a light south-westerly breeze with a slight sea. The helicopter was returning to its station when the lifeboat crew saw it crash into the sea and become partly submerged. The lifeboat went immediately to the scene and picked up all four of the helicopter's crew. The lifeboat then returned to harbour, and the survivors were taken to Manston by ambulance. Fortunately none of them was hurt. The lifeboat reached her station at 6.16 p.m.

12th OCTOBER   ST DAVID'S, PEMBROKESHIRE, **1870**

A new station had been established at St. David's in 1869. The first service was on the 12th October 1870 when the two man crew of the smack *Trout* was rescued.

The Lifeboat Journal of October 1869 describes the rather unusual naming ceremony of the lifeboat *Augusta*. The boat was donated to the Institution by the Earl of Dartmouth and his tenantry and was named after his wife. It was in April 1869 that the boat was taken for exhibition to his lordship's seat at Patshall Park near Wolverhampton en route to St. David's. In the presence of members of his family, many from the surrounding neighbourhood, Lord Dartmouth formally presented the lifeboat

to the Institution, which was represented by the Inspector. The boat was named by Lady Dartmouth and launched into a lake in the Park being manned by an amateur crew of young gentlemen resident in the locality, amongst whom were Lord Dartmouth's two eldest sons, this crew rowing the boat remarkably well. The lifeboat was afterwards forwarded to its station via Haverford West.

13th OCTOBER   DUNBAR, EAST LOTHIAN, **1877**

In the Annual Report for 1877, it was reported with regret 'that on an occasion of the quarterly practice of the lifeboat stationed at Dunbar, it was upset under sail, by carrying an injudicious press of canvas through heavy squalls, on which occasion two of the crew unfortunately perished'. This happened on the 13th October 1877.

The 'Dunbar Lifeboat History' by Ivor B. McPhilips records that *"disaster strikes suddenly at sea and while on rough weather exercise, [the lifeboat] Wallace capsized"*. The lifeboat righted herself almost immediately and eleven men regained the boat. Sadly Coxswain Robert Herkes and former Coxswain Robert Clements were both lost. A local appeal for a dependent's fund met with generous response but Robert Clements' wife, who was ill at the time, died unaware of her husband's fate'.

14th OCTOBER   PORTHOUSTOCK, CORNWALL, **1898**

On the evening of the 14th October 1898, having sailed from London for New York with 97 crew, 60 passengers (53 first class and seven cattlemen) and one stowaway, the 6,889 ton *Mohegan* was badly off course when she passed inshore of the Manacles Bell Buoy, off Manacle Rock, south of Falmouth, Cornwall. She struck Maen Voces Rock in the Varsis Ledge head-on at speed in a moderate east-south-east gale and heavy sea. She immediately took on a port list and sank by the bow after 15 minutes, although some boats got away.

James Hill, Coxswain of the Porthoustock lifeboat *Charlotte* had seen the ship was off course and in danger. He therefore launched the lifeboat and helped save 44 out of 51 survivors of this tragedy.

Lifeboats from Falmouth, Cadgwith and Polpear (Lizard) had

launched but failed to rescue anybody as there were no lights to indicate the ship's position. By the time they located the wreck, the Porthoustock boat had taken off all possible survivors. Some survivors had been picked up from the rocks by a coastguard boat. The Captain and all the officers of the *Mohegan* had drowned. Coxswain Hill was awarded the Institution's silver medal.

15th OCTOBER   LOWESTOFT, SUFFOLK, **1914**

In October 1914, the Germans invaded Belgium, and many refugees fled the country by boat. On the 15th October 1914, about 25 boats had arrived off the coast near Lowestoft. Two of the boats ran aground on the N. E. Newcome sand bank. The Lowestoft Norfolk and Suffolk class lifeboat, *Kentwell*, went out with Coxswain John Swan at the helm. 35 men, women and children were taken off fishing smacks *052* and *0136* and landed safely ashore.

16th OCTOBER   DOVER, KENT; WEYMOUTH, DORSET; SHEERNESS, KENT, **1987**

One silver and eight bronze medals were awarded by the Institution as a result of services by three lifeboats during the hurricane force winds which struck southern England early on the 16th October 1987.

At Dover, Acting Coxswain Roy Couzens received the silver medal and his six crew were each awarded the bronze medal. Three men were rescued from a bulk carrier. During the service, Roy Couzens suffered a heart attack (thankfully surviving after medical treatment).

At Weymouth, Coxswain/Mechanic Derek Sergeant earned the bronze medal for rescuing four people from a catamaran 12 miles south of Portland Bill.

A bronze medal was awarded to Coxswain/Mechanic Robin Castle of Sheerness for going to the rescue of two anglers in a small boat.

17th OCTOBER   MORECAMBE, LANCASHIRE, **1982**

The great increase in pleasure activities around the coasts has resulted in increased calls on the lifeboat service. The rescue of a windsurfer by the Morecambe inshore lifeboat on the 17th October 1982 is an example of the services frequently carried out nowadays, but which were unknown when the RNLI was founded.

With a strong breeze rising to a south by east near gale, a rough sea and confused water, a windsurfer was reported in difficulties in Half Moon Bay, near Heysham, Lancashire. The Morecambe D class inflatable lifeboat was launched at 4.35 p.m., and, with waves breaking right over and filling the lifeboat, Helmsman Keith Willacy steered through a narrow channel towards the open bay and started to search. The windsurfer was discovered 40 feet up an old pier concrete dolphin, a quarter of a mile out to sea. The structure was approached with care, as the man had fixed his board fast to the access ladder blocking his way down and obstructing any approach by the lifeboat. Finally, the man was told to jump into the water where he was quickly lifted into the lifeboat and landed at Heysham at 5.30 p.m.

For this service, Helmsman Willacy was awarded the Institution's silver medal, and crew members Anthony Terence Jolley and Robert A. Coyle received the Thanks of the Institution inscribed on Vellum.

18th OCTOBER   STAITHES, YORKSHIRE, **1989**

Many volunteers are always ready to offer their services to the lifeboat stations. Some start training before their age permits them to join the crew.

The Winter 1989/90 Lifeboat Journal reported the enrolment in the crew of one young member on the 18th October 1989 under the heading 'Youngest Crew Member?'

Jonathan Foster achieved a long-held ambition when he joined the crew of the Staithes lifeboat - the Atlantic 21 Ellis Sinclair - on his 17th birthday. Clem James, Station Honorary Secretary, is quite sure that he has the ability, dedication and physical strength to make a good lifeboatman.

"Jonathan came to every practice and crew night for many months and he has worked hard to achieve the skills needed to be a crewman of an Atlantic 21" he said.

Jonathan was believed to be the youngest crew member aboard a lifeboat and was the first in his family to become a lifeboatman. He was a student at St. Mary's Sixth Form College in Middlesborough studying sport, and hoped to become a physical training instructor in the RAF when he completed his education.

19th OCTOBER   EASTBOURNE and NEWHAVEN, SUSSEX, **1916**

On the 19th October 1916, the Eastbourne self-righting lifeboat *James Stevens No.6* and the Newhaven motor lifeboat *Sir Fitzroy Clayton* were launched to the aid of the liner *Alaunia*. This 14,000-ton Cunarder had been either mined or torpedoed near to the Royal Sovereign light-vessel.

The first boat to reach the crippled liner was a patrol boat which took off 20 people before putting an officer and seven men on

board. The weather conditions deteriorated so that, in view of the damage to the liner, the Eastbourne lifeboat took off the eight men from the patrol boat. The Newhaven boat rescued another six people and also landed the 20 survivors saved by the patrol boat.

20th OCTOBER   HARWICH, ESSEX, **1996**

The first of the RNLI's 25 knot Severn class lifeboats, the *Albert Brown*, entered service at Harwich, and was finally placed 'on station' on the 20th October 1996. The winter 1996/97 Lifeboat Journal reported the views of the lifeboat crews on the new class.

"Although the class suffered from some early teething troubles the design has now been well proven. Coxswain Peter Dawson put things in perspective when he told 'The Guardian' newspaper

The lifeboat Albert Brown - the first of the RNLIs Severn Class.

"We're fully confident in the boat and always have been. You're bound to get problems on prototypes. Give it ten years and they'll thing it's the greatest thing since sliced bread!"

Valentia, on the West Coast of Ireland, was the second station to receive a Severn during October - encountering the tail end of Hurricane Lili while on passage. The station has already confirmed its confidence in the boat, saying: "We've already been to sea in most atrocious conditions - Force 9 and high seas along this most exposed coastline on the edge of the Atlantic Ocean."

21st OCTOBER   POOLE, DORSET, **1908**

The Poole lifeboat station is now one of the busiest in the country, mainly as a result of the increase in pleasure craft attracted to the Harbour. An earlier service by the Watson class lifeboat *City Masonic Club* on the 21st October 1908 is described in the May 1909 Lifeboat Journal.

*"During a strong S. E. gale and heavy sea the ketch **Conquest**, of Bridgewater, proceeded to sea in tow of a tug. When off Studland Bay the Master considered it advisable to return to port as the weather was so heavy, but, whilst in the act of turning, the tow rope carried away, and before another one could be fixed the ketch was driven on to the Sand Banks. The tug then tried to reach the vessel, but the seas were so heavy she could do nothing.*

"The casualty having been reported by the coastguard, the lifeboat was very promptly sent to the assistance of the distressed vessel. Eight of the lifeboatmen were put aboard the ketch to assist at the pumps, and the lifeboat stood by her from soon after noon until 5 p.m., as it was hoped it would be possible to save the craft on the rising tide. At that time it was seen that all efforts were useless. The lifeboatmen were therefore taken into the boat, and the crew, consisting of four hands and a pilot, were rescued and conveyed into safety, the ketch becoming a total wreck. It was very cold at the time, and the men found the exposure very trying."

22nd OCTOBER   RAMSGATE, KENT, **1873**

The Goodwin Sands and the many sandbanks off the entrance to the River Thames have over the years been the scene of many shipwrecks and rescues performed by the nearby lifeboat stations. In his 'Story of the Ramsgate Lifeboats', Jeff Morris describes a particularly gruelling service.

The Ramsgate lifeboatmen had a long and very arduous trip on the 22nd October 1873, after a vessel had been reported aground on the Kentish Knock Sands, N. N. E of Margate. The tug *Aid* towed the lifeboat *Bradford* out of the harbour at 6 o'clock that evening. With Coxswain Charles Fish at the helm, being ably assisted throughout by Second Coxswain Richard Goldsmith, the lifeboat and the tug battled their way through 26 miles of storm tossed seas before reaching the reported area, 5 hours after setting out. But in the appalling conditions, they were unable to find the wreck and so had to lay-to through the night, the lifeboatmen suffering greatly in their open boat, as huge, icy seas repeatedly broke over them.

At day-break, they set off again and eventually found the remains of the barque *Scott*, whose crew of 10 were in a pitiful state, having clung desperately to the top portion of the ship's main mast for over 26 hours. The men were rescued and the *Bradford* returned to Ramsgate, over 17 hours after setting out, her crew being totally exhausted.

As soon as news of this fine service reached RNLI Headquarters in London, the Secretary of the Institution, Mr. Richard Lewis, sent a telegram of congratulations to Coxswain Charles Fish and his very gallant crew.

23rd OCTOBER   TREVOSE HEAD, PADSTOW, CORNWALL, **1967**

The problems involved by the siting of new stations or improving launching facilities at existing lifeboat stations is illustrated by this account of new arrangements made at Padstow which appeared in 'A Short History of the Padstow Lifeboat' compiled by George C. Phillips.

From 1962, Padstow had only one lifeboat which was moored in the Pool outside Padstow Harbour. It became increasingly difficult for the lifeboat to get over the Doom Bar at low tide due to the silting of the Camel estuary, so a new home had to be found for the lifeboat where it could be launched at all states of the tide.

A site for a new boathouse at Mother Ivey's Bay at Trevose Head

The new boathouse at Trevose Head, Padstow. The operational opening took place on the 23rd October 1967 when the new lifeboat James and Catherine MacFarlane was launched down this 240ft long slipway.

was agreed upon after careful recordings taken over a period of two years. These showed that it would always be possible to launch the lifeboat at all states of the tide, but some difficulty might be experienced recovering the lifeboat. The bed rock is slate which is covered by sand and shingle to a depth of 2 to 6 feet. The steel piles which support the access gangway, the boathouse and the slipway were placed in holes drilled through the overlaying sand and shingle into the slate below. The lining tubes of the boreholes were left in position below low water and filled with concrete after the piles had been placed in position. Above low water the piles are encased in concrete in the normal way.

The station was built by E. Thomas & Co., Falmouth, at a cost of

£114,600. The boathouse and slipway were designed and the construction supervised by the RNLI's Consulting Engineers, Messrs. Lewis and Duvivier. The boathouse was built 30 ft above beach level at the bottom of the cliff supported on steel girders encased in concrete, with a slipway 240ft in length and a gradient of 1 in 5.5.

The operational opening of the new boathouse took place on the 23rd October 1967 when the new lifeboat, *James and Catherine MacFarlane*, was launched down the slipway.

24th OCTOBER   SKATERAW, HADDINGTONSHIRE, **1908**

Because of the difficulty of bringing the Dunbar boat overland when needed in the area, a new lifeboat station was established at Skateraw in April 1907, manned by men from the Dunbar station. Skateraw was in fact operational from 1907 until 1943. During that time the Liverpool class lifeboat, *Sarah Kay*, was on service there.

The first service of *Sarah Kay* was on the 24th October 1908 when seventeen men were saved from boats of the s.s. *Prosum* of Christiania (Oslo). The last recorded service was on the 21st December 1927.

25th OCTOBER   CLACTON-ON-SEA, and SOUTHEND-ON-SEA, ESSEX; MARGATE, KENT. **1936**

Before wireless and radio communications came into general use, it was often difficult to locate casualties. Three lifeboats were involved in just such a search on the 25th October 1936. Today one would have been on the scene much quicker - added by technology and more advanced equipment. A description of the service can be found in the March 1937 Lifeboat Journal.

Early on the morning of the 25th, the yacht *Cachalot* of Burnham on Crouch, with one man on board got into difficulties near the Mid-Barrow light-vessel. A moderate S.W. gale was blowing with a very rough sea, and squalls of rain. The man burnt blankets to attract attention, and his signals were seen and repeated by light-vessels in the area. It was not known by those on shore exactly where the casualty was, and three lifeboats were sent out to search.

The Clacton-on-Sea motor lifeboat, *Edward Z. Dresden*, was launched at 6.30a.m.; the Margate motor lifeboat, *Lord Southborough (Civil Service No.1)*, at 6.45a.m.; and the Southend-on-Sea motor lifeboat, *Greater London (Civil Service No.3)*, at 7.25a.m. The Southend boat went to the Nore and Mouse light-vessels, and eventually found the yacht in tow of a collier, near No. 11 Buoy in Barrow Deeps. She took over the tow, took the man on board, and made for her station, arriving at 12.55p.m. The Margate boat saw the other lifeboats, and after searching unsuccessfully for some time, returned to her station at 12.15 p.m. The Clacton boat also made a search and came up just as the Southend lifeboat was taking the yacht in tow. She arrived back at her station at 1 p.m.

26th OCTOBER   MOELFRE, ANGLESEY, **1859**

When the *Royal Charter* was wrecked in Moelfre Bay on the 26th October 1859, 479 persons were sadly drowned out of the 498 on board. The Scottish author, R. M. Ballantyne, was at Liverpool with his brother awaiting the arrival of family members returning on that ship from Australia.

The scenes he witnessed at Moelfre made a great impression on him, and he decided to support the lifeboat cause. His book 'The Lifeboat - A Tale of Our Coast Heroes' was published in 1864. He gave lectures on behalf of the RNLI to raise funds.

In 1866, a lifeboat named *Edinburgh and R. M. Ballantyne* was sent to a new station being established at Port Logan, Wigtownshire (see also 5th November).

27th OCTOBER   SALCOMBE, DEVON, **1916**

The Salcombe Liverpool class lifeboat *William and Emma* set out in a furious gale at about 6 a.m. on the 27th October 1916 to go to the assistance of the Plymouth schooner *Western Lass* which had been driven ashore at Prawle Point. Shortly after the lifeboat had set out, a message was received reporting that life-saving apparatus from the shore had saved the crew of the schooner. In those pre-wireless days, there was no way of getting a recall to the Coxswain.

After finding the wreck deserted, the lifeboat turned back to

Salcombe. Whilst crossing the bar on her return, she was caught by a huge wave which threw her stern in the air. Another sea caught her broadside on before she capsized. Thirteen of the fifteen crew members were drowned.

As the February 1917 Lifeboat Journal reported: *"Shortly after the accident occurred, a Relief Fund was opened for the benefit of the dependant relatives. Wide spread sympathy was aroused and found generous expression, for the Salcombe men were a splendid type of fisher-folk, simple, brave, honest, and self-respecting, and the crew was as good a one as could be found on the coast".* Besides defraying all the funeral and other incidental expenses the Institution at once contributed upwards of £2,200 to the fund.

28th OCTOBER   KILLINCHY, CO. DOWN, **1982**

Money is collected and handed over to the RNLI in many diverse ways. This press release of the 28th October 1982 from the Belfast regional office describes one unusual donation:

"As a result of the recent very successful Hen Island Challenge Race, staff at the Northern Bank, Killinchy, today (Thursday) received for lodgement a golden china hen, in which nestled a cheque for £3,000 being the donation to the RNLI from this event which also benefited the O. Y. C. and Mitchell House."

The Hen was handed over by Mrs. Fiona McCleery, Honorary Secretary of the Comber Branch. Also present were Doctor Barry Bramwell and Mr. David Chamberlain (Chairman Hen Island Challenge Race Committee).

29th OCTOBER   SCARBOROUGH, YORKSHIRE, **1880**

In a period of 24 hours on the 28/29 October 1880, Coxswain John Owston took the Scarborough lifeboat *Lady Leigh* out five times and helped rescue 28 people. For this he was awarded the Institution's silver medal.

The February 1906 Lifeboat Journal relates an incident when King Edward VII, the Patron of the RNLI, met Coxswain Owston:

"When His Majesty the King was staying for a few days at

Londesborough Park last October, John Owston the Coxswain Superintendent of the Scarborough lifeboat, was sent for by Lord Londesborough to assist the shooting parties. After the King had performed the ceremony of planting a tree in the park, he saw Owston standing by, and noticing that he was wearing the silver medal of the Royal National Lifeboat Institution, walked up to him saying, "That's a fine medal you've got my man. It's for saving life." The veteran lifeboatman explained that it had been given him by the Institution, in 1880, for going out in the Scarborough lifeboat five times in one day, and assisting to save 28 lives, each of the five vessels becoming a total wreck.

"The date of the rescues was 25 years to a day prior to his interview with His Majesty. The King asked Owston several questions who in reply stated that he had been the Coxswain of the Scarborough lifeboat since 1872, and that he had been Coxswain longer and saved more lives than any other Coxswain on the Yorkshire coast. "That's good, that's good!" exclaimed the King. His Majesty appeared interested in all that the gallant Coxswain told him, and when he wound up with the remark that he felt it a great honour to stand at the side of his King that day His Majesty laughed heartily and seemed to be pleased."

Coxswain Owston retired on the 31st December 1911 after 41 years in that post.

30th OCTOBER WHITBY, YORKSHIRE, **1914**

One of the great rescues of which much has been written is the wreck of the hospital ship *Rohilla* near Whitby. Among those on board were five nurses all of whom were saved. One of the women rescued was Mrs. K. M. Roberts. This was her second involvement in a famous sinking, for she had also been one of those saved when the *Titanic* sank in 1912. She had been a stewardess in that ill-fated ship.

In the RNLI archives is a letter she wrote back to her husband in Nottingham. The letter is postmarked Queenstown (now Cork) 3.45 p.m. 11 April 1912, and on the reverse Nottingham 7.45 p.m. 12 April 1912. Among the comments she makes are *"the passages length is awful, also stairs......we must be strong and healthy so I dare not show the white feather......I am paying a youth 4/- trip to carry all my soiled dishes away..... I must get some easier boots in New York. These are beggars to pinch."*

Part of the 'Titanic' letter written by Mrs. Roberts

31st OCTOBER LONDON, **1972**

At the Annual General Meeting on the 22nd May 1973, the Chairman, Commander F. R. H. Swann, spoke of a new membership scheme:

"One of the measures we adopted last year to obtain increased regular income was to establish a system of national membership to the Institution. This scheme, which has been given the name 'Shoreline', and came into being on the 31st October 1972, has been designed to give those who may not necessarily want to belong to any of the Institution's active branches or guilds, the opportunity of supporting the lifeboat service with a regular annual donation. His Royal Highness, the Duke of Kent, our President, honoured us by becoming the first member under the new scheme.

'The Yachtmen's Lifeboat Supporters Association', known up to now as the YLA, has been incorporated in to the scheme as from the 1st March. The membership of the YLA has increased to roughly 11,200. I have personally been closely associated with the YLA new national 'membership' as a category known as an 'Offshore Member'.

The YLA had been launched at the International Boat Show at Earls Court on the 2nd January 1969.

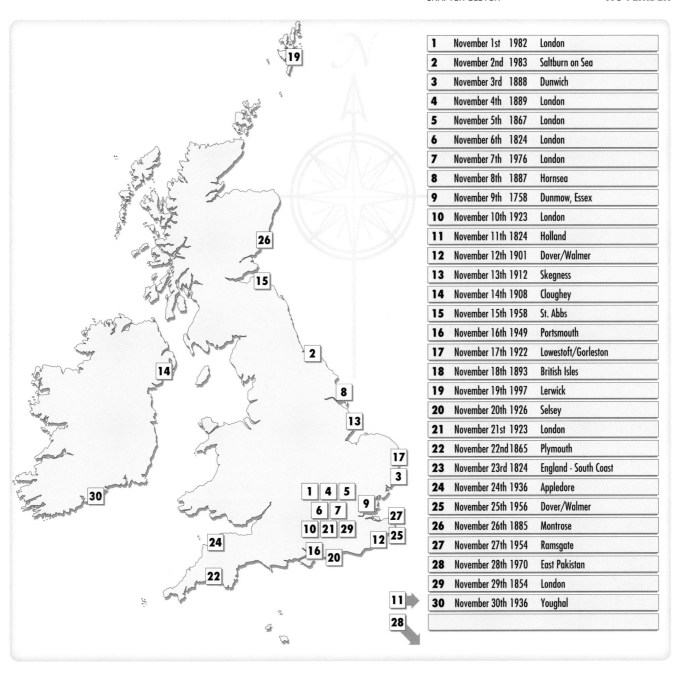

1	November 1st	1982	London
2	November 2nd	1983	Saltburn on Sea
3	November 3rd	1888	Dunwich
4	November 4th	1889	London
5	November 5th	1867	London
6	November 6th	1824	London
7	November 7th	1976	London
8	November 8th	1887	Hornsea
9	November 9th	1758	Dunmow, Essex
10	November 10th	1923	London
11	November 11th	1824	Holland
12	November 12th	1901	Dover/Walmer
13	November 13th	1912	Skegness
14	November 14th	1908	Cloughey
15	November 15th	1958	St. Abbs
16	November 16th	1949	Portsmouth
17	November 17th	1922	Lowestoft/Gorleston
18	November 18th	1893	British Isles
19	November 19th	1997	Lerwick
20	November 20th	1926	Selsey
21	November 21st	1923	London
22	November 22nd	1865	Plymouth
23	November 23rd	1824	England - South Coast
24	November 24th	1936	Appledore
25	November 25th	1956	Dover/Walmer
26	November 26th	1885	Montrose
27	November 27th	1954	Ramsgate
28	November 28th	1970	East Pakistan
29	November 29th	1854	London
30	November 30th	1936	Youghal

1st NOVEMBER   CITY OF LONDON, **1982**

As reported in the Winter 1982/83 Lifeboat Journal, the City of London appeal, which raised £433,485.43 to fund the first prototype 47ft Tyne class lifeboat, was launched by the Rt. Hon. The Earl of Inchcape at Fishmongers' Hall in November 1980.

On Monday the 1st November 1982, the story came full circle when the Lady Mayoress, Lady Leaver, named the impressive new boat *City of London* at Fishmongers' Hall Steps, London Bridge. It was in many ways an historic as well as a splendid occasion. Welcoming the guests, Mr. John Norton, a past Prime Warden of the Fishmongers' Company, reminded them that the RNLI itself had been founded within the City of London in 1824. Also this was the first lifeboat to be named after that great centre of maritime activity, renowned the world over. Among the guests were not only the Lord Mayor and Lady Mayoress, but also representatives of 40 City Livery Companies and other major institutions.

Describing the new lifeboat, Rear Admiral W. J. Graham, Director of the Institution said: *"The RNLI prides itself on being able to put into the hands of our lifeboatmen the best possible tools for the job. You see before you the latest example of our wares which I believe lives up to our traditions of excellence, ingenuity, practicality, ruggedness and, if I may call it such, 'with-it-ness'".*

The *City of London* was placed on station at Selsey on the 21st November 1983.

2nd NOVEMBER   SALTBURN-ON-SEA, CLEVELAND, **1983**

The RNLI is blessed with many devoted fund raisers. Many spend years helping, as the following report clearly indicates.

When Mrs. Doris Longley of Saltburn-on-Sea celebrated her hundredth birthday on the 2nd November 1983, she not only received telegrams from H.M. The Queen and the Secretary of State. There was also greetings from the Humber, Bridlington, Filey, Scarborough, Whitby, Staithes and Runswick, Redcar, Teesmouth and Hartlepool lifeboat stations, as well as from many ladies' guilds along the north east and from the RNLI regional office.

Mrs. Longley was founder member of Saltburn Ladies' Guild and

before that she supported Saltburn lifeboat. She has been helping seafaring charities for 80 years - and still gives her support. She was awarded the RNLI statuette in 1952 and an inscribed clock/barometer from the Shipwreck Mariners Society in 1980.

3rd NOVEMBER   DUNWICH, SUFFOLK, **1888**

On the 3rd November 1888 the Dunwich self-righting lifeboat *Ann Ferguson* launched at 7.20 a.m. to go to the aid of the Swedish barque *Flora*, of Oland, which was wrecked on the Outer Shoal of Sizewell Bank. 14 persons were saved and landed at Sizewell at 8.55 a.m. The lifeboat was unable to return to her station until 4 p.m. on the following day. During the service one of the crew was washed overboard, but he was recovered.

No trace of this station - open from 1873 to 1903 - exists today. The boathouse, along with most of the town, has been washed away by the sea.

4th NOVEMBER   LONDON, **1889**

In the archives at Poole is a slim, manuscript book in which suggestions received from the public were recorded from the 1st January 1887 to September 1922. Very brief details of each proposal are given together with the decision of the relevant committee. Many of these were deemed 'not suitable'.

On the 4th November 1889 a letter was received from a Mr. George Turner of Berwick-on-Tweed. He made a 'suggestion as to making men fast to lifeboats'. This went to the Building Sub Committee and then to the General Committee. The decision recorded states, very tersely, 'Committee do not approve of making men fast to lifeboats'.

5th NOVEMBER   LONDON, **1867**

Between 1860 and 1897, it was the custom for donors, and others, to be given a model of a lifeboat. The Minutes of the Committee of Management and the Finance Committee between those dates record some 300 such presentations.

The majority of models were given to persons or institutions that

THE LIFEBOAT: A TALE OF OUR COAST HEROES.
BY R. M. BALLANTYNE.

Frontispiece to the Lifeboat.

" The first human being placed in the boat was a little child. Its mother, despairing of being saved herself, pressed through the crowd, held her little one over the side, and cried out, ' Save my child ! ' Bax leaped on the air-chamber at the bow of the boat, and, grasping the shoulder of a boatman with one hand, stretched out the other towards the child ; but the boat swooped forward and brought him close under the chains, where a sailor held a woman suspended in his arm, ready to drop her into the boat when it should come close alongside. It did not, however, approach sufficiently near. The next wave carried them back, and enabled Bax to seize the child, and lay it in a place of safety. The mother was soon beside it, and in a short time the boat was quite filled."—PAGE 354. [*Turn over.*]

Part of the original publicity issued by the publishers of R.M. Ballantyne's book.

gave money for specific lifeboats. Amounts given varied but the average was about £500 to £1,000. No definite criteria seem to have been laid down. Some were given to persons as a record for

'services rendered' to the Institution. The Greenwich Museum has the model presented to Captain J.R. Ward RN, the Inspector of Lifeboats on the 7th April 1864.

On the 5th November 1867 the Finance Committee voted a model to 'Master Herbert Marston, The Blind Boy, who collected £100 after R.M. Ballantyne's work on 'The Lifeboat' was read to him. Herbert was the son of the Reverend C. D. Marston, Rector of Kersal, Manchester.

Ballantyne himself (see 26th October) was awarded a model on the 1st May 1866 for his help in collecting £310 for the lifeboat which was named *Edinburgh and R.M. Ballantyne*.

6th NOVEMBER   LONDON, 1824

During the early days of the Institution, many and varied were the suggestions made by the well meaning members of the public (see also 4th November). The Minutes of the Management Committee record that on the 6th November 1824 a letter was read from a Mr. James Thompson.

In this he recommended *"to the consideration of the Committee the importance of causing a Gallon of common Oil to be kept at each station where a Life Boat is established. For by slinging into the sea a quart bottle filled with Oil, in such a way the Oil can escape and expend itself on the surface of the Breakers, it will lay the agitation of the Sea, and allow the men to launch their Boat with less danger than they otherwise would do, - and the same in returning."*

It is not recorded what decision the Committee reached on this suggestion.

7th NOVEMBER   LONDON to BRIGHTON, 1976

A press release from the RNLI describes the participation of a TV personality in the London to Brighton Veteran Car Run on the 7th November 1976:

"Leslie Crowther, the well-known television personality, will be the passenger in a 1904 Wolseley in this year's London to Brighton Veteran Car Run on Sunday the 7th November. The car is being

entered by Ray Rushton to raise money for the Royal National Lifeboat Institution of which Leslie Crowther is a keen supporter.

"Mr. Rushton and his business associates have obtained sponsorship for every mile the car covers and are organising a celebration dinner dance in Wimbledon on the evening of the run. Clive Lloyd, West Indies Cricket captain has accepted an invitation to the dance, also in aid of the RNLI, and has presented a cricket bat, signed by all the members of the West Indies 1976 Touring Team, for auction there.

"The "Lifeboat Car" is a maroon coloured 1904 Wolseley, registration number AH 407 and for the past four years has completed the run, raising money for the RNLI. Last year over £3,000 was raised, and it is hoped to raise more than double the sum this year and provide the funds for an Atlantic 21 inshore lifeboat."

8th NOVEMBER   HORNSEA, YORKSHIRE, **1887**

The May 1888 Lifeboat Journal contained a report on a service by the Hornsea lifeboat carried out on the 8th November 1887:

During a moderate E. gale and a heavy sea, rockets were fired in quick succession by the four masted ship *Earl of Beaconsfield*, of London. Bound from Calcutta to Hull with a cargo of wheat and linseed, she had stranded about two miles S. of Aldbrough, nine miles from Hornsea, during a fog on the previous Sunday morning. The Hornsea lifeboat *Ellen and Margaret of Settle* was launched about 6.10 a.m., reached the stranded vessel at about 9.45 a.m., after more than three hours hard rowing, took off twenty seven men and safely landed them at Aldbrough. The lifeboat returned to her station by road on her carriage, which had been sent out to fetch her.

Hornsea was one of the stations taken over in 1854 from the Shipwrecked Fishermen and Mariners' Royal Benevolent Fund (see 29th November). It remained open until 1924. The lifeboathouse, built in 1879, was converted in 1984 for use as the Hornsea Town Hall.

9th NOVEMBER   DUNMOW, ESSEX, **1758**

Lionel Lukin (see 25th February) was born in Dunmow, Essex in

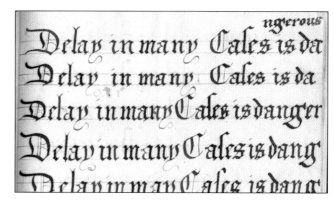

An extract from Lionel Lukin's school book - probably the oldest item in the RNLI archives. The inscription reads 'delay in many cases is dangerous'. (B case).

1742. Probably the oldest item in the RNLI archives is a school copybook in which the young Lionel practiced copper plate handwriting.

Two pages are dated the 9th November 1758. The first reads *"Delay in many cases is dangerous"*. This seems now to be very appropriate to his designing the first lifeboat. On the second page, he writes nine times *"Education is that which makes the man"* - although he does not always complete the phrase in full.

10th NOVEMBER   CITY OF LONDON, **1923**

The RNLI was represented in the Lord Mayor's Show on the 10th November 1923, by a lifeboat and crew drawn by a tractor. For those who were not present, the description in the programme of the show was:

*"The **Ellen and Margaret of Settle** lifeboat, at one time at the Hornsea station, and now a reserve lifeboat, of the self-righting type, 34 feet by 8 feet 6 inches, mounted on a launching carriage, manned by Coxswain Read (a silver medallist of the Institution) and twelve men of the Ramsgate crew, and drawn by a 35 h.p. motor caterpillar tractor, as used for launching lifeboats on flat sandy beaches."*

This was the fourth lifeboat of the same name to be stationed at Hornsea.

11th NOVEMBER   HOLLAND, **1824**

Shortly after the foundation of the RNLI on the 4th March 1824, two lifeboat societies were founded in Holland.

On the 11th November 1824, the Koninklijke Noord en Zuid Hollandsche Redding Maatschappij was formed, followed on the 20th by the Koninklijke Zuid Hollandsche Maatschappij tot Redding, van Schipbreukelingen. On the 18th November 1924, the RNLI awarded each society an honorary gold medal for their centenary, whilst further honorary golds were voted on the 11th September 1974 for their 150th anniversary.

In 1991, the two societies combined to form Koninklijke Nederlandse Redding Maatschappij. Like the RNLI, the Dutch organisation is a completely voluntary organisation. To mark their centenaries in 1924, both organisations had received the prefix Koninklijke (Royal).

12th NOVEMBER   DOVER and WALMER, KENT, **1901**

The Dover lifeboat, *Mary Hamer Hoyle* had been out at 10.30 a.m. on the 12th November 1901 to assist the barge *Jasper* which had parted her towrope and stranded.

In the evening, the lifeboat was called again, and proceeded to the s.s. *Selvio*, of Shields, which was at anchor in the bay in a disabled condition. Her crew of twenty-one men were rescued by the lifeboat which then had to run for Ramsgate.

The boat's rudder having been damaged, she anchored off Deal and burnt flares for assistance, in response to which the Walmer lifeboat *Civil Service No. 4* went out and supplied her with steering gear. She reached Ramsgate at 10.15 p.m. and safely landed the rescued men, who were housed at the Sailors' Home.

13th NOVEMBER   SKEGNESS, LINCOLNSHIRE, **1912**

The Skegness Liverpool class lifeboat *Samuel Lewis* saved the eight-man crew from the Norwegian brig *Azha* which was wrecked during a gale off Sutton-on-Sea. This service was recognised by the King of Norway, as reported in the May 1913 Lifeboat Journal:

"It is our pleasing duty to record, from time to time, the rewards which are conferred on our lifeboatmen by the rulers of foreign countries. The latest instance is a gracious act on the part of H. M. the King of Norway in rewarding the crew of the Skegness lifeboat for their gallant services in saving the crew of the Norwegian brig Azha on 13 November 1912.

"The reward took the shape of money to each of the crew, and His Majesty's recognition will be appreciated by all supporters and of workers of the Institution, and will act as an incentive to all lifeboatmen to maintain, whenever opportunity occurs, those high traditions for which they are justly famous."

14th NOVEMBER   CLOUGHEY, Co. DOWN, **1908**

Not only must a lifeboat save the crew from a wreck, but equally any pets must be saved if at all possible, as a service on the 14th November 1908 exemplified.

At 1.a.m. the coastguard reported that a large barque was ashore on the South Rock. The Cloughey lifeboat *John* was promptly manned and launched, proceeding under sails and oars to the vessel. Owing to the heavy sea considerable difficulty was experienced in getting alongside and rescuing the crew, twenty-six in number, without damaging the lifeboat.

After the men had got into the boat it was found that their pet dog, a half-bred fox terrier, had been left on board, and the men declined to leave their ship without the dog. Eventually the animal was rescued and the lifeboat returned ashore. The barque was the *Croisset* of Rouen, a vessel of 2,783 tons gross, and was bound from New Caledonia to Glasgow with a cargo of nickel ore.

At the Committee Management meeting on the 12th August 1909, it was reported that the President of the French Republic had conferred gold medals on the Coxswain and on the Chief Officer of the coastguard. The crew of the lifeboat received silver medals.

15th NOVEMBER   ST. ABBS, BERWICKSHIRE, **1958**

At 7.57 on the evening of the 15th November 1958, the Coxswain received a message that the motor vessel *Nyon* of Basle was ashore three and a half miles north west of St. Abbs Head. At 8.15 the lifeboat *W. Ross Macarthur of Glasgow* was launched in calm weather and dense fog. The tide was ebbing. The lifeboat went alongside the vessel, and the Coxswain was asked to stand by until high water and to await the arrival of a tug.

The lifeboat stood by throughout the night, and at five o'clock in the morning the tug *George V* sent a wireless message that she was two miles off St. Abbs Head and wanted to be given a course to the casualty. The lifeboat went to meet the tug. The Second Coxswain went aboard her and piloted the tug to the position of the *Nyon*. The lifeboat stood by for a time and then returned to her station, which she reached at 9.30 a.m.

During the next eleven days the lifeboat was launched more than a dozen times and stood by while attempts were made to refloat the *Nyon*. She also conveyed the vessel's crew and their personal belongings to St. Abbs. The *Nyon* was eventually cut in two by the salvage team, and the stern portion of the vessel was refloated by four tugs and towed to the Tyne. The bow portion was abandoned on the rocks.

16th NOVEMBER   PORTSMOUTH, HAMPSHIRE, **1949**

Monies reach the RNLI from a vast variety of sources. The following donation was reported in the December 1949 Lifeboat Journal under the heading 'Linen in Public':

"A naval Lieutenant-Commander stationed at Portsmouth recently received his clean laundry with one pair of socks missing.

He reported the matter, and got this reply from the Laundry:

16 November 1949

Dear Sir,

Re your inquiry regarding a pair of socks, we regret to inform you that they have accidentally been boiled, therefore, in order to settle this matter amicably will you please let us know what you claim as reasonable compensation.....

To this, the Naval Officer replied two days later:

Accidents will happen, even to socks - I should have been very annoyed if my socks had been "fried" or "roasted" or "braised" - give a bob to the Lifeboat Institution.

Action was taken, and further correspondance made a week later:

25 November 1949

Dear Sir,

We would like to thank you for your letter of 18 November, and we appreciate the spirit in which you took this matter.

We have taken you at your word, and enclose a receipt for 5 bob we sent to the Royal National Lifeboat Institution.

We beg to remain, Sir,
The Laundry."

17th NOVEMBER   LOWESTOFT and GORLESTON, SUFFOLK, **1922**

The bronze medal was introduced in March 1917 (see 30th March). Between the first medals voted then and up to November 1922, one hundred and two bronze medals were awarded.

Obverse and reverse views of the Bronze medal, introduced by the Institution in March 1917. The colour of the ribbon is blue.

On the 17th November 1922, the Committee of Management voted gold medals to Coxswain John Swan of Lowestoft and Coxswain William Fleming of Gorleston and silver medals to Commander Edward Carver R. N., District Inspector of Lifeboats and Mechanic Ralph Scott of Lowestoft. The crews of the two lifeboats - 23 men - all received bronze medals. The awards were made for a service extending from late on the 19th to 7 a.m on the 21st October 1922. The s.s. *Hopelyn* had been stranded on North Scroby Sands, off Yarmouth, Norfolk. Finally, twenty-four men - and a black kitten - were rescued.

The awards also included the first instance of a second bronze medal being awarded - to Second Coxswain George Ayers of Lowestoft. He had received the first bronze in 1918 (see 30th September).

18th NOVEMBER   BRITISH ISLES, **1893**

The February 1894 Lifeboat Journal recorded that *"the great gale which visited the British Isles on the 17th November 1893 and practically lasted until the 21st, will long be remembered..... for it was the worst of these exceptional storms ever experienced. North, east, south and west, the lifeboats were called out to the assistance of vessels in distress".*

On the 18th November, lifeboats were out at Broughty Ferry, Fishguard, Tenby, Runswick, Holyhead, Cromer and Redcar. In all they saved 58 lives. Other lifeboats were also called out around the coasts to give assistance.

19th NOVEMBER   LERWICK, SCOTLAND, **1997**

Since the RNLI was founded in 1824, only 119 gold medals have been awarded for outstanding acts of bravery. This medal has became known as the 'lifeboatman's V.C.'.

The first gold medal for several years was awarded on the 21st January 1998 for a service by the Lerwick lifeboat *Michael and Jane Vernon*, on the 19th November 1997.

The refrigerated cargo vessel *Green Lily* had developed engine trouble, and tugs were attempting to take her in tow. The coastguard helicopter had also been scrambled. The Lerwick

lifeboat arrived on the scene at 1.50 p.m. with the casualty only one and a half miles from shore. Then, as the RNLI Divisional Inspector reported:

"Coxswain Clark demonstrated enormous courage, leadership, determination and seamanship. He made the decision to try and rescue the crew after it appeared that all other hope had gone. The towline had parted, the helicopter could not work the casualty. He manoeuvred the lifeboat in limited searoom, which was further reduced with each passing minute, in 15-metre breaking seas and violent Force 11 winds. His incredible skill in handling the lifeboat and taking her alongside the violently rolling casualty ensured his crew were safe and that survivors could be taken off. When he finally drove the lifeboat clear with five survivors on board, there were less than 200 yards to the shore. The crew of the lifeboat were an example of teamwork, courage and tenacity."

Coxswain Peter Hewitt Clark, of the Lerwick lifeboat, who was awarded the RNLIs Gold Medal for a service carried out on the 19th November 1997 by the Michael and Jane Vernon.

Finally, a tug managed to fix a tow and pull the casualty's bow head on to the wind. This enabled the helicopter to rescue the ten remaining crew. Sadly, in doing so, the coastguard winchman, William (Bill) Deacon, was lost overboard when a huge wave had broken over the ship. The five survivors rescued by the lifeboat were landed at Lerwick at 3.20 p.m.

Coxswain Peter Hewitt Clark received the gold medal. His five crew members each received a bronze medal.

20th NOVEMBER   SELSEY, SUSSEX, 1926

In his history of the Selsey lifeboats, Jeff Morris describes a service by the lifeboat and then goes on to explain problems experienced by the station with coastal erosion.

On the morning of the 20th November 1926, the coastguard reported that a vessel was aground on the Mixon Reef. The lifeboat *Jane Holland*, was launched at 8.00 a.m. and, in a severe gale, found the casualty to be the ketch *Roselyn*, of Fécamp. In heavy seas, the lifeboatmen rescued the crew of 8, plus a dog and a cat. Coxswain Barnes decided that the seas were too heavy to attempt to land the survivors at Selsey, and so he made for Portsmouth, where they landed at 11.20 a.m., the lifeboat returning to her station later that day, when the seas had moderated.

It was in the early 1920's that severe coastal erosion was first noticed at Selsey, one theory being that the tidal stream had been altered by the placing of a large number of concrete defence blocks at Spithead during the First World War. Whatever the reason, the fact was that the coast was being eroded at the rate of 20 feet a year. The lifeboat-house, once set back from the top of the beach, was in danger of being undermined, and, by 1925, the situation had become so serious that the RNLI was forced to consider the future of the Selsey Lifeboat Station. The concrete slipway off-shore was still intact and so it was decided to build a new boathouse out over the approach gangway and trolley-track. This boathouse was completed in 1927, at a cost of £5,000 and was funded by the Birmingham Centenary Fund.

21st NOVEMBER   LONDON, 1923

An unusual charity matinée was described in the June 1924 Lifeboat Journal.

"It is a far cry from the snows of Russia to the sands of the Sahara, and as far a cry from the Sahara to the coasts of the British Isles. But experiments are now being made to see if a device originally designed for motor transport over the snows of Russia during the war, and then used with signal success for crossing the Sahara, will be equally effective for launching lifeboats on the coasts of Great Britain.

"This device is the Kegresse track, a self laying track of flexible rubber and canvas creeper bands, which may possibly prove more effective on our coasts than the present tractors which, while they have carried out a number of very prompt launches, have shown that where there is shingle, mud holes or creeping sand, something more powerful is required.

"These facts lend additional interest to a matinée in aid of the funds of the Institution which was given at the Victoria Palace on 21 November last, and which was itself probably unique in the long list of charity matinées in this country.

"Her Majesty the Queen and H.R.H. the Princess Louise, Duchess of Argyll, Patron of the Ladies Lifeboat Guild, were both present, and this matinée, in aid of a great British charity, was given by a Frenchman, M. Citroën, head of the French firm of motor car manufacturers which bears his name, and the whole performance was by French artists."

At the beginning of 1922 an expedition of Citroën cars, fitted with Kegresse track, travelled across the Sahara, from Touggourt to Timbuctoo, a distance of 2,000 miles and back again. The Sahara had never been crossed by automobiles, and the *Citroën* Expedition visited places which no one had ever reached before except on camels. A film was taken of this journey, and it was shown for the first time in England at this matinée. M Citroën came from Paris to be present, and with him were the leaders of the expedition, M. Haardt and M. Audouin Dubreuil.

As the whole expenses of the matinée were borne by M. Citroën every penny of the proceeds, just under £1,000, went to the Institution's funds.

22nd NOVEMBER   PLYMOUTH, DEVON, 1865

A new lifeboat for Plymouth was provided in 1862 thanks to the generosity of the Victorian philanthropist, Miss Burdett Coutts. The boat was built in London by Forrestt and together with her launching carriage was delivered to Plymouth by goods train, free of charge. Three railway companies were involved - Great Western, the Bristol and Exeter, and the South Devon.

The January 1866 Lifeboat Journal recalls one service by the lifeboat which was called the *Prince Consort*:

"On 22 November 1865 a heavy gale from the W.S.W. set in at Plymouth; considerable damage resulted to shipping, a larger number of vessels having been driven ashore than has been known at that port on any previous occasions for many years. The Prince Consort lifeboat was launched at an early hour, and was very actively employed in rendering assistance to wrecked vessels, rescuing eleven men from the Belgian brig Espoir, which had been in collision with another vessel, and bringing them safely ashore. A large concourse of spectators assembled at the pier to see the shipwrecked crew landed by the lifeboat."

23rd NOVEMBER   ENGLAND - SOUTH COAST, **1824**

It would appear that the southern coast of England experienced a violent storm on the 23rd November 1824. Nine separate medal awards were made for rescues between Devonport, Devon and Deal, Kent. In all three gold and fourteen silver medals were voted by the Committee of Management between the 8th December 1824 and the 19th January 1825. A final silver medal was voted on the 30th June 1825.

Two gold and two silver medals were awarded for help given by two coastguards and two naval officers when the transport ship *Admiral Berkeley* was wrecked at Portsmouth. As a result of their efforts, all 195 persons on board were rescued.

From Deal, four Masters put out in their own boats to the vessel Belina, wrecked on the Goodwin Sands. Despite fearful conditions, they were able to save six of the crew before the ship broke up.

24th NOVEMBER   APPLEDORE, DEVON, **1936**

The March 1937 Lifeboat Journal recounted the sad end of an old lady of the seas.

On the 24th November 1936, the ketch Ceres, of Bude, Cornwall, left Swansea for Bude with a cargo of eighty tons of slag. Her crew was a skipper and a mate. They intended to go over Bideford Bar for the night, but at nine p.m. they found water coming in to the engine room. They were then in Croyde Bay, some three miles north of the bar.

They manned the pumps, but the water gained on them. They still hoped to get the ketch over the bar, but she was rolling so badly that they launched their boat in readiness and sent up rockets and flares. When the water was washing the decks they took to the boat and lay in the shelter of the ketch, waiting for the lifeboat.

At 9.45 p.m. their signals had been seen at Appledore, and at 10.15 p.m. the motor lifeboat *V.C.S.* put out. A light breeze was blowing, a moderate sea was running, and there was some fog. At 11.15 p.m. the lifeboat arrived. She took the two men on board and circled round the *Ceres* to see if it were possible to take her in tow, but she was sinking fast. With the ship's boat in tow she reached Appledore again at a quarter of an hour after midnight. When day broke there was nothing of the *Ceres* to be seen.

So had passed away the oldest vessel in service in the British Isles, and probably the oldest in the world. She was built at Salcombe, in 1811, and for 125 years had been engaged in the coastal trade.

25th NOVEMBER   DOVER, KENT, **1956**

A television first was reported in the March 1957 Lifeboat Journal.

On the afternoon of Sunday the 25th November 1956, a lifeboat service was shown for the first time on television screens as it actually took place. The Dover lifeboat *Southern Africa* took part during that weekend in two television programmes arranged by the BBC, one on the Saturday evening and one during children's hour on Sunday afternoon.

She was at sea with the BBC producer, Mr. Peter Webber, the commentator, Mr. Raymond Baxter, BBC engineers and cameras on board. At this point a man in the motor boat *Silver Wings*, anchored near the eastern arm of Dover harbour, shouted to Coxswain John Walker that the local motor boat *Mayflower* needed help near the South Foreland light. There was a moderate sea, a south-westerly breeze was blowing, and the tide was flooding. The lifeboat made for the position and some five minutes later found the *Mayflower*, which had been taking part in an angling contest, very close to the shore at South Foreland.

Her engines were working, but she was unable to make headway against the wind and tide. The BBC's television programmes were interrupted and, watched by millions of viewers on their screens, the lifeboat took the motor boat in tow to Dover, arriving at 4.45 p.m., a quarter of an hour before the children's programme was due to begin.

26th NOVEMBER   MONTROSE, ANGUS, **1885**

David Duncan was the Coxswain of the Montrose No.2 lifeboat *Roman Governor of Caer Hon* from 1876 to 1880, then Coxswain of the No.1 lifeboat *Mincing Lane* from 1880 to 1885. He was awarded the Institution's silver medal on his retirement.

In 1904 he wrote a book on 'Lifeboat Work at Montrose', and in it he describes a service by his successor as Coxswain, James Watt, in the No.2 lifeboat.

For some days an east-south-east gale had been raging, and shortly before eight o'clock on the morning of the 26th November, 1885, a rocket fired from Usan warned those at Montrose that a vessel was off the coast holding north. Not long after, Mr David Clark, the lighthouse keeper, descried a schooner about four miles off, and at once gave the necessary signal for the lifeboatmen to be ready. *The Mincing Lane* (Thomas Watt, Coxswain) was pulled down the river, and lay in readiness inside the bar.

The vessel, however, instead of making for the harbour, as it was expected she would, held off to the north until she disappeared in the haze. Shortly after nine o'clock she was seen again, this time holding to the south. It soon became apparent that the vessel was heading for the shore, and at ten o'clock she struck the Sands opposite the Metal Bridge, fully half a mile north of the South Esk.

By the time the schooner grounded the *Roman Governor* (James Watt, Coxswain), which had been drawn along the Sands by a team of horses, was launched from the beach. After considerable trouble she was on her way to the unfortunate craft, amid the cheers of a large number of spectators on the shore. In a very few minutes the lifeboat was alongside the vessel, and in a short time the crew of four men were taken off and brought to land in safety.

The schooner was the *Familiens Haab*, of Marstall, from Fredrickshaldt for Leven, with pit props. She broke up during the night.

27th NOVEMBER   RAMSGATE, KENT, **1954**

Gales of exceptional force had been blowing for several days off the East Kent coast and, early in the morning of the 27th November 1954, it was noticed that the South Goodwin Light vessel had disappeared. Lifeboats at Ramsgate, Dover and Walmer were warned and, during the night, the first two launched and carried out searches of the Goodwins without success.

At daylight, the vessel was located on her beam-ends, where she had drifted. The Walmer lifeboat launched. The combined efforts of all three boats could not detect any survivors, so a call was made to the 66th Air Rescue Squadron, USAF, which provided a helicopter from its base at Manston, Kent, near Ramsgate.

During a second sortie at 9 a.m., the Captain noticed a solitary figure - a Ministry of Agriculture and Fisheries bird watcher - clinging to the light vessel's superstructure. Ignoring the normal rules, the helicopter was brought down to 30 feet and, in spite of the wreckage and spray, the lone survivor was plucked from his refuge and landed safely at Manston.

Captain Curtis E. Parkins, USAF, was awarded the silver medal of the Institution, the first medal to be awarded to any pilot of any aircraft. The three other members of his crew received the Thanks of the Institution inscribed on Vellum.

Opposite: The wreck of the South Goodwin Lightship. Note the part of the American rescue helicopter on the bottom right corner.

28th NOVEMBER   EAST PAKISTAN, **1970**

The RNLI, following an urgent appeal from the British Red Cross, sent staff and inshore rescue boats to aid victims of the flood disaster in East Pakistan. The cargo of inflatable boats, 20 in all, was air-lifted from Stansted, Essex, to Dacca on the 21st November. The expedition returned to this country on the 8th December.

The expedition which carried it own spares, was led by Lieutenant David Stogdon, Staff Inspector (inshore rescue boats). Mr. Michael Brinton, a mechanic, from East Cowes, accompanied him. They were later joined by two men from the Littlehampton 'Blue Peter' IRB crew, Mr. C.R. Cole and Mr. C.J. Pelham. The RNLI team were part of the international Red Cross relief force which moved in from various parts of the world for work in the south east sector of Bhola Island.

Clive King, who accompanied the expedition, reported: *"On either side of this coastal strip operations were being conducted by the British Royal Navy and the American armed forces respectively, with all the resources of aircraft carriers, landing craft, helicopters, etc. Our expedition received something of a shock on boarding the mv. Bilkis late on the 28th November, to find that the vessel was an antiquated river launch with two totally enclosed decks, six cabins and one latrine, but all 57 of us accepted the conditions philosophically".*

The inflatable boats were used to ferry supplies and medical teams to the devastated area during a week of intense physical effort.

29th NOVEMBER   LONDON, **1854**

On the 29th November 1854, an Extraordinary General Meeting of the Shipwrecked Fishermen and Mariners' Royal Benevolent Society agreed to transfer its lifeboats to the RNLI. The Society had lifeboats at eight stations - Lytham, Rhyl, Portmadoc, Tenby, Llanelli, Teignmouth, Newhaven and Hornsea, as well as one reserve boat. The transfer also included boathouses and carriages.

The lifeboats were all placed on station by the Society between 1851 and 1853. As part of the rationalisation in 1854 the Society then devoted its efforts to caring for the shipwrecked after rescue (see also 20th March).

30th NOVEMBER   YOUGHAL, CO. CORK, **1936**

On the afternoon of the 30th November 1936 the motor lifeboat *Laurana Sarah Blunt* went out on exercise. When near Capel Island, she saw two men in a small fishing boat, about a mile and a half south east of the island, waving for help. She was the motor fishing boat *Point Girl*, of Ballycotton. Her engine had broken down, and she had dropped an anchor. However, this was not holding and she was dragging out to sea. The two men were very wet and cold. The lifeboat towed the *Point Girl* into Youghal harbour and returned to her station at 4.50 p.m.

The lifeboat *Laurana Sarah Blunt* was named at Youghal by Mrs. Cosgrave, wife of the then Irish President, on the 7th July 1931. Present at the ceremony was the 84 year old Bishop of Cloyne. In his address he made the following comments:

"Surely if there is a profession of heroism, it is by eminence the vocation of a lifeboatman. The Holy Father has sent a most special blessing to the sailors of the lifeboats, and in the countries in which lifeboats are maintained, there is not a Bishop or an Archbishop or a Cardinal who has not blessed these men. It is a glorious - a wonderful mission. 'Greater love than this no man hath than he should lay down his life for his friend'."

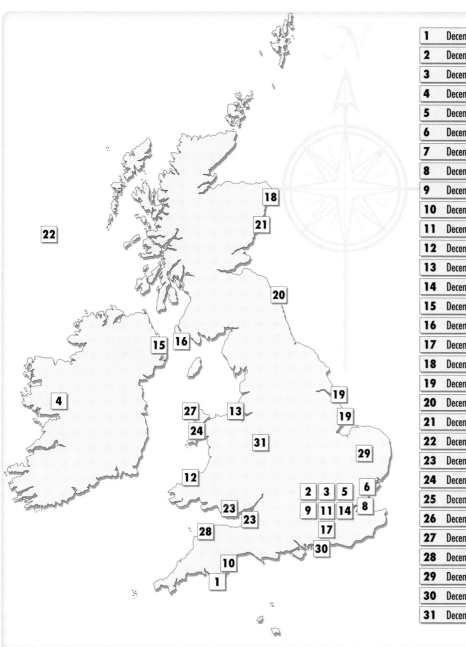

1	December 1st	1896	Hope Cove
2	December 2nd	1869	London
3	December 3rd	1954	London
4	December 4th	1930	Tuam, Co. Galway
5	December 5th	1966	London
6	December 6th	1875	Harwich
7	December 7th	1874	British Isles
8	December 8th	1962	Southend
9	December 9th	1964	London
10	December 10th	1980	Torbay
11	December 11th	1928	London
12	December 12th	1948	New Quay
13	December 13th	1944	New Brighton
14	December 14th	1928	London
15	December 15th	1876	Ballywater
16	December 16th	1867	Port Logan
17	December 17th	1911	London
18	December 18th	1944	Peterhead
19	December 19th	1996	Humber/Skegness
20	December 20th	1925	Boulmer
21	December 21st	1920	Johnshaven
22	December 22nd	1835	Atlantic Ocean
23	December 23rd	1935	Barry/Weston-Super-Mare
24	December 24th	1925	Porthdinllean
25	December 25th	1990	British Isles
26	December 26th	1995	Hedgerly/Maldon
27	December 27th	1902	Holyhead
28	December 28th	1868	Appledore
29	December 29th	1857	Norfolk
30	December 30th	1993	Selsey
31	December 31st	1935	Codsall, Staffs

1st DECEMBER   HOPE COVE, DEVON, **1896**

The 'Salcombe and Hope Cove Lifeboat History' by Malcolm D. Darch describes the arrival of a new lifeboat at Hope Cove and its first service.

The second *Alexandra* was only 34 ft long and 8 ft wide as opposed to the first lifeboat which was 35ft long and 9ft in the beam, but she still rowed ten oars. James Thornton continued as Coxswain.

A period of nine years passed before the new lifeboat was able to perform her first service. On the 1st December 1896 the early Russian steam tanker *Blesk*, on passage from Odessa to Hamburg, got ashore to the east of Graystone Ledge, near Bolt Tail in thick weather after darkness had fallen. Her distress rockets and guns were reported to Coxswain Thornton and the *Alexandra* was launched at 6.45 p.m.

The crew of forty-three were landed in two trips. The paraffin oil, which subsequently escaped from the tanker, created havoc with the local marine life reaching as far afield as the Salcombe estuary. As is common with modern-day oil spillage, the smell alone was enough to make people vomit.

The Hope Cove station was open from 1878 to 1930 and was originally paid for by the United Grand Lodge of Freemasons of England and endowed to celebrate the safe return of the Grand Master, the Prince of Wales, from India. The four lifeboats at the station were all called *Alexandra*.

2nd DECEMBER   LONDON, **1869**

On the 2nd December 1869, the Committee of Management passed a resolution that 'The Royal National Lifeboat Institution, owing to the large and extended support of the British public, having attained a truly National position, no longer requires the assistance it has since 1854 received through the Board of Trade'.

Under the provisions of the Merchant Shipping Act of 1854, the Institution for the first time received a governmental subsidy - at first £2,000 per annum. As a result a degree of governmental control was inevitable. This temporary dependence on the State was found in time to have more disadvantages than advantages.

By 1869 the Institution felt in a secure enough financial position to depend solely on voluntary contributions. And so it remains today.

3rd DECEMBER   LONDON, **1954**

An exhibition of lifeboats through the ages was opened at Lifeboat House, 42 Grosvenor Gardens, London, SW1, by Commodore the Earl Howe, Deputy Chairman of the Institution, on the 3rd December 1954.

The exhibition contains fourteen models of lifeboats ranging in period from 1789 to 1954. The earliest is a model of the *Original*, which was built by Henry Greathead, and the latest is a model of the new St. Peter Port lifeboat. Other models on show are those of a lifeboat designed by George Palmer in 1826; lifeboats sent to Rhoscolyn in 1878, New Romney in 1884, Rhyl in 1896, Padstow in 1899, Walton in 1928, Hastings in 1931, the Lizard in 1934, and Holyhead in 1950. There are also models of a Norfolk and Suffolk boat made in 1890 and a Watson boat made in 1931.

4th DECEMBER   TUAM, CO. GALWAY, **1930**

The following account of support to the RNLI through 'A Working Mens' Dance' was given in the February 1932 Lifeboat Journal. Although no specific date is given, the report has been 'appropriated' to the 4th December 1930.

"A remarkable instance of the enthusiastic support given to the Institution by working men and women was recounted by Mr. R. M. Burke, the Honorary Secretary of the Branch at Tuam, Co. Galway, at the Conference of Honorary Secretaries and Workers in the Irish Free State held in Dublin last September.

"A number of the men employed on his farm approached him one day in December 1930, and said that they wished to arrange a dance in aid of the funds of the Institution. They wanted to do everything themselves, and asked for the loan of a barn. Mr. Burke readily agreed, and the preparations went ahead. Admission was 4d. for men and 3d. for women. For an orchestra, one of the men played a concertina. There were no expenses, and the dance resulted in 15s being handed in to Mr. Burke for the Institution. The evening was so successful that two further dances were

arranged on similar lines, and altogether just over £2 was raised."

Mr. Burke also related that when a number of men on the estate were unemployed he realised some of his investments in order to provide work for them by repairing and improving the cottages of his own employees. He also put up three cottages for poor people who could not afford to build for themselves or pay an economic rent. In order to show their gratitude these men insisted upon contributing to the Institution, and gave donations between 5s. and 10s. each.

BBC tv

BRITISH BROADCASTING CORPORATION
TELEVISION CENTRE WOOD LANE LONDON W12
TELEPHONE 01-743 8000 : CABLES: BROADCASTS LONDON PS4
TELEGRAMS: BROADCASTS LONDON TELEX : TELEX: 22182

"WHAT THE LIFE-BOAT SERVICE MEANS TO US"

To all of us on "Blue Peter" the Life-Boat
Service means our four "Blue Peter" Inshore
Rescue Boats. These boats, stationed at
Littlehampton, Beaumaris, North Berwick and
St. Agnes were bought with thousands of old
paper backed books collected by "Blue Peter"
viewers all over Britain. So far they've
saved 104 lives - 104 people are alive today
thanks to "Blue Peter" viewers who cared!

The letter received from the presenters of the BBC programme 'Blue Peter'.

5th DECEMBER   LONDON, 1966

An appeal was made on BBC TV 'Blue Peter' for 60,000 paper-backed books. The original idea was for them to be sold to provide funds for one inshore lifeboat.

The response was so great that the books, when sold, made enough money to purchase not one, but four in-shore lifeboats. These boats were to be stationed at Littlehampton, Beaumaris, Berwick and St. Agnes, Cornwall.

Since then, further Blue Peter appeals have resulted in there now being seven Blue Peter lifeboats. In addition to the four stations above, in-shore lifeboats are now at Portaferry and Cleethorpes, whilst a Trent class offshore lifeboat *Blue Peter VII* is on station at Fishguard.

6th DECEMBER   HARWICH, ESSEX, 1875

The wreck of the German emigrant steamer *Deutschland*, on the Kentish Knock Sand on the 6th December 1875 drew attention to the need for a lifeboat at Harwich. The site of the wreck was 24 miles from Harwich - out of sight of the port. Signals from various light-vessels finally alerted people on shore, and a tug put out on the morning of the 7th and rescued 173 passengers and crew. Fifty-seven people though, unfortunately, lost their lives.

The Ramsgate lifeboat had been summoned by telegram from Harwich. She was towed 45 miles, arriving after the tug had saved the survivors. The lifeboat then had to be towed 45 miles back. All that time, the fifteen crew sat in their boat, with the seas and spray breaking over them and in a freezing atmosphere.

On the 6th January 1876 the Committee of Management voted *"on the recommendation of the Inspector of Lifeboats, to form a Lifeboat Station at Harwich".*

7th DECEMBER   BRITISH ISLES, 1874

During December 1874, a series of storms struck the British Isles. One of the first lifeboats involved was the Ayr boat, saving five men from the schooner *Princess Helena* on the 7th December.

The February 1875 Lifeboat Journal made a number of observations on the many lifeboat services carried out during the gales:

"To describe them in detail would occupy so much space that we could only present a summary of them; yet would it be ungrateful to the brave men who have so nobly furthered the humane object of the Institution, and upheld the honour and credit of their country, were we to let them pass without a remark.

"In one case a boat had hardly landed with her living freight from the very jaws of death, when she is summoned again to launch, her crew vying with each other once more to face the storm and the crushing surf, whilst others are as eager to displace them and share their glorious work.

"Others have gone forth in the dark night, when the danger and difficulty before them are doubled, nay, often quadrupled, in reply to the distant rocket or booming gun from the lightship near the outlying banks which flank our shore, and, although in most cases successful, yet having the mortification at times to find, on arrival at the spot, that the vessel and crew had been swallowed up together, and that their long hours of risk and exposure had been in vain."

8th DECEMBER   SOUTHEND-ON-SEA, ESSEX, **1962**

Lifeboatmen have to be resourceful, as typified by this summary of a report on a service by the Southend-on-Sea lifeboat *Greater London II (Civil Service and Post Office No. 30)* on the 8th December 1962.

The lifeboat had been called out to the Dutch m.v. *Temar* which was on fire. Other boats had gone to help. Coxswain Peter Gilson circled the Temar, and as he did so a man's head could be seen. He was jammed in a cabin porthole on the starboard quarter. A ship's boat from the tanker *Mobile Enterprise* had already put aboard her chief engineer, her second officer and a deck hand. They had with them an asbestos suit and oxygen breathing apparatus, but they could not reach the man's head either from the deck of the motor vessel or from the ship's boat.

Coxswain Gilson then secured the lifeboat under the Temar's starboard quarter. Two members of the lifeboat crew, Bowman A.

Martin and F. Emery, boarded the motor vessel and took turns at keeping the man's head out of the porthole by pulling his ears. At the same time Coxswain Gilson and Motor Mechanic J. Polkinghorn administered oxygen each time the lifeboat came up on a wave. They were hindered by smoke and could only give the oxygen a few seconds at a time as the lifeboat rose and fell in the swell.

It was then decided to cut away the deck of the *Temar* to allow the man, who was now in a very distressed condition, to be pulled out. This was done with equipment from one of the tugs. As the deck was cut above the cabin a jet of water was played on the man to protect him from the effects of molten metal falling on his back.

When the deck had been cut away, the chief engineer of the *Mobile Enterprise*, dressed in the asbestos suit, pulled the man out from the cabin. He was then taken aboard the lifeboat, which landed him at Southend pier, where a doctor and an ambulance were waiting. During the return journey Bowman Martin, whose skill in bandaging was later commended by the doctor and hospital staff, gave him first aid.

9th DECEMBER   LONDON, **1964**

The Secretary of State for Defence, by Warrant dated the 9th December 1964, authorised lifeboats of the RNLI *"to wear the Red Ensign of Her Majesty with the distinguishing marks of the Institution's House Flag in the Fly thereof".*

The Institution's own flag, however, was designed about 1884 by Miss Leonora Preston, a sister of Mr. Robert Preston who became a member of the Committee of Management. It has been known as the 'house flag' since 1908, and from 1920 onwards it became the custom to have it painted on the bows of all lifeboats.

In an item in the magazine of the Lifeboat Enthusiasts Society, Grahame Farr wrote about the house flag. It all started on the afternoon of the 24th October 1882, when signals of distress came from the Gull lightship. The Ramsgate lifeboat *Bradford* went out in tow of the harbour tug *Aid* and the light vessel keeper told them a vessel was ashore on the S.E. part of the Goodwins. The lifeboat was slipped, anchored and veered down to the yacht *Arab*, of Poole, bound from Boulogne for Dover, which was becoming a total wreck.

The Red Ensign and Institution flags fluttering in the breeze from Shoreham's Tyne Class. The Red Ensign is not flown on this lifeboat as a matter of course, but more commonly when the crew are 'flying the flag'. This would include occasions when important personalities are present, for publicity or during open days. One other point of interest is the third flag - that of the oil company 'Texaco'. 'Texaco' has an oil terminal at Shoreham Harbour, and since 1934 have granted the various lifeboats stationed there petrol and diesel free of charge. (By kind permission of Mr. D. Cassan).

Nine people were taken off and then put aboard the tug for the trip back to Ramsgate. The yacht was owned by Alderson Berthon of London, and among those saved was the owner himself and his step-son, Robert A.B. Preston. Mr. Preston was probably in the legal profession for he later resided at The Temple. In gratitude for his rescue he gave the lifeboat *Arab*, a 34 ft. self-righter, which was stationed at Padstow in 1883.

Mr. Preston took a great interest in lifeboat affairs thereafter and was elected to the Committee of Management, upon which he served until 1908.

10th DECEMBER   TORBAY, DEVON, **1980**

After a service by the Torbay lifeboat *Edward Bridges (Civil Service and Post Office No. 37)* to a diving work boat, the Honorary Secretary received the following letter of appreciation:

On Wednesday 10 December 1980, our diving boat Kermit, named

after a famous frog, decided to roll over on her back in an attempt to swim like her namesake. She found, however, although floating in this position was easy, unlike a frog her means of propulsion did not work totally submerged and upside down. This position did not suit her crew who were not too politely deposited into the sea between Berry Head and Sharkham Point.

Kermit has been severely reprimanded for taking such action, and on behalf of her crew, of which I myself was a member, may I offer our very sincere thanks to the Coxswain and crew of the lifeboat for their speedy action on that day, and as a more practical expression of our appreciation we enclose a cheque in aid of RNLI funds.

Once again many thanks for your prompt assistance on that fateful day. - J. G. Errington, Director, Keliston Marine Ltd, Orwell Quay, Duke Street, Ipswich, Suffolk.

11th DECEMBER   LONDON, **1928**

A Royal Lifeboat Matinée was held at the Lyceum on the 11th December 1928. Mr. Louis N. Parker wrote a special one-act play called 'Their Business in Great Waters'. He was able to arrange for such stars as Tallulah Bankhead and Leslie Howard to appear. The entire rights in the play were presented to the Ladies' Lifeboat Guild. The play was described in the March 1929 Lifeboat Journal.

"There are eight parts, four women and four men. The scene of the play is in the living room of a lifeboat Coxswain's cottage on a wild night. A signal of distress is heard, and the Coxswain and his son, the Second Coxswain, hurry to the boathouse. From the window of the room the Coxswain's wife watches the lifeboat's searchlight, as she goes out, sees it disappear, believes the lifeboat to be lost with all her crew, and waits in agony until the Coxswain and his son return triumphant with the whole crew saved.

The play is a noble expression of the unaffected courage and the deep humanity of the lifeboat service. It moves naturally, inevitably, and without any exaggeration, from a simple human interest to a tense atmosphere created by the storm, increasing from anxiety to terror and anguish and culminating in a noble close, where the joy and thankfulness at lives rescued from death, men returned in safety from a terrible ordeal, and a family reunited, finding expression in the words from the Bible which the Coxswain reads, "And He arose, and rebuked the wind, and said unto the sea, Peace, be still, and the wind ceased, and there was a great calm"."

THEIR BUSINESS IN GREAT WATERS

A PLAY IN ONE ACT

Written for and presented to the Ladies' Life-Boat Guild of the
Royal National Life-Boat Institution

By LOUIS N. PARKER

CHARACTERS :

John Colson (a Life-Boat Coxswain) . . .	EDMUND GWENN
Jack, his Son (Second Coxswain) . . .	LESLIE HOWARD
Martha, John's Wife . . .	LENA ASHWELL
Joan, engaged to Jack . . .	MARJORIE MARS
Old Mrs. Colson, John's Mother . . .	SARA ALLGOOD
Millie, a typical flapper . . .	TALLULAH BANKHEAD
Gerald, a young Londoner . . .	FRANK LAWTON
Jim, a sailor . . .	EDGAR NORFOLK

Scene.—The living room in John's cottage.

The Play produced by . . .	NORMAN PAGE
Honorary Stage Manager . .	GEORGE DESMOND

The programme of the royal matinée held at the Lyceum in London on the 11th December 1928.

12th DECEMBER   NEW QUAY, CARDIGAN, **1948**

The April 1949 Lifeboat Journal described the end of an era when the last sailing lifeboat was replaced by a motor lifeboat.

At half past eight in the morning of Sunday, 12th December 1948, a new motor lifeboat, the *St. Albans*, arrived at New Quay, Cardigan, from the building yard at Cowes. She replaced the last of the pulling and sailing lifeboats in the Institution's fleet. The *St. Albans* is a Liverpool boat, 35 feet 6 inches long, with a beam of 10 feet 8 inches, and is driven by two 18hp engines. She carries a crew of eight, and with gear and crew on board weighs 8¼ tons. She is a gift to the Institution from the people of St. Albans.

The last sailing boat, which that day came to the end of her service, was the *William Cantrell Ashley*. She was a Liverpool

boat, 35 feet long, with 10 feet beam. She was rigged with jib, fore lug and mizzen, and had twelve oars. She carried a crew of fifteen, and with crew and gear on board weighed just over 5 ½ tons. She was a gift to the Institution from Mr. Charles Carr Ashley, who died in 1906, leaving £65,000 to provide and endow five lifeboats. She was built in 1907 and had spent her forty-one years at New Quay. There she was launched on service 18 times and rescued 10 lives.

The first of all lifeboats, the *Original*, built at South Shields in 1789, had only oars. The first sailing lifeboat was built by the London coach builder Lionel Lukin for the Suffolk Humane Society in 1807, so that sailing lifeboats have served on our coasts for 141 years.

When the *St. Albans* arrived at New Quay the *William Cantrell Ashley* sailed out to meet her and a BBC television unit filmed the two boats. They were the first lifeboats to be televised.

The last of the sailing lifeboats - The William Cantrell Ashley sails away from New Quay, Cardigan, and into a place in the history of the RNLI.

13th DECEMBER   NEW BRIGHTON, CHESHIRE, **1944**

In his 'Story of the New Brighton Lifeboats', Jeff Morris describes an unusual service by their lifeboat.

During the war, lifeboats from all around our coast were called out scores of times to aircraft ditched in the sea. Just occasionally, survivors would be rescued, but often, all that was found was wreckage or patches of oil. However, on the 13th December 1944, the *Edmund and Mary Robinson* saved an aircraft!

It was 2 o'clock that afternoon that the coastguard reported that an aeroplane had come down in the River Mersey, off the Gladstone Dock. The lifeboat set out 10 minutes later, in dense fog and found a Walrus amphibious aeroplane. The pilot had been forced down through shortage of fuel and so the lifeboat took the plane in tow and returned to her moorings at 5 o'clock. During the next 5 days, the lifeboatmen helped to refuel the plane and she was then able to take off and return to her base.

14th DECEMBER   LONDON, **1928**

On the 14th December 1928, H.M. Queen Mary unveiled the memorial which had been erected on Tower Hill, to the 12,649 men of the Merchant Navy and Fishing Fleets who gave their lives in the Great War and who have no grave but the sea.

During the War, from August 1914, to the signing of peace in June 1919, besides the lifeboatmen who lost their lives when serving with the navy, twenty-three lifeboatmen lost their lives on lifeboat service.

At the ceremony on Tower Hill twenty-four lifeboatmen were present. Wearing full lifeboat dress, they were drawn from the stations at Southend, Margate, Ramsgate, Eastbourne, Newhaven and Worthing. These men, on behalf of the whole service, paid their last tribute to their own comrades and to the men of the Mercantile Navy and Fishing Fleets who died in the Great War.

15th DECEMBER   BALLYWALTER, CO. DOWN, **1876**

The clergy, particularly in Ireland, have frequently been prominent in helping the lifeboat service. On the 15th December 1876, during the night, the brigantine *Jennie Lind*, of Whitehaven, laden with coal, was driven on the Pladdie Rocks off Ballywalter. A strong S.E. gale was blowing, with a very heavy sea, and the night very dark. It was therefore felt to be a

very dangerous service, and for some time a sufficient number of volunteers could not be obtained to man the lifeboat *Admiral Henry Meynell*. After a while, however, and encouraged by Rev. Henry Wilson, son of the Rector of Ballywalter, who accompanied them as one of the crew of the boat, she proceeded on her dangerous mission. In a little more than an hour they reached the stranded vessel, taking her crew of five men on board, and afterwards landed them safely at Ballywalter. This was altogether a very gallant and praiseworthy service.

The Rev. Wilson was voted the Thanks of the Institution inscribed on Vellum for his part in this service.

16th DECEMBER   PORT LOGAN, WIGTOWNSHIRE, **1867**

A 'singular coincidence' was reported in the October 1868 Lifeboat Journal. The new lifeboat for Port Logan, the *Edinburgh and R.M. Ballantyne* (see 26th October), was exhibited in Glasgow on the 16th December 1866 whilst on its way to the station. The wife of the Master of the Glasgow barque *Strathleven* took her children to see the boat and put some money in the collecting box.

Exactly one year later, her husband's vessel was wrecked in a gale about seven miles from Port Logan. The *Edinburgh and R.M. Ballantyne* was launched and rescued the fifteen crew and brought them safely to shore. So it just goes to show how you never know when your donation to the RNLI may come in useful!

17th DECEMBER   LONDON, **1911**

At times the Lifeboat Journal waxed lyrical about the need to guide children in the need to support charitable works. On the 17th December 1911, a young girl wrote to the Institution from Belsize Park:

Dear Sir John Lamb,

I got this money through having a small sale of work in our nursery. I had one last year, and spent the money on toys for the hospital. This year I would like to give it to the lifeboat at Criccieth in North Wales.

I enclose the £3.10s. which I earned, and, if possible, could you send it to Criccieth?

Your sincere little friend,
BARBARA M. LEWIS GLOVER

That letter appeared in the February 1912 Lifeboat Journal. Perhaps Barbara's mother had been influenced by the article which appeared in August 1905:

A SUGGESTION
TO THOSE IN CHARGE OF THE YOUNG

Character never alters, but it may be influenced, instructed and guided, and never so well as in the days of childhood and early youth. Whilst it is of the utmost importance that the young should be encouraged to be industrious, thrifty and unselfish, it is no less important that they should learn the clear duty of being frank, open and generous. Every child should be taught to exercise consideration for others, and that every gift received and each present bestowed is not to be used exclusively for the benefit of self, but that it should be also employed in doing good or giving pleasure to others. We would suggest that an excellent way of engaging the interest of the young in the well -being of others and of encouraging, if not promoting, in them generous impulses would be for parents, and, indeed, any placed in a position of authority over children, whether for purposes of education or otherwise, to urge them to contribute - say a penny a week, or even a penny a month - to the Royal National Lifeboat Institution - an object which has undoubtedly for very many years been a thoroughly attractive one to the young having a decided flavour of romance coupled with a good dash of sentiment. Schoolmasters and schoolmistresses might do much by this means to help and encourage the great life-saving work of the Institution. The Secretary will be delighted to co-operate by supplying, on application, pretty contribution boxes in the shape of a lifeboat to any proposing to adopt our suggestion. Apply to the Secretary, Royal National Lifeboat Institution, 20 Charing Cross Road, London WC.

18th DECEMBER   PETERHEAD, ABERDEENSHIRE, **1944**

During the war fishermen still went out to distant waters despite the threat from hostile enemy forces. Unfortunately they also had

to contend with the forces of nature as this report of a service by the Peterhead lifeboat illustrates.

At 7.20 on the evening of the 18th December 1944 the coastguard telephoned that a vessel was ashore on the North Head at the harbour entrance. A light south-west wind was blowing, with a ground swell. Visibility was poor. The motor lifeboat *Julia Park Barry of Glasgow* put out at 7.40 p.m. and within a few minutes had found the motor vessel *Finlande* hard aground.

She was a French trawler of 1,300 tons, working from Hull, to which port she was bound with a cargo of fish from Iceland - reported to be worth £10,000. Her crew numbered thirty-six, and she was said to be the largest fishing trawler in the world. As she was leaking badly, and was fast on the rocks her crew had decided to abandon her. The swell was heavy, but the crew were able to jump aboard the lifeboat. One man fell into the sea, but he was quickly pulled out. The lifeboat reached harbour again at 8.30 p.m.

19th DECEMBER   HUMBER & SKEGNESS, **1996**

A 'long tow in difficult conditions' is how the next rescue might be described. The Skegness and Humber lifeboats were both involved in a long service when conditions became too severe for a classic 1920s-built motor yacht on a delivery passage from Great Yarmouth to Amble on the 19th December 1996.

With winds freshening to Force 9 her skipper was having difficulty keeping control and, also worried for the safety of his 17-year-old son, put out a 'Peter Pan' call. Humber coastguard who asked Skegness Mersey *Lincolnshire Poacher* to launch received the call.

Both of the yacht's crew were affected by seasickness so, despite the risks in the high winds and heavy sea, it was necessary to put two lifeboatmen aboard her. This was achieved after a couple of attempts and the motor yacht was then able to make about 6 knots down sea towards Grimsby. However, after about half an hour the casualty's steering failed and she had to be taken in tow - an operation which took several attempts as the lifeboat crew aboard the yacht were working on a wave-swept and very slippery foredeck.

Just after 07.00 *Lincolnshire Poacher* handed over the tow to

Humber's Arun *Kenneth Thelwall* - again a tricky task as the crew members and the drogue used to steady the yacht had to be recovered. The Humber lifeboat in turn put a crew member aboard and continued the tow towards the Humber River, making slow progress in the gale force easterly wind and heavy seas.

By 10.15 a.m. she was able to find some shelter under Spurn Head where Dave Steenvoorden, the crew member aboard, and the yacht's owner were able to make temporary repairs to the casualty's steering. By 10.30 a.m. she was under way again, eventually leaving the yacht in the safety of Grimsby's Fish Dock Marina.

20th DECEMBER   BOULMER, NORTHUMBERLAND, **1925**

The March 1926 Lifeboat Journal tells of a remarkable service by the Alnmouth and Boulmer lifeboats on the 20th December 1925 to the collier *Amble* wrecked in Alnmouth Bay.

The Alnmouth lifeboat was launched with great difficulty but was unable to reach the wreck. Meanwhile the Boulmer lifeboat had also gone to the scene of the wreck. It was not only blowing very hard, but the weather was very cold, with hail, snow and sleet.

So fierce and bitter was it that the horse drawing the cart

The Runswick women launching their lifeboat on the 12th April 1901, when it went to the aid of local fishing cobles caught in a heavy sea. This picture provides a graphic illustration of the conditions that both crew and launchers faced.

containing stores and lowering gear refused to go on, and a motor had to be obtained. In face of this blizzard, the sixty one launchers, of whom thirty five were women, dragged the lifeboat for a mile and a quarter, along a road so narrow that the wheels were continually sinking in the ditches. It was only with the utmost difficulty that the boat and her carriage, weighing altogether nearly 11 tons, were got along at all.

The women launchers at Boulmer, Northumberland.

The boat was not actually launched, but the launchers stood by, keeping her in position for launching, until the Alnmouth lifeboat returned to shore at 9 p.m. They had been out on duty in the height of this gale on a December night for over six hours.

The village of Boulmer consists of less than fifty houses and has a population of about 150 people. On this night this little place manned both the lifeboats, (the Alnmouth, with a crew of 14, and the Boulmer, with a crew of 13); provided the launching party of 61 for the Boulmer boat; and manned the life-saving apparatus with a crew of 27. It was by these means that the crew of the *Amble* were actually brought ashore. Thus four-fifths of the people of Boulmer were engaged that night in efforts to rescue the *Amble's* crew.

In recognition of the magnificent courage and endurance of the women-launchers the Institution has awarded them its Thanks inscribed on Vellum.

21st DECEMBER   JOHNSHAVEN, KINCARDINESHIRE, **1920**

The Johnshaven lifeboat, *James Marsh*, succeeded in taking off the nine crew of the Danish schooner *Fredensborg*, during a whole gale on the 21st December 1920. In attempting to make the very difficult entrance to the harbour, the lifeboat heeled over so far that all on board were thrown into the water. Although she righted herself at once, two of the crew of the schooner and one of the lifeboatmen were drowned.

The King of Denmark presented to Coxswain John McBay and to each of the eleven members of the crew, a silver cup with the following inscription:

"Awarded by the Royal Danish Government, in recognition of bravery and self sacrifice on the occasion of the rescue of the crew of the schooner Fredensborg, of Korsör, wrecked in St. Cyrus Bay, on 21 December 1920."

The King also made a monetary award to Mrs. Jane McBay, the widow of James McBay, the member of the crew who lost his life.

22nd DECEMBER   ATLANTIC OCEAN, **1835**

Medals are normally awarded for services on the coasts of the United Kingdom and Ireland. Some exceptions have been made, as in the case described here.

On the 22nd December 1835 and five days out from St. John's, Newfoundland, the brig *Angerona* came across the *Francis Sparght*, dismasted and waterlogged, 800 miles east of Newfoundland. A strong gale was blowing and a tremendous sea running, breaking over the vessel frequently. Noticing a number of people on the poop, Captain Jellard, with three other men, lowered their only boat and made for the wreck.

In two trips they took off eleven survivors who, miserable and helpless, had been without provisions and water for 19 days.

Three men had been washed overboard when the vessel first became a wreck. On the 15th day lots were drawn for a victim to satisfy their hunger, and ultimately in four cases 'human blood had been shed for the sustenance of the survivors'.

On the 7th January 1836 the survivors were landed at Falmouth.

Captain William John Jellard was awarded the Institution's gold medal and the three men who went with him each received the silver medal.

23rd DECEMBER
WESTON-SUPER-MARE, SOMERSET; BARRY DOCK, GLAMORGAN, **1935**

It is not unusual for lifeboats to stand by casualties through the night. On the 23rd December 1935 two lifeboats did just that.

On the night of 23rd December the Greek steamer *Michalis Poutous*, of Piraeus, bound light from Rouen to Barry Dock, ran on to the rocks in Bridgwater Bay, near Burnham. She carried a crew of twenty-nine. A moderate easterly breeze was blowing, with showers of snow and sleet. A moderate sea was running and there was a dense fog.

The Weston-Super-Mare motor lifeboat *Fifi and Charles* was launched at 9.30 p.m., and found the steamer two hours later. Her back was breaking. The lifeboat stood by until the tide had turned sufficiently to enable her to get alongside. Then twenty-seven of the crew left the steamer and took to the ship's boats and the lifeboat. The Captain and steward remained on the part of the wreck which was not in immediate danger.

The Barry Dock motor lifeboat *Prince David*, which had put out at 10.15 p.m., arrived later, and closed with the Weston-Super-Mare boat. Both lifeboats then stood by the steamer until daylight in order to see how much she was damaged, and then, soon after 7 a.m. they made for Barry, each towing a ship's boat, leaving the Captain and steward on board. They arrived at Barry at about 10 a.m. on the 24th. The Weston-Super-Mare lifeboat left again soon afterwards, and reached her station at noon. She had been on service for about fifteen hours and the Barry Dock lifeboat for twelve. The *Michalis Poutous*, her back broken, was eventually salved by tugs, and taken into Barry Roads, with the Captain and the steward still on board.

24th DECEMBER
PORTHDINLLAEN, CAERNARVON, **1925**

The September 1929 Lifeboat Journal described the exploits of

one of the Institution's engineers who exchanged his normal duties to become a lifeboatman.

"While the engineers of the Institution were engaged in constructing the new launching slipway at Porthdinllaen, in Caernarvonshire, for the motor lifeboat which was sent to the station in March last, the foreman in charge of the new works Mr. T.A. Hooper, twice went out and helped to save life from shipwreck."

On the 4th August 1925, he and three of his men manned the lifeboat's boarding boat and saved two men who were in a sinking punt, and but for his prompt help would have lost their lives.

On the 24th December 1925, he formed one of the crew of the Porthdinllaen lifeboat when she went out in a whole gale, with a very heavy sea, and helped to save the s.s. *Matje*, of Hull, and her crew of six. The *Matje* had anchored, but was dragging slowly towards the rocks. Some of the lifeboat crew were put on board, and with their help the steamer was brought safely into Porthdinllaen Bay. In recognition of these services the Institution presented Mr. Hooper with an inscribed Aneroid Barometer.

25th DECEMBER
BRITISH ISLES, **1990**

Christmas Day is no different from any other day in the lifeboat service. The volunteer crew members willingly put to sea at any time to save lives. The crews of eight lifeboats the length and breadth of the country left their family festivities to put to sea to help others on Christmas Day 1990, and no less than 15 lifeboats were launched between Christmas Eve and Boxing Day.

The crew of Angle's lifeboat were awakened by their pagers before dawn on Christmas morning when the tanker *Thuntank 9* went aground in Milford Haven. The lifeboat stood by the stricken vessel while a helicopter lifted off some of her crew, and then stayed at the scene in severe conditions to pass a tow line to tugs. She was at sea for more than five hours in winds gusting to 40 knots until the tanker was safely secured in port.

The six-man crew of the Lerwick lifeboat found themselves at sea in storm force winds (gusting to 60-70 knots) instead of sitting down with their families for Christmas lunch. The lifeboat was launched at 1.35 p.m. when a rig supply vessel was hit by a giant wave which knocked out her electrical supply, steering and engine. The lifeboat was at sea for more than four hours, standing by while the crew of the casualty were evacuated and only returning to Lerwick when they were safely aboard a rescue helicopter.

Lifeboats were also called out at Appledore, Penlee, Salcombe, Newhaven, Longhope and Tenby.

26th DECEMBER   HEDGERLY, BERKSHIRE AND MALDON, ESSEX, **1995**

Boxing Day is a popular time for intrepid souls to take to the water, and the spring 1996 Lifeboat Journal described two ways in which the RNLI benefited.

A dip in Black Park Lake on Boxing Day by the Apollo Venture Unit from Hedgerley, near Slough raised £300 for lifeboat coffers. Some fifteen stalwarts in festive fancy dress grouped around a campfire on the bright, frosty morning, and while collectors rattled their tins, some 100 supporters gathered on the wooded shores of the lake as the bathers plunged into the icy waters with barely perceptible hesitation!

Naughty nuns, cheeky St. Trinians girls, Mary Quant look-alikes and Sergeant Peppers braved bitterly cold conditions on Boxing Day 1995, to take part in the Maldon, Essex rowing event to raise money for the RNLI. More than 35 boats, with over 100 rowers, took part in the 5-kilometre row on the river Blackwater, which has become an annual event at Christmas or New Year for 25 years. The Maldon Little Ship Club runs the event and thousands are raised for charity every year. A total of £6,000 was raised this time and the trophy for the boat sponsored for the most money went to the all-ladies group, the Hythe Hookers. The inshore lifeboat from West Mersea was in attendance.

27th DECEMBER   HOLYHEAD, ANGLESEY, **1902**

The steam lifeboat *Duke of Northumberland* did excellent service whilst at Holyhead from 1892 to 1893 and 1897 to 1922. In all she "launched" 131 times and saved 248 lives. One of her services, on the 27th December 1902, was described in the May 1903 Lifeboat Journal.

"During the afternoon a large four masted barque was observed

being taken in tow by a tug, but it was noticed that very little progress had been made when darkness came on. Shortly after 9 p.m. a distress signal was sent, upon which the steam lifeboat was at once ordered out. Upon arrival they found the **Lord Shaftesbury***, of Liverpool, a vessel of over 2,000 tons, anchored but still attached by a hawser to a tug.*

"She was then about 500 yards from a lee shore, and in spite of everything was dragging into greater danger. It was blowing a strong gale from W.S.W., and a very heavy sea was running; the Captain therefore thought it advisable to abandon his vessel, and the crew of 29 hands were accordingly taken into the lifeboat. This feat was fortunately accomplished without mishap, and the Captain of the vessel spoke in terms of the highest praise of both the lifeboat and her crew, stating it was quite the smartest piece of work he had ever seen performed."

Amazingly, the barque did not end up on the rocks, and the crew were able to get back aboard on the 30th and so save the ship.

The steam lifeboat The Duke of Northumberland that was stationed at Holyhead, Anglesey, from 1892 to 1893, and again from 1897 to 1922.

28th DECEMBER   APPLEDORE, DEVON, **1868**

Very occasionally, in the early days of the Institution, double medal awards were made. For a service at Appledore on the 28th December 1868, Coxswain Joseph Cox was awarded second and third clasps to the silver medal he received in 1861. The Second Coxswain, Joseph Cox Junior, and Crew Member John Kelly each received a silver medal. The service is described in the book 'Lifeboat Gallantry'.

Information was received that a vessel was embayed near Appledore, Devon. When it was confirmed that she had grounded, the self righting lifeboat *Hope* was dragged to the nearest point and launched over Pebble Ridge into a terrific surf, reached the Austrian barque *Pace*, and made fast to her. The Master refused to let his crew leave, except that one boy ran to the side and dropped into the boat. After another five minutes, eight men rushed forward and dropped into the water from where all were saved just before a tremendous sea struck the lifeboat and drove her under the barque's counter.

With the lifeboat's rudder carried away, the Coxswain bruised (his cork lifebelt saved him from serious injury or death), the boat returned to shore after another unsuccessful appeal to the barque's crew. Cox, the elder, raised another crew with his son, which again included Mr. Kelly. They set off once more, young Cox using an oar to steer. Just short of the wreck, they were swept by a huge sea which threw all the crew into the water. After some difficulty everybody regained the boat which returned to the shore, where other crews volunteered.

However, it was decided not to make any further rescue attempt in the lifeboat. The barque's Master and two men were taken off when the tide fell; three more had perished.

The Emperor of Austria awarded the three men the Silver Cross of Merit and made awards to others involved in the rescue.

29th DECEMBER   NORFOLK, **1857**

On the 29th December 1857, the lifeboats of the Norfolk Association were taken over by the RNLI. Lifeboats at Mundesley, Cromer, Bacton, Palling, Winterton, Caister and Yarmouth were transferred to the Institution.

Many of the boats were old and in bad condition. The Mundesley boat was noted as being 'very old and worn out' and, worse, 'very leaky'. Similarly, the Cromer boat was '28 years old'. On the other hand the Caister boat, a '42 ft., double banked one, built by Bramford of Yarmouth' was, with the *gear and house in good order, a large sum having recently been expended on them'.*

Mundesley was operational until 1895; Bacton to 1882; Palling to 1930 and Winterton 1924. Caister was closed by the RNLI in 1969 but now has a very active independently run lifeboat, operated by the Caister Volunteer Rescue Service. The ex-Norfolk Association station at Cromer is still very active.

The Association's station at Great Yarmouth was operational until 1919, and in 1926 the nearby RNLI station at Gorleston was renamed Great Yarmouth and Gorleston.

30th DECEMBER   SELSEY, SUSSEX, **1993**

The RNLI is renowned for never saying no to those requiring assistance on water. However one call, on the 30th December 1993, to Barnham in West Sussex, stretched the interpretation a little - as it is 15 miles by road from Selsey and 8 miles inland!

Chaos reigns in Uckfield, East Sussex, on the 12th October 2000. The conditions that faced the lifeboat crews were almost identical to those endured by the Selsey lifeboat on the 30th December 1993. Note the proliferation of dangerous obstacles littering the water. The D Class in the foreground is that from Eastbourne, whilst in the background is Brighton's Y Class. The latter is mainly used in the confines of Brighton Marina, whilst their Atlantic 75 is the main rescue boat. (By kind permission of Mr. D. Cassan.)

Two people were marooned in a car by flash floods and a complex of homes for the elderly, which housed 200 people, were also giving cause for concern. Sussex Fire Services asked the Solent coastguard for assistance and they in turn alerted the Selsey and Shoreham lifeboat stations.

Selsey's Honorary Secretary, Clive Cockayne, and Coxswain Mike Grant mustered the crew and loaded the D class lifeboat onto a lorry, having made sure that a full crew was left to man the all-weather lifeboat.

On arrival at Barnham they ferried 40 elderly people to safety, plus other civilians, although the lifeboat was 'stranded' for a while on top of a street bollard. When checking a coach for casualties, with water almost up to the top of the windows, the lifeboat bumped into a car which had been swept down by the flood, crashing into the coach which had been swung sideways across the road.

During its searching one of the lifeboat's sponson compartments was punctured - by a *"Keep Left"* sign under the railway bridge - but with everyone accounted for the lifeboat was released after three hours.

When the River Lavant burst its banks at Chichester on the 9th January 1994, Selsey again gave help. Over the next few days a total of 575 hours of continuous service were clocked up.

31st DECEMBER   CODSALL, STAFFORDSHIRE, **1935**

To end the lifeboat year, a warming story appeared in the December 1937 Lifeboat Journal.

Although told here one day early (author's licence!) it makes a pleasant antidote to stories of rescues from storm tossed seas, whilst illustrating the efforts of helpers throughout the country to support lifeboatmen.

Mrs. Edith Manby, of Codsall, Staffordshire, completed, on New Year's Day 1936, a task which she began in April 1935, of knitting woollen scarf helmets for the lifeboat crews around our coasts. Mrs. Manby had the help of 491 knitters and subscribers, and the work cost £250, of which she herself contributed over £100. As the scarf helmets were finished they were sent to the coast, and at many stations special presentation ceremonies were arranged.

The following figures will show the enormous task that Mrs. Manby and her helpers had successfully completed. The number of scarves knitted was 1,525. They were each nearly two yards long, so that, if laid end to end, they would stretch over 3,000 yards or nearly a mile and three quarters.

The wool weighed over a quarter of a ton, and was 580,850 yards, or over 330 miles long. Over 60,400 pieces of fringe were used, and over 4,550 initials were worked on the scarves!

INDEX OF LIFEBOAT STATIONS FEATURED IN A LIFEBOAT YEAR

Johnshaven	26 Mar., 3 Oct., 21 Dec.
Killybegs	24 Aug.
Kilmore	20 Feb., 19 Mar.
Kirkcudbright	11 Jul.
Kirkwall	29 Jan., 12 Jul
Lerwick	5 Mar., 19 Nov., 25 Dec.
Littlehampton	28 Nov., 5 Dec.
Lizard	17 Mar., 31 Mar., 14 Oct.
Lizard - Cadgwith	7 Jul.
Llandudno	26 Feb., 10 Aug.
Llanelli	29 Nov.
Longhope	25 Dec.
Lowestoft	30 Sept., 15 Oct., 17 Nov.
Lynmouth	12 Jan., 17 Aug.
Lytham	29 Nov.
Lytham St. Anne's	6 Jun.
Margate	9 Jun., 25 Oct.
Minehead	23 Jul.
Moelfre	7 Feb.
Montrose	26 Mar., 26 Nov.
Morecombe	17 Oct.
Mumbles (The)	27 Jan., 23 Apr., 28 Jun.
Mundesley	29 Dec.
Newbiggin	14 Sept.
New Brighton	1 Jan., 28 May, 31 May, 4 Jun., 21 Sept., 1 Oct., 13 Dec.
Newhaven	24 Mar., 18 Sept., 19 Oct., 29 Nov., 25 Dec.
Newquay, Cornwall	17 Apr., 28 Jun., 30 Jul.
New Quay, Cardigan	5 Sep., 12 Dec.
North Deal	31 Jan., 3 Aug.
North Sunderland	18 Feb., 29 Jun.
Oban	7 May
Padstow	24 May, 10 Jul., 29 Aug., 6 Sept., 23 Oct
Palling	29 Dec.
Penarth	10 Apr.
Penlee	3 Jan., 21 Jan., 18 Mar., 19 Sept., 25 Dec.
Peterhead	18 Dec.

Plymouth	19 Jul., 9 Aug., 22 Nov.
Poole	27 Mar., 21 Apr., 30 May, 27 Jul., 21 Oct.
Portaferry	5 Dec
Port Erin	11 Mar.
Porthdinllaen	5 Oct., 24 Dec.
Porthleven	17 Mar.
Porthoustock	21 May, 14 Oct.
Port Isaac	13 Apr.
Port Logan	26 Oct., 16 Dec.
Portmadoc	29 Nov.
Portpatrick	13 Jan.
Port St. Mary	6 Aug.
Portsmouth	23 Sept.
Pwllheli	29 Apr.
Queensferry	25 Jan.
Ramsey	8 Feb.
Ramsgate	6 Jan., 31 Jan., 8 Oct., 11 Oct., 22 Oct., 27 Nov., 6 Dec.
Redcar	14 Aug., 18 Nov.
Rhyl	26 Feb., 17 Sept., 29 Nov.
Rosslare Harbour	21 Mar., 24 Jun., 21 Sept.
Runswick	20 Sept., 18 Nov.
Rye Harbour	27 Sept.
St. Abbs	15 Nov.
St. Agnes, Cornwall	5 Dec.
St. David's	26 Apr., 22 Aug., 12 Oct.
St. Ives	23 Jan., 8 Apr., 29 Jul.
St. Mary's	18 Mar., 21 Mar.
St. Peter Port	5 Feb., 28 Mar., 19 Apr.
Salcombe	9 Jul., 27 Oct., 25 Dec.
Scarborough	11 Jun., 29 Oct.
Selsey	9 Jun., 1 Nov., 20 Nov., 30 Dec.
Sheerness	9 Jun., 16 Oct.
Sheringham	15 Mar., 18 Apr.
Shoreham Harbour	24 Jan., 9 Dec.
Sidmouth	29 Mar.
Skateraw	24 Oct.
Skegness	19 Aug., 13 Nov., 19 Dec.
Southend-on-Sea	27 Feb., 25 Mar., 30 Jun., 25 Oct., 8 Dec.

South Shields	30 Jan.	Varne Lightvessel	13 May
Staithes	18 Oct.	Walmer	20 May, 27 Aug., 12 Nov., 27 Nov.
Stromness	14 Feb., 15 Apr., 1 May, 4 May, 4 Oct.	Walton and Frinton	27 May, 10 Jul.
		Wells	5 May, 19 May, 8 Jul.
Stronsay	15 Apr., 1 May	West Kirby	14 Jan.
Swanage	23 May, 28 Aug, 16 Sept.	West Mersea	26 Jan.
		Weston-Super-Mare	10 Apr., 2 Jun., 13 Sept., 23 Dec.
Teesmouth	28 Jun.	Wexford	20 Feb., 25 Mar.
Teignmouth	1 Oct., 29 Nov.	Weymouth	16 Oct.
Tenby	3 Apr., 29 Sept., 18 Nov., 29 Nov., 25 Dec.	Whitby	17 Jan., 19 Jan., 9 Apr., 1 Aug., 4 Sept.
Thurso	15 Apr., 31 Aug.	Wick	18 Jan.
Tobermory	3 May	Winterton	29 Dec.
Torbay	9 Jul., 7 Aug., 15 Aug., 10 Dec.		
Tynemouth	11 Jan., 1 May, 10 May, 4 Jul.	Yarmouth, (Isle of Wight)	14 Jun., 5 Jul., 12 Aug., 26 Aug.
Valentia	20 Oct.	Youghal	30 Nov.

GENERAL INDEX